Autodesk Revit
Management:
Template and Family Creation

ASCENT – Center for Technical Knowledge®

autodesk®
authorized author

Publications

SDC Publications
P.O. Box 1334
Mission KS 66222
913-262-2664
www.SDCpublications.com
Publisher: Stephen Schroff

ISBN-13: 978-1-58503-883-1
ISBN-10: 1-58503-883-0

Printed and bound in the United States of America.

Table of Contents

vi

© 2014, ASCENT - Center for Technical Knowledge®

Preface

Building Information Modeling (BIM) is an approach to the entire building life cycle. Autodesk® Revit® Architecture, Autodesk® Revit® MEP, and Autodesk® Revit® Structure are powerful BIM programs that support the ability to coordinate, update, and share design data with team members throughout the design construction and management phases of a building's life. A key component in managing the BIM process is to establish a company foundation for different types of projects by creating standard templates and custom elements. Having this in place makes the process of any new project flow smoothly and efficiently.

The objective of the *Autodesk® Revit® 2015 BIM Management: Template and Family Creation* training guide is to enable students who have worked with the software to expand their knowledge in setting up office standards with templates that include annotation styles, preset views, sheets, and schedules, as well as creating custom element types and families. The class can be taught in any one or a mix of all of the software programs using practices specific to each discipline.

Students learn how to:

- Create custom templates with annotation styles, title blocks, and custom element types.

- Create schedules, including material takeoff schedules with formula.

- Create custom wall, roof, and floor types as well as MEP system families.

- Set up a family file.

- Create family geometry.

- Create family types.

- Create specific families, including in-place families, profiles, annotations, and parameters.

The training guide contains additional discipline-specific practices for families including doors, windows, railings, pipe fittings, light fixtures, gusset plates, and built-up columns.

Information about creating object styles, fill patterns, and materials as well as some basic User Interface customization is included in Appendix A.

Icon Reference Chart

The following icons are used throughout this training guide to help you to quickly and easily find helpful information.

	Indicates the Learning Objectives that are covered in the current chapter or section of the training guide.
Enhanced in 2015	Indicates items that have been enhanced in the Autodesk Revit 2015 software.
New in 2015	Indicates items that are new in the Autodesk Revit 2015 software.
	Indicates items that are related to the Autodesk Revit 2015 Certification Exam Professional topics and objectives.
	Indicates items that are related to the Autodesk Revit 2015 Certification Exam User topics and objectives.

Appendix B includes a list of the Autodesk Certification topics and objectives for the Autodesk Revit software (Autodesk Revit Architecture only.). References to content in this training guide have been included to assist you in preparing for the certification exam.

Students and Educators can Access Free Autodesk Software and Resources

Autodesk challenges you to get started with free educational licenses for professional software and creativity apps used by millions of architects, engineers, designers, and hobbyists today. Bring Autodesk software into your classroom, studio, or workshop to learn, teach, and explore real-world design challenges the way professionals do.

Get started today - register at the Autodesk Education Community and download one of the many Autodesk software applications available.

Visit www.autodesk.com/joinedu/

Free products are subject to the terms and conditions of the end-user license and services agreement that accompanies the software. The software is for personal use for education purposes and is not intended for classroom or lab use.

Class Files

To download the Class Files that are required for this training guide, type or click the following in the address bar of your web browser:

SDCpublications.com/downloads/978-1-58503-883-1

Setting Up the Interface

The Autodesk® Building Design Suite version of the Autodesk® Revit® software is designed to be used with all building disciplines but the interface can be modified to suit each user's need. In this topic you learn how to modify the discipline-specific interface that is used in this training guide.

Customizing the Interface

The Autodesk Revit software has three disciplines: Architecture, Structure, and MEP (Mechanical, Electrical, and Plumbing, which is also know as Systems). When using the Autodesk Building Design Suite, all of the tools for these disciplines are installed in one copy of the software. By default, all of the tools, templates, and sample files are available, as shown in Figure 1. Most users only need access to their specific set of tools and the interface can be customized to suit those needs.

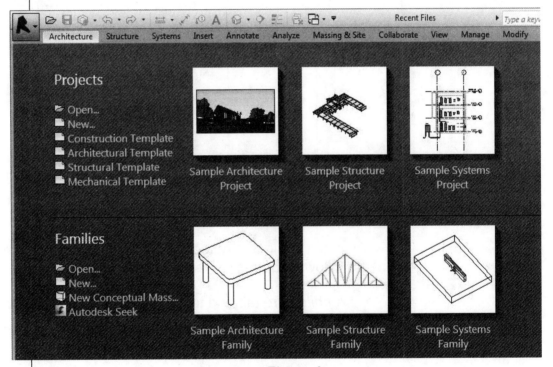

Figure 1

- The following steps describe how to customize the suite-based software with special reference to the layout of the discipline-specific software. If you are using the discipline-specific software, you do not need to make any changes.

- This training guide covers all the three disciplines and you can work through each without making any changes to the interface.

Hint: Setup the Autodesk Revit Interface by Discipline

1. In the upper left corner of the screen, expand (Application Menu) and click Options.

2. In the Options dialog box, in the left pane, select **User Interface**.

   In the *Configure* area, under *Tools and analyses* (as shown in Figure 2), clear all of options that you do not want to use.

You are not deleting these tools, just removing them from the current user interface.

Figure 2

- To match the Autodesk Revit Architecture interface, select only the following options:

  - *Architecture* tab and tools
  - *Structure* tab and tools (but not Structural analysis and tools)
  - *Massing and Site* tab and tools
  - Energy analysis and tools

- To match the Autodesk Revit Structure interface, select only the following options:

  - *Architecture* tab and tools
  - *Structure* tab and tools including Structural analysis and tools
  - *Massing and Site* tab and tools

- To match the Autodesk Revit MEP interface, clear only the following option:

  - *Structure* tab and tools

3. You can also specify which templates display when starting a new project. In the left pane, select **File Locations**.
4. In the right pane (as shown in Figure 3), select and order the templates that you want to display. Typically, these are set up by the company.

Project template files: The first five project templates will appear as links on the Recent Files page.

Name	Path
Construction Tem...	C:\ProgramData\Autodesk\RVT 2015\Tem...
Architectural Temp...	C:\ProgramData\Autodesk\RVT 2015\Tem...
Structural Template	C:\ProgramData\Autodesk\RVT 2015\Tem...
Mechanical Templ...	C:\ProgramData\Autodesk\RVT 2015\Tem...

Figure 3

- To match the Autodesk Revit Architecture interface, select **Architectural Template** and move it to the top of the list. Remove the **Structural Template** and **Mechanical Template**.

- To match the Autodesk Revit Structure interface, select **Structural Template** and move it to the top of the list. Remove the **Architectural Template**, **Construction Template**, and **Mechanical Template**.

- To match the Autodesk Revit MEP interface, remove the **Construction Template, Architectural Template**, and **Structural Template**. Add the **Electrical Template (Electrical-Default.rte)** and **Systems Template (Systems-Default.rte)** found in the RVT 2014>Templates>*<appropriate units>* folder.

5. Click **OK**. The interface and template locations update for this installation of the software.

- You might also need to move the tabs to a different order. To do so, select the tab, hold down <Ctrl>, and drag the tab to the new location.

- To match the Autodesk Revit Architecture interface you are not required to modify the tab locations.

- To match the Autodesk Revit Structure interface, select the *Structure* tab and drag it to the front of the tabs.

- To match the Autodesk Revit MEP interface, select the *Systems* tab and drag it to the front of the tabs.

Chapter 1

Creating Custom Templates

In this chapter you learn how to prepare project templates, create preset annotation styles, create title blocks, and create and apply view templates. You also review settings for structural, mechanical, and electrical projects.

This chapter contains the following topics:

- **Preparing Project Templates**
- **Customizing Annotation Styles**
- **Creating Title Blocks**
- **View Templates**
- **Settings for Mechanical and Electrical Projects**
- **Settings for Structural Projects**

1.1 Preparing Project Templates

Learning Objectives

- Create project templates that include basic information and settings.
- Customize units, snap settings, temporary dimension settings, and typed in shortcuts.

A project template is an existing file that contains preloaded families, settings, views, sheets, schedules, and sometimes geometry, that can be used to create a new project. You can have several project templates for different types of projects or building types, such as residential, commercial, and industrial. If you do a lot of work for a specific client (e.g., a school system), you can also create a template specifically for their projects with associated title blocks and other information. The aim is to save time with standards so that you can concentrate on the design.

- Defining *Levels* in a project template is helpful. They could be just a few basic levels for a residential project, as shown in Figure 1–1, or 100 stories for a high-rise.

Figure 1–1

How To: Create a Project Template File

1. In the Application Menu, expand (New) and click (Project).
2. In the New Project dialog box, select a template file to build from or select **None** to use a blank project file.

Project template files have the extension .RTE.

3. In the *Create new* area, select **Project template**, as shown in Figure 1–2.

Figure 1–2

4. Click OK .
5. If you select <None> in the Template file list, you are prompted to specify the initial unit system for the project: **Imperial** or **Metric**, as shown in Figure 1–3.

Figure 1–3

6. Add settings, families, views, etc., as needed to the new file.
7. Save the project template file.

• To save time, use an existing project or template that includes some of the basics you need rather than starting from scratch.

Managing Settings

Most of the settings stored in a template file are found in the *Manage* tab>Settings panel as shown in Figure 1–4. These settings include Units, Snaps, Temporary Dimensions, Object Styles (Lineweights, Line color, and Line patterns), Line Styles, Materials, Fill Patterns, etc.

Figure 1–4

- Specific Structural Settings, MEP Settings, and Panel Schedule Templates are also included in this grouping.

System Families

Walls, Wall Foundations, Floors, Slabs, Ceilings, and Roofs as well as Duct, Pipe, Cable Tray and Conduit types are created by duplicating and modifying an existing type as shown in Figure 1–5. These are considered System Families because they are created in the system rather than in a separate family file. Annotation Styles for Text and Dimensions are also system families and are modified in Type Properties as well.

To open Type Properties, select a type and, in the Modify tab >Properties panel, click

(Type Properties) or in Properties, click

(Edit Type).

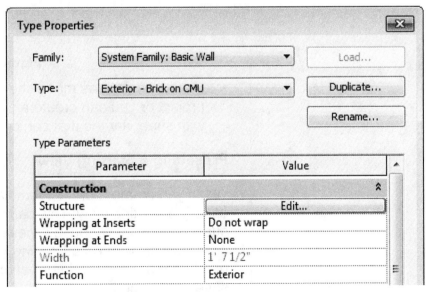

Figure 1–5

- System Families can also be added when a project is in process, but it helps to have company standards created in the template.

- Component Families, such as furniture, trees, beams, columns, mechanical equipment, and electrical devices can be loaded directly in a template file if there are types and sizes that are used frequently. Otherwise, they can be loaded from a library as the project progresses.

Views and Sheets

Additional items that you can setup in a template include Views and Sheets. You can place empty views on sheets that are going to be filled in as you proceed through a project. Views can be a few basic floor and/or ceiling plans for a residential project, as shown on the left in Figure 1–6, or a more complex mix of Mechanical, Electrical, and Plumbing categories as shown on the right in Figure 1–6

Figure 1–6

- You can create as many sheets as are typically used in a project or you can create a sheet schedule and populate it with sheet names that can be used as placeholder sheets.

Presetting a Starting View

When you create a project template or project, it can help to specify a starting view. This can be any of the standard views, such as plan, elevation, 3D view, or one that is specifically created. This is often a Drafting View (as shown in Figure 1–7), or a Legend View with information about the project or the cover sheet for the project.

Figure 1–7

How To: Set a Starting View

1. Set up the view or sheet that you want to use as the starting view.

2. In the *Manage* tab>Manage Project panel, click 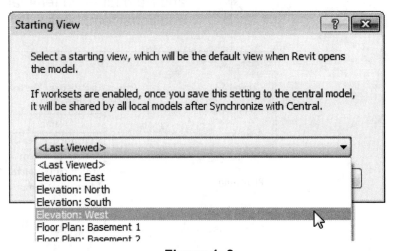 (Starting View).

3. In the Starting View dialog box, select the view or sheet that you want to use as shown in Figure 1–8.

Figure 1–8

4. Click OK .

5. Save the project or project template. The file opens to this view, when it is next opened.

Setting Default Template Files

If your company uses several different templates, you can create a list that displays in the New Project dialog box, as shown in Figure 1–9. The top five templates also display on the Recent Files page.

Figure 1–9

- To set the project template file list, in the Application Menu, click Options . In the Options dialog box, in the left pane, select **File Locations**, as shown in Figure 1–10. Specify the *Name* and *Path* for each template. Use ✛ (Add Value) to select additional templates.

Figure 1–10

- Use ↑E (Move Rows Up) and ↓E (Move Rows Down) to order the templates. Move the templates that are used most often to the top.

- If you do not require a template anymore, select it and click ▬ (Remove Value).

Specifying Units

Even though you select Imperial or Metric units when you create the project template, you can set up the Project Units with specific formats and options. For example, if you are working on a Civil project where everything is set up in feet, you specify **Decimal Feet** as the Length Format. For an international metric project, you can specify the length units as Meters, Centimeters, or Millimeters.

How To: Set Up Project Units

1. In the *Manage* tab>Settings panel, click (Project Units) or type **UN**.
2. In the Project Units dialog box, as shown on the left in Figure 1–11, in the *Format* column, click the button next to the unit type that you want to modify. The related Format dialog box opens, as shown on the right in Figure 1–11.

Figure 1–11

3. Set the *Units*, *Rounding*, and other options as needed.
4. In the Project Units dialog box, you can also select the *Discipline* (**Common** by default) and change the Unit format for each discipline. The other options are **Structural**, **HVAC**, **Electrical**, **Piping**, and **Energy**. The options vary according to the discipline-specific software in use.

5. Click OK to close each dialog box.

Format Options

Each unit has specific formatting options. The option is grayed out if it is not applicable to that unit type.

Units	Select the type of units in the Units drop-down list, as shown in Figure 1–12. **Figure 1–12**
Rounding	Specify how precisely you want the dimensions to be rounded. The options depend on the *Units* you selected.
Unit Symbol	If you are using metric units, you can select a unit symbol, such as **cm** for centimeters or **None**.
Suppress trailing 0's	(For decimal-based units) If selected, this option removes any trailing 0s. For example, it displays 1.5 instead of 1.50 if you are using two decimal places.
Suppress 0 feet	(Imperial Units only) If selected, this option removes the 0 in front of a dimension in inches only. For example, the dimension displays as 0'-4", rather than 4".
Use digit grouping	If selected, the unit uses the Decimal symbol/digit grouping specified in the Project Units dialog box, as shown in Figure 1–13. **Figure 1–13**
Suppress spaces	(Imperial Units only) If selected, this option removes the spaces between the feet and inches, so that a dimension reads 1'-2", rather than 1' - 2".

- The **Use project settings** and **Show + for positive values** options are grayed out when setting units for the project. This dialog box is used when creating dimension styles or specifying label formats when the options are available.

Snap Settings

The Snaps dialog box controls *Dimension Snaps,* which are the increments you see in temporary dimensions, and *Object Snaps*, which are the points on elements that you can select. In the

Manage tab>Settings panel, click (Snaps) to open the dialog box, as shown in Figure 1–14.

Figure 1–14

- Snap overrides are listed as keyboard shortcuts in parentheses, next to the corresponding snap. When a snap override is used, the cursor finds that specified snap type in your view until something is selected.

- Snap overrides can be used while inside a command by right-clicking and selecting **Snap Overrides** and then selecting the one that you want to use from the list.

Keyboard shortcuts, such as the ones listed here, are part of the User Interface and apply to all projects.

Temporary Dimension Settings

Temporary dimensions display when you draw or edit building elements in the software. By default, they measure from the center lines of walls to the center lines of openings, as shown in Figure 1–15.

Figure 1–15

- When you move a witness line to another element or part of an element, the location is remembered within the current session of program.

You can control where temporary dimensions are placed by default. In the *Manage* tab>Settings panel, expand ⚒ (Additional Settings) and click ⊢⊚ (Temporary Dimensions) to open the Temporary Dimension Properties dialog box, as shown in Figure 1–16.

Figure 1–16

- Temporary dimensions can be measured from the **Centerlines**, **Faces**, **Center of Core** or **Faces of Core** of walls and the **Centerlines** or **Openings** of doors and windows.

- You can set up these properties in the project template file or modify them at any time. They do not affect existing elements in your project.

- You can control the size of the temporary dimension text in the Options dialog box in the *Graphics* area.

1.2 Customizing Annotation Styles

 Learning Objectives

- Create standard text and dimension types for use in your project templates.
- Modify callout, elevation, and section tags and specify which tags are loaded.

You can customize Annotation styles in your project template file including dimensions, text types, and tags, as shown in Figure 1–17.

Figure 1–17

Text, Dimensions, and Arrowheads are all system families. This means they have a standard set of parameters, which you can modify and save as a type. Callout, Section, and Elevation tags can be modified within the Autodesk Revit software. Most other tags are created using families.

Creating Text Types

Text types are used to standardize text formatting (such as the font, text height, etc.), as shown in Figure 1–18. They can be created for to both annotative text and Model Text.

A FANCY FONT AT 1/4"

A HAND LETTERING FONT AT 1/8"

A HAND LETTERING FONT AT 3/32"

Figure 1–18

- The **Text** command places text at the height you need for the final plot. The view scale controls the height of the standard text in the views.

- The **Model Text** command places text that is typically used on the building, such as the signage shown in Figure 1–19. Text types for Model Text should be the full height of the text and are not affected by the view scale.

Figure 1–19

How To: Create a Text Type

1. Start the **Text** command. In Properties, click ⊞ (Edit Type) or in the *Annotate* tab>Text panel title, click ⌄ (Text Types). For **Model Text** you first have to place an instance, select it, and modify the type properties.

2. In the Type Properties dialog box, click [Duplicate...].

3. Type a new name and click [OK].The new type is activated.

4. Modify the parameters as needed for the new type, as shown for annotation text in Figure 1–20.

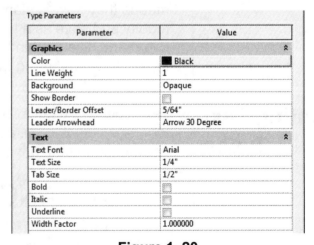

Figure 1–20

5. Click [OK] to finish.

Dimensions

Dimensions are one of the more complex system families in terms of the number of parameters you can modify. You can create types for each dimension method.

How To: Create Dimension Types

1. In the *Annotate* tab>Dimension panel, expand the Dimension panel title (as shown in Figure 1–21), and click ⚒ next to the dimension type you want to create.

Figure 1–21

2. In the Type Properties dialog box, click [Duplicate...].

3. Type a new name and click [OK]. The new type is activated.

4. Modify the parameters as needed for the new type.

5. Click [OK] when you are finished.

Dimension Type Options

The dimension type parameters include the *Graphics* of the dimension (such as **Tick Mark** and **Line Weight**), as shown in Figure 1–22, for Linear dimensions, and the *Text* formatting (scroll down in the Type Parameter dialog box to view).

Values for parameters (such as text size, witness line extension, etc.) are the actual plot size for these elements. The view scale controls how large they are in the specific view.

Figure 1–22

- For Linear dimensions, you can specify a *Leader Type, Shoulder Length, Leader Tick Mark, and Show Leader When Text Moves* that is used when the text is pulled away from the dimension string. You can also specify the text inserted for **Equality Text** (the default is still EQ).

- You can specify a *Text Background* option. If you set the value to **opaque**, it automatically masks any elements behind the text. If it is set to **transparent**, anything the text overlaps is still visible.

- If you are dimensioning doors and windows by their widths rather than their centers, you can also have the opening height displayed with the dimension. Select the **Show Opening Height** option.

Arrowheads

A variety of arrowhead types are supplied with the Autodesk Revit software, including open and filled arrow styles, tick marks, and dots. You can also create custom styles by duplicating an existing style and defining the parameters, such as the *Arrow Style* shown in Figure 1–23. In the *Manage* tab>Settings panel, expand ✐ (Additional Settings) and click ⇄ (Arrowheads) to open the dialog box.

Type Parameters	
Parameter	Value
Graphics	☆
Arrow Style	Arrow
Fill Tick	☐
Arrow Width Angle	30.000°
Tick Size	1/8"
Heavy End Pen Weight	7

Figure 1–23

- Arrowheads are used by both text (with a leader) and dimensions.

- The MEP templates include loop leaders that can be set as *Tick Mark* for dimensions and *Leader Arrowhead* for text, as shown in Figure 1–24. You can also create an Arrow Style using Loop in the Arrowhead settings.

ALL-THREAD WITH ISOLATORS

Figure 1–24

Callout, Elevation, and Section Tags

Callout, Elevation, and Section tags can be modified to suit an office standard. Using these tags is frequently a two-step process. Set up the tag itself and then associate it with a related command.

How To: Create Callout, Elevation, and Section Tags

1. In the *Manage* tab>Settings panel, expand 🔧 (Additional Settings) and click ⌖ (Callout Tags), ⌂ (Elevation Tags), or ⌀ (Section Tags).

2. In the Type Properties dialog box, click [Duplicate...].

3. Type a new name and click [OK]. The new type is activated in Type Properties.

4. Modify the parameters as needed for the new type. In the example of an Elevation Tag shown in Figure 1–25, a new type was created and a new Elevation Mark was selected.

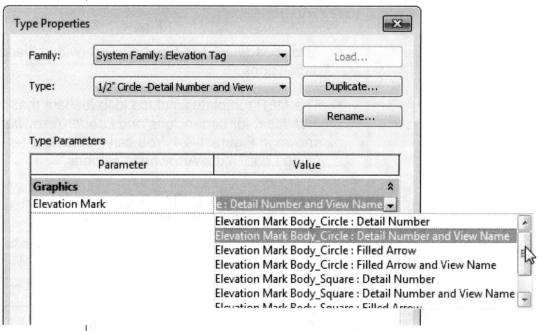

Figure 1–25

5. Click [OK] when finished.

6. Click ⌖ (Callout), ⌂ (Elevation), or ⌀ (Section) as required.

7. In Properties, click ⊞ (Edit Type).

8. In the Type Properties dialog box, duplicate and name the new view type.

9. Specify the related tag(s) values. When you select the value click ⎣…⎦ (Browse). This opens the Type Properties for the tag in which you can select a different type, as shown in Figure 1–26. (You can also create tag types in this dialog box.)

Figure 1–26

10. Click ⎣ OK ⎦ to apply the tag type.

11. Modify the other parameters as needed and click ⎣ OK ⎦ to close the Type Properties dialog box and continue using the command.

Type Specific Tag Parameters

The **Callout Tags** parameters specify a *Callout Head* and the *Corner Radius* of the callout box, as shown in Figure 1–27.

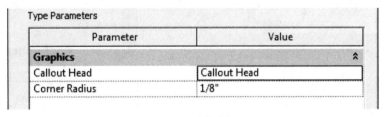

Figure 1–27

The **Elevation Tags** parameter is the *Elevation Mark*. You can select from a variety of types that come with the Autodesk Revit software, as shown in Figure 1–28. For example, you might want to set the exterior elevation mark to display a square body and the detail number on the sheet where it is placed.

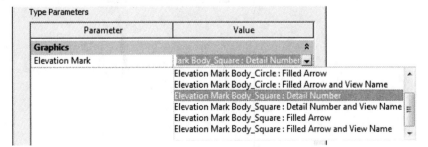

Figure 1–28

The **Section Tags** parameters include both the *Section Head* and *Section Tail*, as well as the *Broken Section Display Style*, as shown in Figure 1–29.

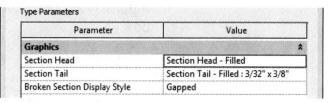

Type Parameters	
Parameter	Value
Graphics	☆
Section Head	Section Head - Filled
Section Tail	Section Tail - Filled : 3/32" x 3/8"
Broken Section Display Style	Gapped

Figure 1–29

Loaded Tags

You can load tags, such as door, window, and wall tags (as shown in Figure 1–30), from the libraries that are included with the software in the *Annotations* folder, or from a specified network drive, into a project template. Having the specific tags required for your projects increases adherence to company standards.

Figure 1–30

Tags are created as separate family files (RFA) and stored in the assigned library (frequently on a network drive). In the Loaded Tags and Symbols dialog box (shown in Figure 1–31), you can easily load the tags you need from the Library into the project template Therefore, when you start the **Tag** command, the one you need is available.

Figure 1–31

- Some elements, such as Floors and Structural Fabric Reinforcement, have both tags and symbols. They can both be specified in this dialog box.

How To: Specify Loaded Tags

1. In the *Annotate* tab>Tag panel, expand the panel title and click 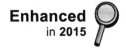 (Loaded Tags).
2. In the Tags dialog box, Use the *Filter* field to limit the types of tags you are looking for by discipline.
3. Click Load Family... .
4. In the Load Family dialog box, navigate to the appropriate library and folder.
5. Select the required tags and click Open . Hold down <Ctrl> or <Shift> to select multiple tags.
6. When you have loaded all of the tags that you typically need for a project, click OK .

Practice 1a

Prepare Templates - All Disciplines

 Learning Objectives

- Create a new project template file and specify the units and levels.
- Setup text and dimension types and load tags.

Estimated time for completion: 15 minutes

In this practice you will create a new project template file, modify the units, snaps, temporary dimensions, and add several new levels. You will create several text types, add a dimension style that uses arrows (as shown in Figure 1–32), and load typical tags into the project template file.

1/8" Arial   *1/8" Hand*

3/32" Arial   *3/32" Hand*

1/4" Title

Figure 1–32

Task 1 - Establish a project template file.

1. In the Application Menu, expand ☐ (New) and click ⬚ (Project).

2. In the New Project dialog box, select an existing template file and Project template and click [OK].

3. In the Quick Access Toolbar, click 🖫 (Save) and save the template in your class directory as **Midrise-Template.rte**.

4. In the *Manage* tab>Settings panel, click 📟 (Project Units) or type **UN**.

5. In the Project Units dialog box, set the *Length* formats as follows:

Length:

Units	Feet and Fractional Inches
Rounding	To the nearest 1/16"
Suppress 0 feet	Check

Angle:

Rounding	0 decimal places

6. Click [OK] to close the Units dialog box.

7. Set the Snaps and Temporary Dimensions as needed.

8. Open an elevation view.

9. Change Level 2 to **16'-0"**. Add three more levels above the current levels at **12'-0"** apart. Add two levels below Level 1 and set them **10'-0"** apart. Rename them as **Basement 1** and **Basement 2**, as shown in Figure 1–33.

Figure 1–33

- If you draw the levels using ⊕ (Level), you can select the **Make Plan View** option in the Options Bar to create the associated views.

- If you copy the existing levels, you need to create the plan views and ceiling plan views. In the *View* tab>Create panel, expand ▧ (Plan Views) and click ▢ (Floor Plan), ▤ (Structural Plan), and/or ▦ (Reflected Ceiling Plan).

- **MEP only:** Rename above ground levels and corresponding views to match the other levels in the HVAC sub-discipline (3 - Mech, 4 - Mech, etc) and expand the ??? node and select all of the new ceiling plans. In Properties, change the *Sub-Discipline* to **HVAC**.

10. Switch back to the original plan view and save the project template.

Task 2 - Preset annotation types.

1. Create the following text types:

1/8" Arial	Use the default, but set the *Height* to **1/8"**.
1/8" Hand	Use a hand-lettering *Font*, such as **Comic Sans MS**, and select *Italic*.
3/32" Hand	Same as above with a *Height* of **3/32"**.
1/4" Title	Use the font of your choice, in bold.
1" Title	Duplicate **1/4" Title** and change the *Height* to **1"**

2. Create or modify a Linear Dimension type and change the Units Format *Rounding* to the **nearest 1/8"**. Modify the angular dimension type to use arrowheads. Modify other parameters if required. You can create an additional arrow type if time permits.

3. Load the following tags from the Revit Library into the discipline-specific project template:

Architecture:

Folder	Tag Name
Architectural	Casework, furniture, and furniture systems
Civil	Parking and planting

MEP:

Folder	Tag Name
Fire Protection	Sprinkler
Electrical	Lighting fixture and panel name

Structure:

Folder	Tag Name
Architectural	Wall and Floor
Structural	Select any different Structural tags you might want to use in place of those already loaded.

4. Save the project template.

1.3 Creating Title Blocks

Learning Objectives

- Create title blocks including detail lines, text, labels, symbols, regions, and revision schedules.
- Create sheets and sheet list schedules.
- Specify a starting view for the project.

Title blocks contain information about the company and consultants designing the project, project information, and sheet-specific information, as shown in Figure 1–34. This information might include but is not limited to the following: the project name, address, number, sheet number, revisions, and other parameters. Some of these parameters never change, some are project-specific, and some are sheet-specific.

Labels and Revision Schedules are specifically used in title blocks.

Figure 1–34

- Create the title block by sketching detail lines and adding text, symbols, and regions, as well as image files for company logos. The variable information is stored in labels.

How To: Create a Title Block

1. In the Application Menu, expand ⬚ (New) and click ⬚ (Title Block).

2. In the New Title Block - Select Template File dialog box, select a template file size from the list and click [Open]. A new family file opens and the Family tools display in the Ribbon, as shown in Figure 1–35.

You can select from several preset sizes or create a custom size.

Figure 1–35

- If you select a template with a standard size, a rectangle of that size displays in the view.

- If you select **New Size**, a rectangle with dimensions displays. Edit the dimensions to modify the size.

3. Add lines, filled regions, symbols, text, labels, etc., as needed.

4. Save the file and close it.

- You can use dimensions to help place the elements in the title block family, they are not displayed when the title block is inserted.

Adding Labels

Labels are not just text but elements that are assigned to specific parameters and can be added to title blocks or tags. They can change without modifying the rest of the elements. For example, you would use annotation text for the words **Drawn By:** and a label for the initials of the person who did the work (by default displaying DRW in Figure 1–36), because that varies from sheet to sheet.

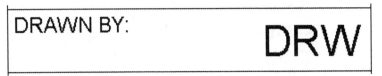

DRAWN BY: DRW

Figure 1–36

- The title block template comes with one text type and one label type already defined. You can create additional types in Properties by duplicating types. The **Text** and **Label** parameters are similar, but you must create separate types for each of them.

How To: Create a Label

1. In the Family Editor, in the *Create* tab>Text panel, click (Label).

2. In the *Modify | Place Label* tab>Format panel, specify the alignments: **Left**, **Center**, **Right**, **Top**, **Center Middle**, or **Bottom**, as shown in Figure 1–37.

Figure 1–37

3. Click in the view window to place the label, as shown in Figure 1–38.

Figure 1–38

4. In the Edit Label dialog box shown in Figure 1–39, select a label in the *Category Parameters* list and double-click or click (Add parameter(s) to label). You can select more than one by holding down <Ctrl> or <Shift>.

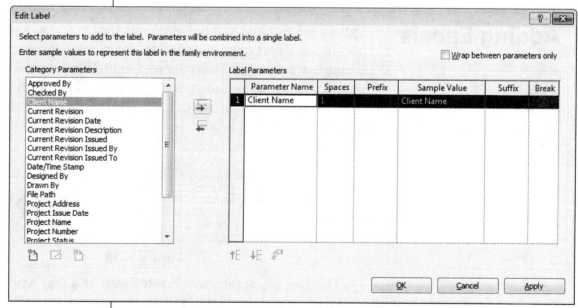

Figure 1–39

5. Enter the *Sample Value* and specify any other options as needed.

- If you are using several parameters in one label, select **Wrap between parameters only** and **Break** (in column) options to separate them while still permitting a word wrap.

- Click (Add Parameter) to create a new parameter for the project.

- Click ⬆E (Move parameter up) and ⬇E (Move parameter down) to reorder multiple parameters.

- If you select a numerical parameter, click ⚲ (Edit parameter's units format) to change, if necessary.

6. Click [OK] when you have finished editing the label.
7. While still placing the label, rotate or stretch it as needed (as shown in Figure 1–40), or select a point for an additional label.

•DRW ↻
•

Figure 1–40

8. Click ↖ (Modify) or press <Esc*-++*-**-+66> twice to finish the command.

- You can also rotate or stretch a label once it has been placed in the title block.

Adding Revision Schedules

A table of revisions included in a project and/or sheet is typically added to a company title block, as shown in Figure 1–41. In the Autodesk Revit software, you can create a Revision Schedule that is then linked to the Revision Table in the project.

No.	Description	Date

Figure 1–41

How To: Add Revision Schedules to Title Blocks

1. In the Family Editor, in the *View* tab>Create panel, click
   (Revision Schedule).
2. In the Revision Properties dialog box, select the fields you want to use. Several are already selected for you, as shown in Figure 1–42.

Figure 1–42

3. Modify the options in the *Sorting/Grouping* and *Formatting* tabs as needed.
4. In the *Appearance* tab, select how you want to build the schedule: from the **Top-down** or **Bottom-up**. You can also set the *Height* to **Variable** or **User-Defined**.

5. Click ⌐ OK ¬. The schedule view displays.
6. In the Project Browser, open the Sheet view (it has no name).

7. Drag and drop the schedule onto the sheet and modify the controls, as shown in Figure 1–43.

*If the height is set to **User-Defined**, an additional control is displayed at the bottom of the schedule. Use it to set the height of the schedule.*

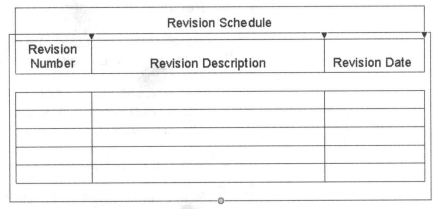

Figure 1–43

- In the Options Bar, you can change the *Rotation on the Sheet* to **None**, **90° Clockwise**, or **90° Counterclockwise**.

Adding Sheets to Project Templates

You can set up project templates using the custom title block in two ways. Add all or most of the sheets typically needed for a project, or create a Sheet List Schedule that can be used to automatically create sheets when they are needed.

In most cases, it is best to create sheets that are always used in projects in the template and even put typical views on them, as shown in Figure 1–44. Note that the view is empty in the template, but as you draw elements in the project they automatically display in the view and on the sheet.

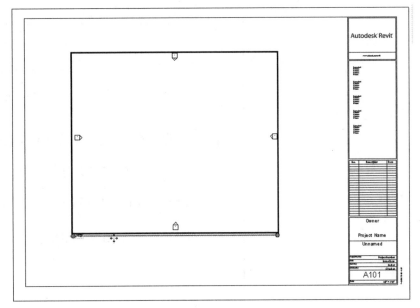

Figure 1–44

How To: Load a Title Block into a Project Template

1. Open the project template.
2. Return to the custom title block family. In the Family Editor panel, click 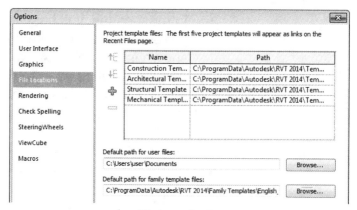 (Load into Project).
3. In the Load into Projects dialog box, select the project you want the title block loaded into and click [OK]. If only one project is open, it is loaded into the project automatically.
4. The title block is now available when you create a sheet.

- If the title block family is not open, select *Insert* tab>Load from Library panel and click (Load Family) to access it, or click [Load...] in the New Sheet dialog box.

- When you save a title block, it should be on the network where everyone has access to it. That way, it is not deleted if someone reinstalls the Autodesk Revit software. Set the default location for the family template files in the Options dialog box, in the *File Locations* tab, as shown in Figure 1–45.

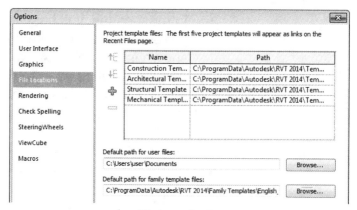

Figure 1–45

How To: Create a Sheet List Schedule

1. Open a project template file (or a project).

2. In the *View* tab>Create panel, expand (Schedules) and click (Sheet List).

3. In the Sheet List Properties dialog box, in the *Fields* tab, select the **Sheet Number** and **Sheet Name** and add them to the *Scheduled fields* list as shown in Figure 1–46.

Figure 1–46

4. Depending on the complexity of your sheet naming scheme, you can also modify items on the *Filter* and *Sorting/Grouping* tabs.

5. Click OK when you are finished.

6. You are placed in the schedule view with the two parameters displayed. Stretch out the columns as shown in Figure 1–47.

If sheets are already in the project, they display here.

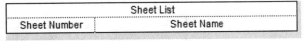

Figure 1–47

7. In the *Modify Schedule/Quantities* tab>Rows panel, expand

(Insert) and click (Data Row) as shown in Figure 1–48.

Figure 1–48

Sheet lists are often used by architects to display all of the sheets in a building project including consultant sheets that are not in the Autodesk Revit project file. In that case, they would only be in the Sheet List schedule and not created as actual sheets.

8. A new row is added below the schedule names. If no sheets are in the project, it comes in automatically as **A101** and **Unnamed**.

9. Add as many rows as you have sheets. If you are using a numbering scheme such as A1xx for site plans, A2xx for Floor Plans, A3xx for Detail plans, etc., then you should rename the sheet number for the first row of a set before creating more rows so that they increment automatically.

10. Enter the name of each sheet. Once you have added a new name, it is available in the drop-down list, as shown in Figure 1–49.

Figure 1–49

How To: Use Sheet List Tables

1. Create a new sheet. In the Sheet List Schedule view, in the *Modify Schedule/Quantities* tab>Create panel, click (New Sheet), You can also access the command on the *View* tab or right-click on *Sheets* in the Project Browser.

2. In the New Sheet dialog box, select the placeholder sheets you want to use, as shown in Figure 1–50. To select more than one, hold down <Ctrl> or <Shift> as you select.

Figure 1–50

3. Click [OK]. The new sheets are created in the project.

• This sheet list is available in all projects based on the project template where it was created.

• You can import the sheet list schedule into another project, but it does not import the associated sheets. That is because they are part of the project, not the schedule view.

Practice 1b

Create Title Blocks - All Disciplines

 Learning Objectives

- Draw a custom title block including detail lines, text, labels, and a revision table.
- Setup sheets in the template using the new title block and create a sheet list.

Estimated time for completion: 15 minutes

In this practice you will create a new title block by adding lines, text, labels, logo, and a Revision Schedule similar to Figure 1–51. You will then load it into a project template file and create several standard sheets as well as a Sheet List Schedule.

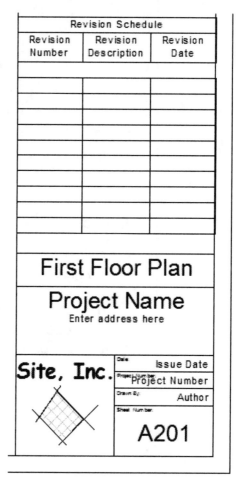

Figure 1–51

Task 1 - Create a title block.

1. In the Application Menu, expand ⬜ (New) and click ⬓ (Title Block).

2. In the New Title Block - Select Template File dialog box, select **D - 36 x24.rft** and click [Open] .

3. In the *Create* tab>Detail panel, click ⌐ (Line) and create lines on the inside of the existing rectangle **1/4"** away from the top, bottom, and right sides. Draw a line **1"** away on the left margin. Trim the lines as needed.

4. Draw lines in the lower right corner of the title block, as shown in Figure 1–52.

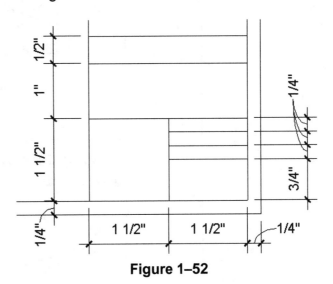

Figure 1–52

5. In the *Create* tab>Text panel, click **A** (Text).

6. In Properties, click ▦ (Edit Type) and create the following Text types:

Type Name	Font	Size	Bold	Background
Arial 1/16"	Arial	1/16"	No	Transparent
Title	Comic SansMS	1"	Yes	Transparent
Logo	Your choice	1/4"	Yes	Transparent

7. In the *Create* tab>Text panel, click ... (Label).

8. In Properties, click (Edit Type) and create the following Label types:

Type Name	Font	Size	Bold	Background
Arial 1/8"	Arial	1/8"	No	Transparent
Arial 1/4"	Arial	1/4"	No	Transparent

9. Create a graphic and company name of your own design in the lower left box, for example Jepson+Johnson Architects. as shown in Figure 1–53. Using the following steps, add text, labels, and graphics to the title block.

Figure 1–53

- Use **A** (Text) with the *text type* **Arial 1/16"** to add text in the lower right spaces for the *Date*, *Project Number*, *Drawn By*, and *Sheet Number*.

- Use (Label) with the *label type* **Arial 1/4"** and (Align Center) justification to add the *Sheet Name*, *Project Name*, and *Sheet Number*. Move and stretch the labels to fit in the title block.

- Using the *label type* **Arial 1/8"** and ≣ (Align Center) justification, add the *Project Address* below the *Project Name*.

- Using the *label type* **Arial 1/8"** and ≣ (Align Right) justification, add the *Project Issue Date*, *Project Number*, and *Drawn By*.

- Add the **Logo** text in the box on the lower left side, shown as Site, Inc. in the title block. Draw lines and add a filled region for a graphic logo as needed.

10. Save the title block in your class directory with the name **TBLK-D.rfa**.

Task 2 - Add a Revision Schedule.

1. In the title block Family Editor, in the *View* tab>Create panel, click (Revision Schedule).

2. In the Revision Properties dialog box, *Fields* tab, set up the fields as shown in Figure 1–54.

Figure 1–54

3. Accept the defaults for the *Sorting/Grouping* and *Formatting* tabs.

4. Select the *Appearance* tab and change the *Height* to **User defined**.

5. Click OK.

6. In the Project Browser, expand *Views (all)* to display the *Schedules* and *Sheets (all)* areas, as shown in Figure 1–55. In the *Sheets (all)* area, open the - view.

Figure 1–55

7. Drag and drop the Revision Schedule onto the sheet.

8. Move it above the sheet name and resize it to display several lines, as shown in Figure 1–56.

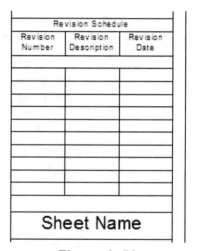

Figure 1–56

9. Save and close the title block.

Task 3 - Set up sheets in a project template using the new title block.

---

1. Open the project template **Midrise-Template.rte** that you created in the previous practice. If you did not complete the previous practice, open the template found in your class files folder:

   • /Architectural/**Midrise-Template-A.rte**

   • /MEP/**Midrise-Template-MEP.rte**

   • /Structural/**Midrise-Template-S.rte**

2. In the *View* tab>Sheet Composition panel, click ⬚ (Sheet).

3. In the New Sheet dialog box, click [Load...].

4. In the Load Family dialog box, navigate to your class files folder, select **TBLK-D.rfa** (that you just created), and click [Open]. If you did not complete the previous task, open the title block found in your class files folder:

   - /Architectural/**TBLK-D-A.rfa**
   - /MEP/**TBLK-D-MEP.rfa**
   - /Structural/**TBLK-D-S.rfa**

5. Select the title block that you just loaded and click [OK].

6. In the Project Browser, select the sheet and rename it as **CS000 – Cover Sheet**.

7. Using the **Title** text type, add placeholder text for the project name and address, as shown in Figure 1–57.

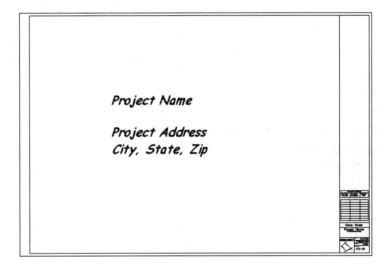

Figure 1–57

8. In the *Manage* tab>Manage Project panel, click ⬚ (Starting View).

9. In the Starting View dialog box, select **Sheet: CS000 - Cover Sheet** as shown in Figure 1–58.

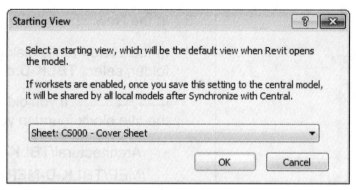

Figure 1–58

10. Create another sheet with the new title block and name it according to your discipline:

*   **A201 – First Floor Plan**
*   **M201 - First Floor Plan Mechanical**
*   **E201 - First Floor Plan Electrical**
*   **P201 - First Floor Plan Plumbing**
*   **S201 - First Floor Plan Structural**

11. Open this sheet view. Drag the associated **Level 1** floor plan view onto the sheet, as shown in Figure 1–59.

Figure 1–59

No elements are on the view, but it acts as a placeholder on the sheet. Elements are displayed as they are drawn.

Task 4 - Create a Sheet List.

1. In the *View* tab>Create panel, expand 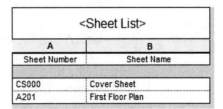 (Schedules) and

   click ▢ (Sheet List).

2. In the Sheet List Properties dialog box, in the *Fields* tab, select the **Sheet Number** and **Sheet Name** and add them to the *Scheduled fields* list, as shown in Figure 1–60.

Figure 1–60

3. Click ▢ OK ▢.

4. The Sheet List schedule opens with the two existing sheets listed. Stretch out the columns, as shown for an architectural project in Figure 1–61.

<Sheet List>	
A	**B**
Sheet Number	Sheet Name
CS000	Cover Sheet
A201	First Floor Plan

Figure 1–61

5. In the *Modify Schedule/Quantities* tab>Rows panel, expand

   ⊐ᵗᴇ (Insert) and click ▦ (Data Row).

6. Add floor plans to match the levels, as shown for an architectural project in Figure 1–62.

<Sheet List>	
A	**B**
Sheet Number	Sheet Name
CS000	Cover Sheet
A201	First Floor Plan
A202	Second Floor Plan
A203	Third Floor Plan
A204	Fouth Floor Plan
A205	Fifth Floor Plan
A206	Sixth Floor Plan

Figure 1–62

7. In the *Modify Schedule/Quantities* tab>Create panel, click 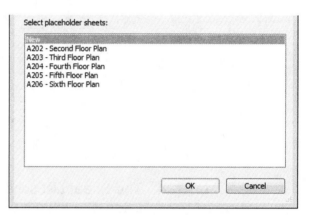 (New Sheet). The list displays the plans you added to the Sheet List display, but the sheets already in the project do not, as shown in Figure 1–63.

Select placeholder sheets:

New
A202 - Second Floor Plan
A203 - Third Floor Plan
A204 - Fourth Floor Plan
A205 - Fifth Floor Plan
A206 - Sixth Floor Plan

OK   Cancel

Figure 1–63

8. Close the dialog box.

9. Open the Cover Sheet.

10. Drag and drop the Sheet List schedule, as shown in Figure 1–64, onto the sheet.

Sheet List	
Sheet Number	Sheet Name
A101	Site Plan
A201	1st Floor Plan
A202	2nd Floor Plan
A203	3rd Floor Plan
A204	4th Floor Plan
A205	5th Floor Plan
C000	Cover Sheet

Figure 1–64

11. Add another sheet or two that are not on the sheet list.

12. Return to the Cover Sheet. The new sheets are added to the sheet list as shown in Figure 1–65.

Sheet List	
Sheet Number	Sheet Name
A101	Site Plan
A201	1st Floor Plan
A202	2nd Floor Plan
A203	3rd Floor Plan
A204	4th Floor Plan
A205	5th Floor Plan
C000	Cover Sheet
S201	Structural Plan
M202	Mechanical Plan

Figure 1–65

13. If time permits, create additional sheets for various other views.

14. Save the project template.

1.4 View Templates

 Learning Objectives

- Apply and set view templates to views.
- Create view templates.
- Setup Visibility/Graphic override filters for various categories of elements.

View templates enable you to specify all of the view properties and visibility options for a view by selecting another view or a view template as a base. For example, you can create a furniture plan view template that sets the scale, detail level, and visibility of objects so that everything except the furniture displays in halftone, as shown in Figure 1–66.

Figure 1–66

View templates can be applied to specific views when you create a project template file and as you work in a project. You can also specify a view template in view properties that restricts you from making changes, such as the Detail Level shown in Figure 1–67. This is useful for views that have been setup for printing.

Figure 1–67

Applying View Templates

There are two typical ways to use view templates. The first is while you are working to display different view parameters in the same view. For example, you might want to display the spaces in a section and use a view template to switch to the mechanical layout in the same section, as shown in Figure 1–68. You can continue to make changes to the views even after the view template has been applied. The other way is to preset a view using a default view template so you cannot make changes to it.

Figure 1–68

How To: Apply a Temporary View Template Override

1. Select one or more views in the Project Browser. (Hold down <Ctrl> or <Shift> to select multiple views.)
2. Right-click in the Project Browser and select **Apply Template Properties**, or on the *View* tab>Graphics panel, expand

   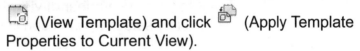 (View Template) and click (Apply Template Properties to Current View).

3. In the Apply View Template dialog box, select the view template you want to use from the *Names* list, as shown in Figure 1–69. Several standard view templates are available when you create a project using one of the Autodesk Revit project templates.

Figure 1–69

4. If you do not want the entire view template to be applied to the selected view, clear the check mark in the *Include* column for the parameters you do not want to include. You can also create overrides to the view template by changing parameter values.

5. Click [OK] to finish.

• To limit the number of view templates that display, filter the list by selecting an option in the Discipline filter and View type filter drop-down lists, as shown in Figure 1–70.

Figure 1–70

- You can apply view templates to any view as many times as needed only if it is not set as the default template in the view properties.

- If you want to start a new view template based on an existing view, select **Show Views**. The *Names* list expands to include all of the related views in the project.

How To: Set the Default View Template for a View

1. Select one or more views in the Project Browser. (Hold down <Ctrl> or <Shift> to select multiple views.)
2. In Properties, in the *Identity Data* section, click the button next to *View Template*, as shown in Figure 1–71. The name on the button varies according to any template that has already been applied.

Figure 1–71

3. In the Apply View Template dialog box, select the appropriate template and click OK.
4. The view is now locked using the parameters setup in the view template.

- View Templates can also be set by the type properties of a view. For example, in a view's Type Properties, duplicate a view type, such as Space Plan shown in Figure 1–72. Apply the appropriate template and select **New views are dependent on template**.

Figure 1–72

- When you use the View type, the view modifies to match the view template and is also placed in its own group in the Project Browser, as shown in Figure 1–73.

Figure 1–73

Creating View Templates

Many view templates come with the Autodesk Revit software, but you might need to create your own custom view types that are best applied by view template. You can create a view template from the view settings in an existing view or through the View Template dialog box.

How To: Create a View Template from an Existing View

1. Set up a view the way you want it with *Scale*, *Detail Level*, *Visibility Graphic Overrides*, and other *View Settings*.
2. In the Project Browser, right-click on the view and select **Create View Template from View** or, on the *View* tab> Graphics panel, expand ⬛ (View Template) and click ⬛ (Create Template from Current View).
3. In the New View Template dialog box, type a name for the view template.
4. Click ⬛ OK .
5. In the View Template dialog box, make other adjustments as needed and click ⬛ OK .

How To: Create a View Template

1. In the *View* tab>Graphics panel, expand ⬛ (View Template) and click ⬛ (Manage View Templates).
2. In the Apply View Template dialog box, in the *Names* list, select a view similar to the one you want to create and click ⬛ (Duplicate).

3. In the New View Template dialog box, type a new name for the view template and click OK .

4. Select the new view template as shown in Figure 1–74, and modify the View Properties parameter values as needed.

Figure 1–74

5. Click OK to finish.

• Not all view types have the same view parameters. For example, 3D views have options for Rendering and Perspectives that plans do not have. When you apply a view template across view types, only the options that are mutual are updated.

• The only parameter saved to a view template for schedule views is the appearance of the schedule.

Hint: Setting the View Scale-to-detail Level Correspondence

One of the parameters in views is the *Detail Level*. There are three options: **Coarse**, **Medium**, and **Fine**. You can modify the table of scales that are related to the levels. In the *Manage* tab>

Settings panel, expand 🔧 (Additional Settings) and select **Detail Level**. The View scale-to-detail level correspondence dialog box opens, as shown in Figure 1–75.

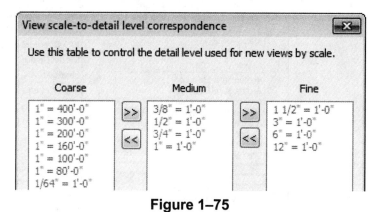

Figure 1–75

Visibility/ Graphic Overrides Filters

Visibility/Graphic Overrides filters can speed up the process of specifying categories that are modified in View Templates. You might want to display certain elements in halftone, or with a different color or lineweight in specific views. For example, a fire evacuation plan might have walls with different fire ratings that display with thicker lineweights, as shown in Figure 1–76. By creating these filters and then applying them in a view template, you can reuse them without having to recreate them each time.

Figure 1–76

How To: Create Filters

1. In the *View* tab>Graphics panel, click (Filters). The Filters dialog box opens as shown in Figure 1–77.

Figure 1–77

2. In the *Filters* area, click ⬆ (New) or ⬆ (Duplicate). Name the new filter and click ⟦ OK ⟧ .

3. In the *Categories* area, filter the list by discipline and then select the categories to include in the filter. Use ⟦ Check All ⟧ and ⟦ Check None ⟧ to help select the categories.

4. In the *Filter Rules* area, select what you what to *Filter by*, the filter operator(s), and the value for the filter. If more than one category is selected, the *Filter by* list is limited to parameters shared by the categories you selected. You can create more than one filter rule. They are applied in order. Set *Filter by* to **None** if you do not want to filter by parameters. Filter operators are shown in Figure 1–78.

Figure 1–78

5. Click ⟦ Apply ⟧ to save the changes and remain in the dialog box, or click ⟦ OK ⟧ to finish.

How To: Apply Visibility/Graphic Overrides Filters

1. Type **VG** or **VV** or in the *View* tab>Graphics panel, click

   (Visibility/Graphics) to open the Visibility/Graphic Overrides dialog box. Select the *Filters* tab, as shown in Figure 1–79.

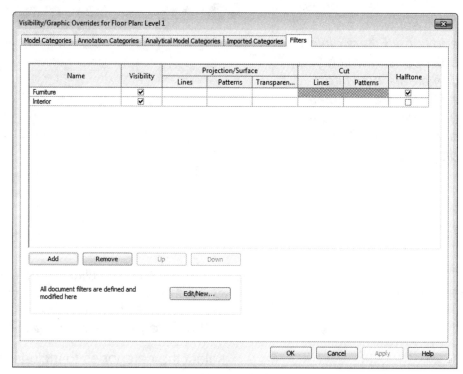

Figure 1–79

2. Click [Add] to add a filter to the list.
3. In the Add Filters dialog box, select the filter(s) you want to

   add and click [OK].

   - If the filter you want is not defined, click [Edit/New...] to open the Filters dialog box, where you can define a new filter or edit an existing one.

4. In the Visibility/Graphic Overrides dialog box, assign the overrides you want for the filter. For example, you might want items to be **Halftone**, as shown in Figure 1–80.

Name	Visibility	Projection/Surface			Cut		Halftone
		Lines	Patterns	Transparen...	Lines	Patterns	
Furniture	✔						✔
Interior	✔						☐

Figure 1–80

5. Click [OK].

Practice 1c

View Templates for Architectural and Structural Projects

 Learning Objectives

- Create visibility filters.
- Create a view template and apply it to several views.

Estimated time for completion: 15 minutes

In this practice you will create filters that you will use in a structural view template, and apply the view template to several structural plan views, as shown in Figure 1–81. When the filter is working correctly you can add the same information to a project template file.

Figure 1–81

Task 1 - Create filters.

1. Open the project found in your class files folder:

   - /Architectural/**Office-A.rvt**
   - /Structural/**Office-S.rvt**

2. In the *View* tab>Graphics panel, click ⬚ (Filters).

In the non-discipline specific Autodesk Revit software, an additional Filters dialog box opens.

Click [New...] *and name the new filter. Select* **Define Criteria** *and click* [OK]. *This opens the full Filters dialog box.*

3. In the Filters dialog box, click ⬚ (New), name the new filter **All But Structural**, and click [OK].

4. In the *Categories* area, set the *Filter list* to **Architecture** and **Structure**.

5. Click [Check All], and clear **Columns**, all categories starting with **Analytical**, **Structural**, and **Walls**. Click [Apply].

6. Click ⬚ (New). Name the new filter **Non-Structural Walls** and click [OK].

7. In the *Categories* area, click ⬚Check None⬚ and select **Walls**.

8. In the *Filter Rules* area, set *Filter by* to **Structural Usage**, **equals**, and **Non-bearing**, as shown in Figure 1–82.

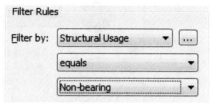

Figure 1–82

9. Click ⬚ OK ⬚ to close the Filters dialog box.

Task 2 - Create a View Template.

1. In the Project Browser, in the Floor Plans area, right-click on the **Level 1** view and select **Create View Template From View**.

2. Name the new view template **Structural Plan** and click ⬚ OK ⬚.

3. In the View Templates dialog box, set the *View Scale* to **1/16"=1'-0"** and the *Detail Level* to **Coarse**.

4. Next to **V/G Override Filters**, click ⬚ Edit... ⬚ The Visibility/Graphic Overrides dialog box opens with the *Filter* tab selected.

5. Click ⬚ Add ⬚.

6. In the Add Filters dialog box, select the two filters you just created and click ⬚ OK ⬚.

7. Place a check mark in the *Halftone* column for both filters. Continue working in the Visibility/Graphics Overrides dialog box.

8. In the *Annotation Categories* tab, turn off everything except Grids and all Structural annotations and tags.

9. In the *Model Categories* tab, turn off items, such as **Casework**, **Furniture**, **Furniture Systems** and **Plumbing**, and **Mechanical equipment**.

10. Click [OK] to close the Visibility/Graphic Overrides dialog box, and click [OK] to complete the view template.

Task 3 - Apply a View Template to several views.

1. In the *Floor Plans* area, use *Duplicate with Detailing* on the **Level 1**, **Level 2**, **Level 3**, and **Level 4** views. Rename them as **Level 1 - Structural**, **Level 2 - Structural**, **Level 3 - Structural**, and **Level 4 - Structural**.

2. Select the new Structural views.

3. Right-click and select **Apply View Template**.

4. In the Apply View Template dialog box, select the **Structural Plan** view template you just created and click [OK] to apply it.

5. Look at the different views and compare them to the standard floor plan views. Finish with the **Level 1** view.

6. Save the project.

Practice 1d

Estimated time for completion: 15 minutes

View Templates for MEP Projects

 Learning Objectives

- Create visibility filters.
- Create a view template and apply it to several views.

In this practice you will create velocity based filters for ductwork that you will use in a mechanical view template, and apply the view template to a duplicated plan view, as shown in Figure 1–83. When the filter is working correctly, you can add the same information to a project template file.

Figure 1–83

Task 1 - Create filters.

1. Open the project /MEP/**Office-MEP.rvt** found in your class files folder.

2. In the *View* tab>Graphics panel, click ⬚ (Filters).

3. If you are using the non-discipline specific version of the Autodesk Revit software, an additional Filters dialog box opens. Click [New...], name the new filter, select **Define Criteria**, and click [OK]. This opens the full Filters dialog box.

4. If you are using the Autodesk Revit MEP software, in the Filters dialog box, click ⬚ (New), name the new filter **Mechanical - Low Velocity**, and click [OK].

5. In the *Categories* area, set the *Filter list* to **Mechanical**. Select **Ducts** and **Flex Ducts**.

6. In the *Filter Rules* area, set *Filter by* to **Velocity**, **is less than or equal to**, and **900 FPM**, as shown in Figure 1–84.

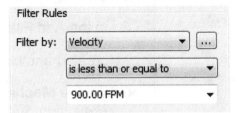

Figure 1–84

7. Click [Apply] and remain in the Filters dialog box.

8. Select the new **Mechanical-Low Velocity** filter and click (Duplicate). Right-click on the duplicated filter and click (Rename). In the Rename dialog box type

   Mechanical-Medium/High Velocity and click [OK].

9. In the *Filter Rules* area, set *Filter by* to **Velocity**, **is greater than**, and **1900 FPM**, as shown in Figure 1–85.

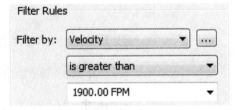

Figure 1–85

10. Click [OK] twice to close the Filters dialog boxes.

Task 2 - Create a View Template.

---

1. In the Project Browser, in the *Mechanical>Floor Plans* area, right-click on the **1 - Mech** view and select **Create View Template From View**.

2. Name the new view template **Velocity Duct Plan** and click [OK].

---

3. Next to **V/G Override Filters**, click [Edit...] The Visibility/Graphic Overrides dialog box opens with the *Filter* tab selected.

4. Click [Add].

5. In the Add Filters dialog box, select the two filters you just created and click [OK].

6. For the **Mechanical-Low Velocity** filter, in the *Projection/Surface>Lines* column, select **Override**.

7. In the Line Graphics dialog box, change *Weight* to **6** and the *Color* to an orange, as shown in Figure 1–86. Click [OK].

Figure 1–86

8. Repeat for the **Mechanical-Medium/High Velocity** filter and set the *Weight* to **6** and the *Color* to a green. Click [OK].

9. In the Visibility/Graphics Overrides dialog box, move the new filters to the top of the list. For **Mechanical-Exhaust**, in the *Visibility* column, clear the checkbox as shown in Figure 1–87.

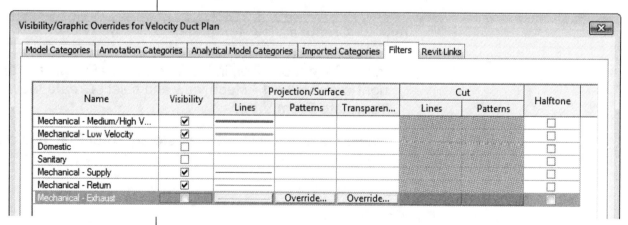

Figure 1–87

10. Click [OK] to close the Visibility/Graphic Overrides dialog box, and click [OK] to complete the view template.

Task 3 - Apply a View Template the views.

1. In the Project Browser, use *Duplicate with Detailing* to duplicate the **1 - Mech** view. Rename it **1 - Mech - Velocity.**

2. Right-click and select **Apply View Template**.

3. In the Apply View Template dialog box, select the **Velocity Duct Plan** view template you just created and click [OK] to apply it.

4. Compare the new floor plan view with the existing 1 - Mech view.

5. Duplicate the 2 - Mech view, rename it as **2 - Mech - Velocity**, and apply the same view template to it.

6. Finish with the **1 - Mech** view.

7. Save the project.

1.5 Settings for Mechanical and Electrical Projects

Learning Objective

- Review Mechanical settings for ducts and pipes and Electrical settings for wiring, cable trays, and conduit.

In addition to the standard settings common to all Autodesk Revit projects, the Autodesk Revit MEP software also has specific Mechanical and Electrical settings that can be setup in a template or a project.

- In the Autodesk Revit MEP software, the settings are found in the *Manage* tab>Settings panel. Expand (MEP Settings) and click (Mechanical Settings) or (Electrical Settings).

- Additional types of settings include Load Classifications, Demand Factors, and Building/Space Type Settings.

Mechanical Settings

Mechanical settings enable you to preset many items relating to duct and pipe sizes, conversion settings, and other key defaults, as shown in Figure 1–88.

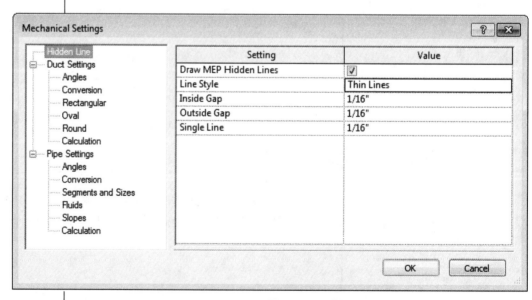

Figure 1–88

Hidden Line

If the **Draw MEP Hidden Lines** option is selected, hidden lines are displayed to indicate pipes and ducts that are below other pipes and ducts, as shown in Figure 1–89.

Figure 1–89

The **Line Style**, **Inside Gap**, and **Outside Gap** options enable you to specify how the hidden lines are displayed.

Angles

In the *Angles* category you can specify the limits on the angles that can be used as ducts or pipes are being drawn, as shown in Figure 1–90. This is most often used with piping.

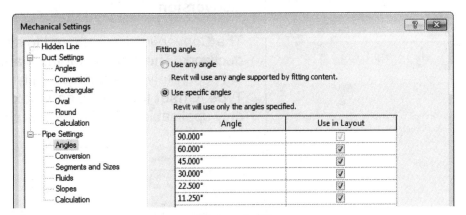

Figure 1–90

- The **Duct Settings>Angles** options also include **Set an angle increment** for determining the angle values.

Duct Settings

For the **Single Line Fittings** option, the first two settings relate to how fittings are displayed in a single line view, as shown in Figure 1–91. If the **Use Annot. Scale for Single Line Fittings** option is selected, the single line fittings are displayed at the same size on every sheet, regardless of the view scale. The **Duct Fitting Annotation Size** option enables you to specify the size at which the fittings should be displayed.

Setting	Value
Use Annot. Scale for Single Line Fittings	☑
Duct Fitting Annotation Size	1/8"
Air Density	0.0751 lb/ft^3
Air Viscosity	0.02 cP
Rectangular Duct Size Separator	x
Rectangular Duct Size Suffix	
Round Duct Size Prefix	
Round Duct Size Suffix	ø
Duct Connector Separator	-
Oval Duct Size Separator	/
Oval Duct Size Suffix	
Duct Rise / Drop Annotation Size	1/8"

Figure 1–91

The **Air Density** and **Air Viscosity** options are used when sizing the ducts. The remaining options set the separators and suffixes that are used for duct objects.

Conversion

The *Conversion* area is used to set the routing solutions for ductwork. The settings for the **Main** and **Branch** options can be set separately for each system type. You can specify the **Duct Type**, **Offset** from level, and **Flex Duct Type** settings (this is only applicable to branches), as shown in Figure 1–92.

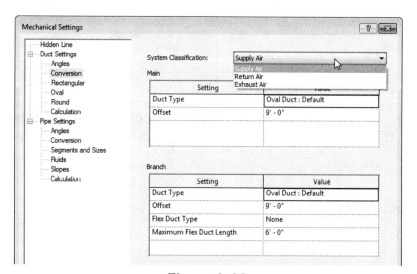

Figure 1–92

Rectangular, Oval, and Round

The **Rectangular, Oval,** and **Round** options enable you to adjust the sizing tables. The *Size* column lists all of the sizes.

You can click New Size... to add a size to the list and Delete Size to remove sizes from the list.

In addition, you can specify whether a size is displayed in the size lists (to be available when you place a new duct or select existing ducts) or if the size is used by the sizing routine (automatic sizing of duct branches and systems), as shown in Figure 1–93.

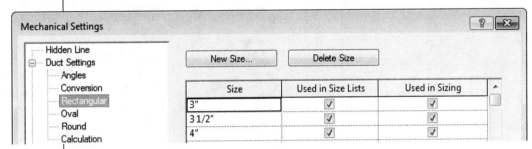

Figure 1–93

- For example, if you do not want the sizing routine to use any odd numbered sizes, clear the **Used in Sizing** option for all odd-numbered sizes.

Pipe Settings

Most of the options in the *Pipe Settings* area are identical to or similar to those in the *Duct Settings* area.

Pipe Segments and Sizes

Pipe segment and size settings are more complex due to the many different materials and connections available. Each material has its own roughness, connection types, schedule/types, and sizes that correspond to each combination, as shown in Figure 1–94. For example, Schedule 40 Carbon Steel with a Flanged Connection can have different sizes than Schedule 80 Carbon Steel with a Flanged Connection.

Figure 1–94

The actual size lists are identical in function to those for ducts, except for the inclusion of the **ID** (inside diameter) and **OD** (outside diameter) parameters.

- Click ⬚ (Create New Pipe Segment) to open the New Segment dialog box (as shown in Figure 1–95), where you specify new Material, and/or Schedule/Type for the segment.

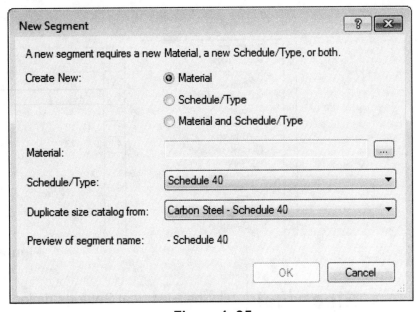

Figure 1–95

- To delete a segment, click ⬚ (Delete Pipe Segment).

Fluids

The *Fluids* area enables you to specify the viscosity and density of fluids at different temperatures, as shown in Figure 1–96. You can add or delete fluid types, and for each type, add or delete temperatures.

Figure 1–96

Slopes

In the *Slopes* area, you can add or delete typical slopes used in a project, as shown in Figure 1–97.

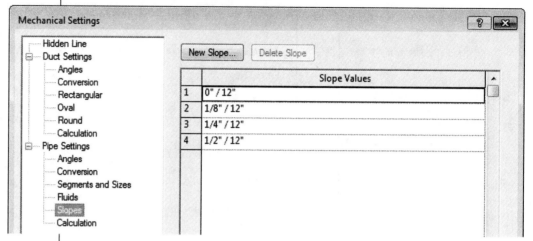

Figure 1–97

Electrical Settings

In the Electrical Settings dialog box, you can preset many options relating to wiring, voltage, cable trays and conduits as well as Load Calculations and Panel Schedules, as shown in Figure 1–98. Setting these up in the template for all of the commonly used electrical settings, saves time for individual projects and increases consistency.

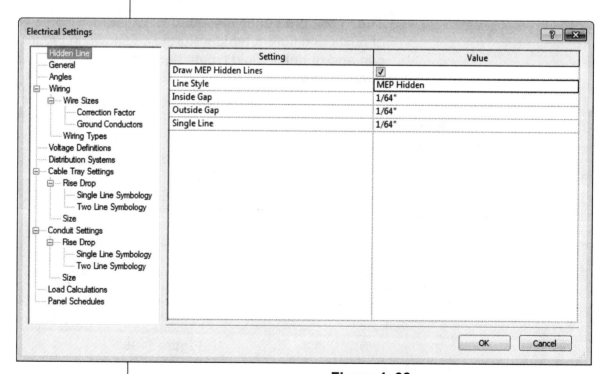

Figure 1–98

General

The parameters in the *General* area affect the display of electrical information. The **Electrical Data Style** option sets how the power information is displayed in the **Electrical Data** parameter in the Instance Properties of the electrical component. The **Circuit Description** option sets the formatting of the circuit description.

Wiring

The *Wiring* area enables you to specify the ambient temperature for wiring and some annotation settings related to wiring. The **Tick Mark** families need to be preloaded into the template so that they can be selected in this area, as shown in Figure 1–99.

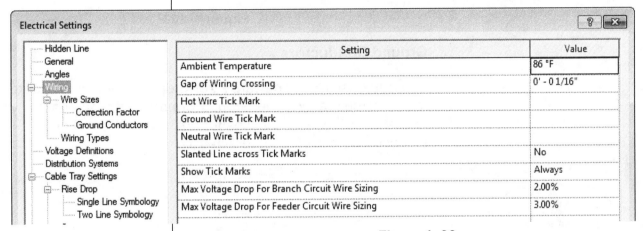

Figure 1–99

Wire Sizes

The Wire Size settings enable you to create new wire materials, temperature ratings, and insulation types. You can then specify the ampacity, size, diameter, and if the size is used by the wire sizing tools.

- The functionality in the *Wire Sizes* area is similar to that in the *Pipe Sizes* and *Fluids* areas.

Correction Factor

The *Correction Factor* area enables you to specify the correction factors for different temperatures and for each wire type, as shown in Figure 1–100.

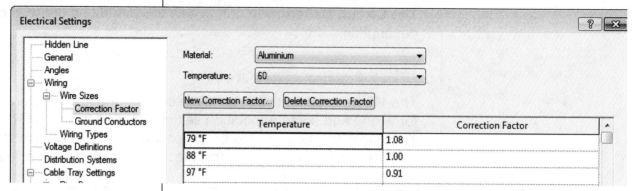

Figure 1–100

Ground Conductors

The Autodesk Revit software sizes ground conductors according to their circuit rating. The *Ground Conductors* area enables you to customize the sizes it uses for each wire material and ampacity, as shown in Figure 1–101.

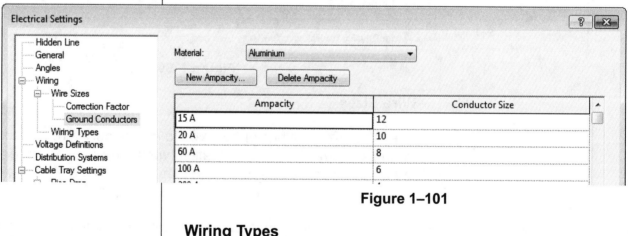

Figure 1–101

Wiring Types

The *Wiring Types* area enables you to create wiring types by clicking Add and to delete them by clicking Delete. You can also specify their properties.

Voltage Definitions

In the *Voltage Definitions* area, you can specify the minimum and maximum voltages of devices that can be added to the distribution systems of a specified voltage. For example, the Autodesk Revit software permits devices ranging from 110V to 130V on a 120V distribution system, as shown in Figure 1–102. You can also add or delete definitions.

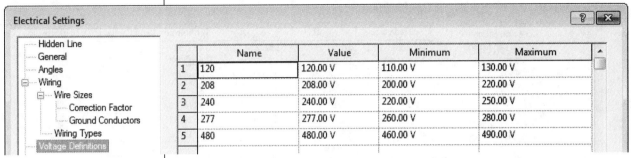

Figure 1–102

Distribution Systems

The *Distribution Systems* area sets the distribution systems that are available in your project, as shown in Figure 1–103. You can edit the names by selecting them. The options for *Phase* are preset and affect the options that are available in the *Configuration* and *Wires* columns and whether L-L Voltage is available. You can add more systems and delete existing systems if they are not assigned to devices in the current project.

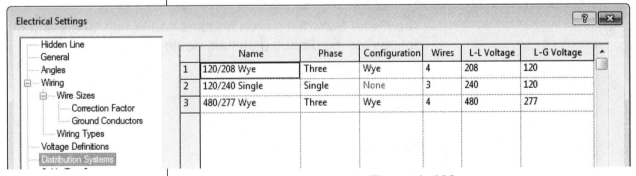

Figure 1–103

Cable Tray and Conduit Settings

Cable Trays and Conduits settings include annotation, Rise Drop Symbology, and sizing, as shown in Figure 1–104.

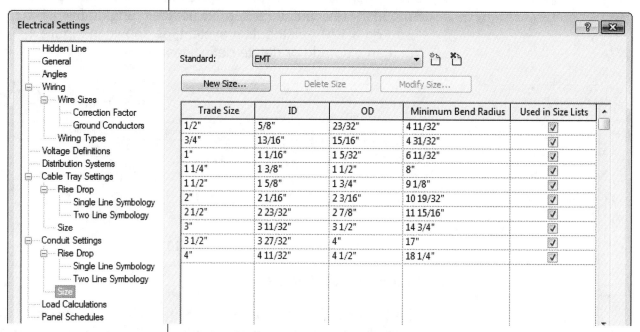

Figure 1–104

Load Calculations and Panel Schedules

The *Load Calculations* area gives you access to additional dialog boxes where you can setup Load Classifications and Demand Factors.

The *Panel Schedules* area enables you set up labels and other options for the default panel schedule.

1.6 Settings for Structural Projects

Learning Objective

- Review structural specific settings including symbolic representation, load cases and combinations, analytical model settings, and boundary conditions.

In addition to the standard settings common to all Autodesk Revit products, the Autodesk Revit Structure software has structural settings that need to be customized. To access them, click

 (Structural Settings) in the *Manage* tab>Settings panel.

Symbolic Representation

There are several tabs at the top of the Structural Settings dialog box, as shown in Figure 1–105. The first tab, *Symbolic Representation Settings*, contains options that are mainly used for the graphical model and the common defaults.

Figure 1–105

The **Symbolic Cutback Distance** setting represents the distance that cuts a framing member back from a column or into another framing member. This cutback distance is symbolic and does not affect the 3D view. For example, in plan, beams do not extend into the column and there is a gap between them, as shown in Figure 1–106. The same connection in 3D displays the beams back from the column, which is more consistent with a real-world situation.

Figure 1–106

The *Brace Symbols* and *Connection Symbols* areas enable you to specify the kinds of symbols that are shown for the braces in plan, and for frame and shear connections. For many of these items, only one symbol is loaded into the default template.

Load Cases and Load Combinations

Two tabs are related to setting up Load Cases and Load Combinations. These vary by project and by region and typically requires the input of a company's engineer.

Analytical Model Settings

The process of modeling a building simultaneously creates a digital model and its corresponding analytical model. As this is done, the software can check for consistency between these two models. The *Analytical Model Settings* tab contains settings for automatic checks, tolerances, and checks, as shown in Figure 1–107.

Figure 1–107

It is a best practice not to enable **Automatic Checks** in the template, as in the early stages of design there might be many elements that are not supported, causing many warning boxes to open. Automatic Checks are very useful when most of the structure has been modeled and should be enabled at that time.

The values in the *Tolerances* area informs the kind of tolerance that is permitted for supports, differences between the analytical and physical distance, adjusting, and auto-detects. For example, when the **Analytical Model** parameters for a wall are set to auto-detect, the software adjusts the analytical lines, provided it can do so within the specified tolerances.

The *Analytical/Physical Model Consistency Check* area enables you to specify the kinds of consistencies to be checked for.

Boundary Condition Settings

In the last tab, you can select the family symbols used for boundary conditions, as shown in Figure 1–108 (from left to right: **Fixed**, **Pinned**, **Roller**, and **User**).

Figure 1–108

The structural templates typically include four boundary condition families: **Fixed**, **Pinned**, **Roller**, and **Variable**. They are assigned to the corresponding boundary conditions, as shown in Figure 1–109.

Figure 1–109

- You can create new boundary condition families, load them into the template, and select them from the drop-down lists as needed.

Chapter Review Questions

1. Which of the following items are NOT setup in a template file?

    a. Units

    b. Annotation Types

    c. Title blocks

    d. Keyboard Shortcuts

2. What is a label?

    a. A text type used in title blocks.

    b. A dimension with text instead of numbers.

    c. A type of text with variable information.

3. When you want to create new Text Types, such as those shown in Figure 1–110, you need to copy an existing one.

A FANCY FONT AT 1/4"

A HAND LETTERING FONT AT 1/8"

A HAND LETTERING FONT AT 3/32"

Figure 1–110

    a. True

    b. False

4. Which of the following enables you to assign a view template consistently to a view so that no changes can be made to the view parameters?

    a. In the View Status Bar, lock the view.

    b. In Properties, select a View Template.

    c. In the Project Browser, right-click on the view and select **Lock**.

    d. In the Apply View Template dialog box, select a template.

5. Which of the following parameters are included in a View Template (as shown in Figure 1–111)? (Select all that apply.)

Figure 1–111

a. View Scale

b. V/G Overrides

c. Project Units

d. Detail Level

Command Summary

Button	Command	Location
Templates		
	Callout Tags	• **Ribbon:** *Manage* tab>Settings panel> expand Additional Settings
	Elevation Tags	• **Ribbon:** *Manage* tab>Settings panel> expand Additional Settings
	Floor Plan	• **Ribbon:** *View* tab>Create panel> expand Plan Views
	Loaded Tags	• **Ribbon:** *Annotate* tab>Tag panel> expand the panel title
	Project Units	• **Ribbon:** *Manage* tab>Settings panel • **Shortcut:** UN
	Section Tags	• **Ribbon:** *Manage* tab>Settings panel> expand Additional Settings
	Temporary Dimensions	• **Ribbon:** *Manage* tab>Settings panel> expand Additional Settings
Annotation		
	Arrowheads	• **Ribbon:** *Manage* tab>Settings panel> expand Additional Settings
	Dimension Types • **Linear** • **Angular** • **Radial** • **Spot Elevation** • **Spot Coordinate** • **Spot Slope**	• **Ribbon:** *Annotate* tab>Dimensions panel>expand the panel title
A	**Text**	• **Family Editor** • **Ribbon:** *Create* tab>Text panel
Title Blocks		
	Label	• **Family Editor** • **Ribbon:** *Create* tab>Text panel
	New Title Block	• **Application Menu:** expand New> Title block
	Revision Schedule	• **Family Editor** • **Ribbon:** *View* tab>Create panel
View Templates		
	ApplyTemplate Properties to Current View	• **Ribbon:** *View* tab>Graphics panel> expand View Templates • **Project Browser:** (*right-click on a view*) **Apply Template Properties...**

		Create View Template From View	• **Ribbon:** *View* tab>Graphics panel> expand View Templates • **Project Browser:** (*right-click on a view*)
		Manage View Templates	• **Ribbon:** *View* tab>Graphics panel> expand View Templates
Settings			
		Electrical Settings	• **Autodesk Revit MEP** • **Ribbon:** *Manage* tab>Settings panel expand MEP Settings
		Mechanical Settings	• **Autodesk Revit MEP** • **Ribbon:** *Manage* tab>Settings panel expand MEP Settings
		Structural Settings	• **Autodesk Revit Structure** • **Ribbon:** *Manage* tab>Settings panel
	Options	**Options**	• **Application Menu**

Chapter 2

Schedules

In this chapter you learn how to create building component schedules and to modify their appearance. You then learn about key schedules and material takeoff schedules. Finally, you learn to use advanced schedule options, including creating parameters, formulas, and conditional formatting, as well as embedding schedules (in the Autodesk® Revit® MEP software only).

This chapter contains the following topics:

- **Introduction to Schedules**
- **Creating Building Component Schedules**
- **Modifying Schedule Appearance**
- **Creating Key Schedules**
- **Advanced Schedule Options**
- **Creating Material Takeoff Schedules**

2.1 Introduction to Schedules

Learning Objective

- Identify types of schedules that can be created in the Autodesk Revit software.

Schedules can be created at any point in a project or included in template files. Each schedule is a separate view and can be inserted on a sheet, as shown in Figure 2–1.

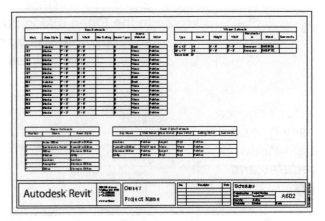

Figure 2–1

You can create the following types of schedules:

(Schedule/ Quantities)	Generates schedules using parameters available at category level. There are two types of Schedule/ Quantities schedules: **Building Component** and **Key**.
(Material Takeoff)	Generates schedules from information about materials in a project and can be used to do quantity takeoffs.
(Sheet List)	Generates schedule from sheet information including who has designed and checked the sheet.
(Note Block)	Generates schedules that keep count of all of the symbols used in the project.
(View List)	Generates schedules that keep count of all of the views in the project, including their scale, phase, and use on sheets.
(Graphical Column Schedule)	(Autodesk Revit Structure only) Generates graphical schedules displaying heights of all columns in a project compared to levels.

Importing and Exporting Schedules

Schedules are views and can be copied into your project from other projects. Only the formatting information is copied; the information about individually scheduled items is not included. That information is automatically gathered from the elements in the current project. You can also export the schedule information to be used in spreadsheets.

How To: Import Schedules

1. In the *Insert* tab>Import panel, expand 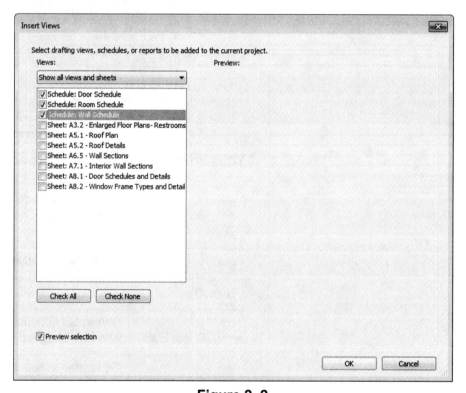 (Insert From File) and click (Insert Views From File).
2. In the Open dialog box, locate the project file containing the schedule that you want to use.
3. Select the schedules that you want to import, as shown in Figure 2–2.

*If the referenced project contains many types of views, change Views: to **Show schedules and reports only**.*

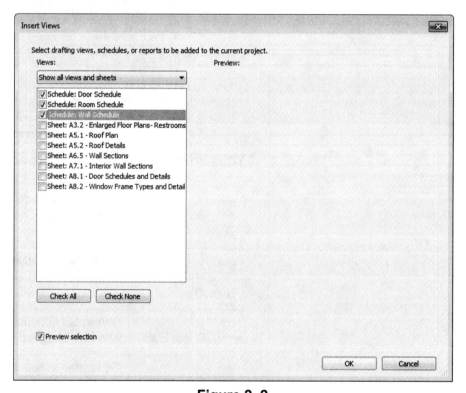

Figure 2–2

4. Click OK .

How To: Export Schedule Information

1. Switch to the schedule view that you want to export.

2. In the Application Menu, expand (Export), expand (Reports), and click (Schedule).

3. In the Export Schedule dialog box, select a location and name for the text file and click Save .

4. In the Export Schedule dialog box, set the options in the *Schedule appearance* and *Output options* areas that best suit your spreadsheet software, as shown in Figure 2–3.

Figure 2–3

5. Click OK . A new text file is created that you can open in a spreadsheet, as shown in Figure 2–4.

Figure 2–4

2.2 Creating Building Component Schedules

Autodesk Certification Topics & Objectives

Pro.   User

Views

• Organize and sort items in a schedule   ✓

 Learning Objectives

• Schedule building components based on type and instance parameters of elements.
• Setup schedule tables using filters, sorting/grouping, formatting, and appearance.
• Access the Schedule Properties dialog box from the Properties palette.

A Building Component schedule is a table view of the type and instance parameters of a specific element category. You can specify the parameters (fields) you want to include in the schedule. All of the parameters found in the type of element category you are scheduling are available to use. For example, a door schedule (as shown in Figure 2–5) can include instance parameters that are automatically filled in (such as the **Height** and **Width**) and type parameters that might need to have the information assigned in the schedule or element type (such as the **Fire Rating** and **Frame**).

<Door Schedule>

A	B	C	D	E	F	G	H
Mark	Height	Width	Fire Rating	Frame Type	Frame Material	Finish	Function
2	7' - 0"	10' - 0"	A	A	Steel	Brushed	Exterior
3	6' - 8"	3' - 0"	B	B	Wood	Paint	Interior ▼
4	6' - 8"	3' - 0"	B	B	Wood	Paint	Interior
5	6' - 8"	3' - 0"	B	B	Wood	Paint	Interior
6	6' - 8"	3' - 0"	B	B	Wood	Paint	Interior

Figure 2–5

How To: Create a Building Component Schedule

1. In the *View* tab>Create panel, expand (Schedules) and
   click (Schedule/Quantities) or in the Project Browser, right-click on the Schedule/Quantities node and select **New Schedule/Quantities**.
2. In the New Schedule dialog box, select the type of schedule you want to create (e.g., Columns) from the *Category* list, as shown in Figure 2–6.

In the Filter list drop-down list, you can specify the discipline(s) to show only the categories that you want to display.

Figure 2–6

3. Type a new *Name*, if the default does not suit.
4. Select **Schedule building components.**
5. Specify the *Phase* as required.
6. Click [OK].
7. Fill out the information in the Schedule Properties dialog box. This includes the information in the *Fields, Filter, Sorting/Grouping, Formatting,* and *Appearance* tabs.
8. Once you have entering the schedule properties, click
    . A schedule report is created in its own view.

Schedule Properties – Fields Tab

In the *Fields* tab, you can select from a list of available fields and organize them in the order in which you want them to display in the schedule, as shown in Figure 2–7.

Figure 2–7

How To: Fill out the Fields Tab

You can also double-click on a field to move it from the Available Fields to the Scheduled Fields list.

1. In the *Available fields* list, select one or more fields you want to add to the schedule and click [Add -->]. The field(s) are placed in the *Scheduled fields (in order)* list.
2. Continue adding fields as required. If you add one you did not want to use, select it in the *Scheduled fields* list and click [<-- Remove] to move it back to the *Available fields* list.
3. Use [Move Up] and [Move Down] to change the order of the scheduled fields.

Other Fields Tab Options

Select available fields from	Enables you to select additional category fields for the specified schedule. The available list of additional fields depends on the original category of the schedule. Typically, they include room information.
Include elements in linked files	Includes elements that are in files linked to the current project, so that their elements can be included in the schedule.
Add Parameter...	Adds a new field according to your specification. New fields can be placed by instance or by type.
Calculated Value...	Enables you to create a field that uses a formula based on other fields.
Edit...	Enables you to edit custom fields. This is grayed out if you select a standard field.
Delete	Deletes selected custom fields. This is grayed out if you select a standard field.

Schedule Properties – Filter Tab

In the *Filter* tab, you can set up filters so that only elements meeting specific criteria are included in the schedule. For example, you might only want to show information for one level, as shown in Figure 2–8. You can create filters for up to eight values. All values must be satisfied for the elements to display.

Figure 2–8

- The parameter you want to use as a filter must be included in the schedule. You can hide the parameter once you have completed the schedule, if required.

Filter by	Specifies the field to filter. Not all fields are available to be filtered.
Condition	Specifies the condition that must be met. This includes options such as **equal**, **not equal**, **greater than**, and **less than**.
Value	Specifies the value of the element to be filtered. You can select from a drop-down list of appropriate values. For example, if you set *Filter By* to **Level**, it displays the list of levels in the project.

Schedule Properties – Sorting/Grouping Tab

In the *Sorting/Grouping* tab, you can set how you want the information to be sorted, as shown in Figure 2–9. For example, you can sort by **Mark** (number) and then **Type**.

Figure 2–9

Sort by	Enables you to select the field(s) you want to sort by. You can select up to four levels of sorting.
Ascending/ Descending	Sorts fields in **Ascending** or **Descending** order.
Header/Footer	Enables you to group similar information and separate it by a **Header** with a title and/or a **Footer** with quantity information.
Blank line	Adds a blank line between groups.
Grand totals	Selects which totals to display for the entire schedule. You can specify a name to display in the schedule for the Grand total.
Itemize every instance	If selected, displays each instance of the element in the schedule. If not selected, displays only one instance of each type, as shown in Figure 2–10.

Enhanced
in 2015

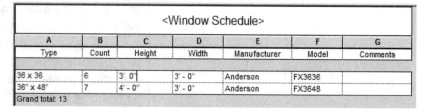

Figure 2–10

Schedule Properties – Formatting Tab

In the *Formatting* tab, you can control how the headers of each field display, as shown in Figure 2–11.

Figure 2–11

Fields	Enables you to select the field for which you want to modify the formatting.
Heading	Enables you to change the heading of the field if you want it to be different from the field name. For example, you might want to replace **Mark** (a generic name) with the more specific **Door Number** in a door schedule.
Heading orientation	Enables you to set the heading on sheets to **Horizontal** or **Vertical**. This does not impact the schedule view.
Alignment	Aligns the text in rows under the heading to be **Left**, **Right**, or **Center**.
Field Format...	Sets the units format for the length, area, volume, angle, or number field. By default, this is set to use the project settings.
Conditional Format...	Sets up the schedule to display visual feedback based on the conditions listed.
Hidden field	Enables you to hide a field. For example, you might want to use a field for sorting purposes, but not have it display in the schedule. You can also modify this option in the schedule view later.
Show conditional format on sheets	Select if you want the color code set up in the Conditional Format dialog box to display on sheets.
Calculate totals	Displays the subtotals of numerical columns in a group.

Schedule Properties – Appearance Tab

In the *Appearance* tab, you can set the text style and grid options for a schedule, as shown in Figure 2–12.

Figure 2–12

Grid lines	Displays lines between each instance listed and around the outside of the schedule. Select the style of lines from the drop-down list; this controls all lines for the schedule, unless modified.
Grid in headers/footers/ spacers	Extends the vertical grid lines between the columns.
Outline	Specify a different line type for the outline of the schedule.
Blank row before data	Select this option if you want a blank row to be displayed before the data begins in the schedule.
Show Title/Show Headers	Select these options to include the text in the schedule.
Title text/Header text/Body Text	Select the text style for the title, header, and body text.

Schedule Properties

Schedule views have properties including the *View Name*, *Phases* and methods of returning to the Schedule Properties dialog box as shown in Figure 2–13. In the *Other* area, select the button next to the tab that you want to open in the Schedule Properties dialog box. In the dialog box, you can switch from tab to tab and make any required changes to the overall schedule.

Figure 2–13

Filtering Elements from Schedules

When you create schedules based on a category you might need to filter out some of the element types in that category. For example, in the Autodesk Revit software, doors (and windows) in curtain walls are automatically added to a door schedule, as shown at the top in Figure 2–14, but are typically estimated as part of the curtain wall rather than as a separate door. To remove them from the schedule, as shown at the bottom in Figure 2–14, assign a parameter that identifies them and then use that parameter to filter them out of the schedule.

| | Door Size | | | Frame | | Door Schedule- 1st |
Door Type	Width	Height	Thickness	Frame Type	Frame Material	Head Detail
	8' - 3 1/2"	9' - 4 1/4"				
	3' - 0"	7' - 0"	0' - 2"	A	Aluminum	
	3' - 0"	7' - 0"	0' - 2"	B	Aluminum	
	3' - 0"	6' - 8"	0' - 2"	C	Aluminum	

| | Door Size | | | Frame | | Door Schedule- 1st |
Door Type	Width	Height	Thickness	Frame Type	Frame Material	Head Detail
	3' - 0"	7' - 0"	0' - 2"	A	Aluminum	
	3' - 0"	7' - 0"	0' - 2"	B	Aluminum	
	3' - 0"	6' - 8"	0' - 2"	C	Aluminum	
	3' - 0"	6' - 8"	0' - 2"	C	Aluminum	

Figure 2–14

* This type of filtering can be used for any schedule in any discipline.

Create a type specifically for this if you are using one that is also used elsewhere.

How To: Filter Elements in a Schedule

1. Select an element (such as a door used in curtain walls) and modify the Type Parameters. Add a value to one of the parameters that you are not otherwise using in your schedule. For example, set *Construction Type* to **CW**, as shown Figure 2–15

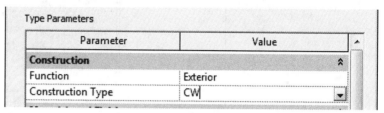

Figure 2–15

2. Create a schedule and include the field, such as *Construction Type*.
3. Modify the *Filter* of the schedule so the parameter does not equal the specified value. In the example shown in Figure 2–16, *Construction Type* **does not equal CW**. Any types that match this filter are excluded from the schedule.

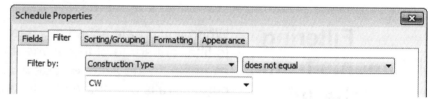

Figure 2–16

4. In the final schedule, the elements display with the specified value. Right-click on the column header and select **Hide Column(s)**, as shown in Figure 2–17. It is just used as a filter and not part of the final schedule.

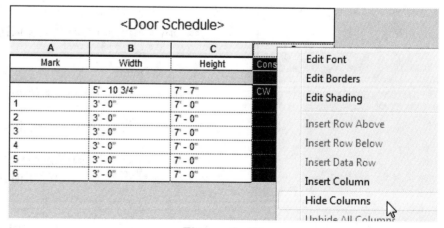

Figure 2–17

Practice 2a

Create Schedules for Architectural Projects

Learning Objectives

- Create a door schedule and a window schedule.
- Filter out curtain wall doors from the door schedule.
- Fill in additional information in the door schedule.
- Place the schedules on a sheet.

Estimated time for completion: 15 minutes

n this practice you will create Door and Window schedules and place them on a sheet, as shown in Figure 2–18.

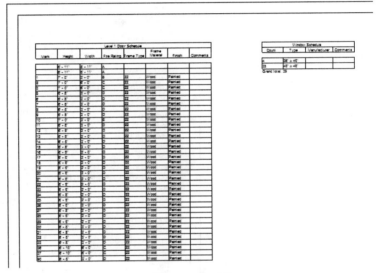

Figure 2–18

Task 1 - Create a Door schedule.

1. Open the project **Clark-Hall-Schedules-Create-A.rvt** found in the *Architectural* folder of your class files folder.

2. In the *View* tab>Create panel, expand ▦ (Schedules) and click ▦ (Schedule/Quantities).

3. In the New Schedule dialog box, set the *Filter List* to **Architecture** only to limit the number of categories and then set the *Category* to **Doors.**

4. Name the schedule **Door Schedule-Level 1**. Click .

5. In the Schedule Properties dialog box, in the *Fields* tab, add the following fields, as shown in Figure 2–19:

- *Level*
- *Mark*
- *Height*
- *Width*
- *Fire Rating*
- *Frame Type*
- *Frame Material*
- *Finish*
- *Comments*
- *Construction Type*

Figure 2–19

6. Click [OK] to create the schedule. Note that Level 1, Level 2, and Level 3 doors are included.

7. In Properties, in the *Other* category, next to **Filter**, click [Edit...]. The Schedule Properties dialog box opens with the *Filter* tab selected. Set *Filter by* to **Level - equals - Level 1**.

8. In the dialog box, in the *Sorting/Grouping* tab, sort the doors by **Mark**, and click [OK] to update the schedule.

9. Save the project.

Task 2 - Remove the Curtain Wall Doors from the schedule.

1. Continue working in the new **Door Schedule-Level 1** view, The doors in the curtain walls do not display with a **Mark**, as shown in Figure 2–20. Additionally, they are not included in door schedules and need to be removed.

A	B	C	D
Level	Mark	Height	Width
Level 1		6' - 11"	5' - 11"
Level 1		6' - 11"	5' - 11"
Level 1	1	7' - 0"	3' - 0"
Level 1	2	7' - 0"	6' - 0"
Level 1	3	7' - 0"	6' - 0"
Level 1	4	6' - 8"	3' - 0"
Level 1	5	6' - 8"	3' - 0"

Figure 2–20

2. In Properties, in the *Other* category, next to **Filter**, click [Edit...].

3. In the Schedule Properties dialog box, in the *Filter* tab, add the additional Filter: **Construction Type - does not equal - CW** as shown in Figure 2–21, and click [OK].

*You need to type **CW** because the option does not yet exist in the project.*

Figure 2–21

4. In the Schedule, next to one of the curtain wall doors, in the *Construction Type* column, type **CW**. An alert displays prompting you that this is a type property. Click [OK] and the curtain wall doors are no longer included in the schedule, as shown in Figure 2–22.

A	B	C	D
Level	Mark	Height	Width
Level 1	1	7' - 0"	3' - 0"
Level 1	2	7' - 0"	6' - 0"
Level 1	3	7' - 0"	6' - 0"
Level 1	4	6' - 8"	3' - 0"

Figure 2–22

5. Save the project

Task 3 - Fill in additional information in the Door Schedule

1. Continue working in the new **Door Schedule-Level 1** view,

2. In the *Fire Rating* column, type a letter for one of the door types. Because the door type controls the **Fire Rating** parameter, an alert box opens, as shown in Figure 2–23. Click [OK].

Figure 2–23

3. Repeat with the other doors until they all have a fire rating.

4. Open the Floor Plans>**Level 1** view and select one of the interior single doors.

5. Right-click and select **Select All Instances>In Entire Project** in Properties. Set the following parameters:

   • **Frame Type:** 22
   • **Frame Material:** Wood
   • **Finish:** Stained

6. Switch back to the schedule to verify that it has updated with the new information.

7. In the schedule view, set the rest of the doors to the following parameters:

- **Frame Type:** 21
- **Frame Material:** Aluminum
- **Finish:** Brushed

8. Right-click on the *Level* header and select **Hide Columns**. Repeat the procedure with the *Construction Type* header. This removes the columns from the schedule as shown in Figure 2–24, while still enabling you to use the fields as filters.

<Door Schedule-Level 1>							
A	B	C	D	E	F	G	H
Mark	Height	Width	Fire Rating	Frame Type	Frame Material	Finish	Comments
1	7' - 0"	3' - 0"	A	21	Aluminum	Brushed	
2	7' - 0"	6' - 0"	A	21	Aluminum	Brushed	
3	7' - 0"	6' - 0"	A	21	Aluminum	Brushed	
4	6' - 8"	3' - 0"	B	22	Wood	Stained	
5	6' - 8"	3' - 0"	B	22	Wood	Stained	
6	6' - 8"	3' - 0"	B	22	Wood	Stained	
7	6' - 8"	3' - 0"	B	22	Wood	Stained	
8	6' - 8"	3' - 0"	B	22	Wood	Stained	

Figure 2–24

9. Save the project.

Task 4 - Create a Window schedule.

1. Create a new window schedule with the following fields: **Count**, **Type**, **Manufacturer**, and **Comments**.

2. In the *Sorting/Grouping* tab, sort the windows by **Type**. Toggle on **Grand totals** and toggle off **Itemize every instance**.

3. Click 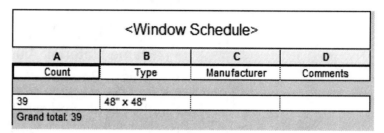 to create the schedule. It lists the total count for a single type (only one type is used in the project), as shown in Figure 2–25.

<Window Schedule>			
A	**B**	**C**	**D**
Count	Type	Manufacturer	Comments
39	48" x 48"		
Grand total: 39			

Figure 2–25

4. In the Floor Plans>**Level 1** view, select the three windows in the Conference Room in the office wing. In Properties change the type to **Fixed with Trim: 36" x 72"**.

5. Switch back to the schedule view. A change should display in the schedule that reflects the new window type, as shown in Figure 2–26.

<Window Schedule>			
A	**B**	**C**	**D**
Count	Type	Manufacturer	Comments
3	36" x 72"		
36	48" x 48"		
Grand total: 39			

Figure 2–26

6. Open the **A601- Schedules** sheet. Drag and drop the schedules to this sheet. Modify the width of each field as needed.

7. Save the project.

Practice 2b

Create Schedules for MEP Projects

 Learning Objectives

- Create a duct system schedule.
- Create a plumbing fixture schedule.
- (Optional) Create electrical circuit and lighting fixture schedules.

Estimated time for completion: 15 minutes

In this practice you will create schedules for two types of typical MEP schedules: a system schedule and a fixture schedule. In this case, they will be for duct systems and plumbing fixtures. If you have time, you will also create schedules for electrical circuits and lighting fixtures. You will then place the schedules on a sheet, as shown in Figure 2–27.

Duct Systems		
System Name	Comments	Flow
Exhaust Air		
Mechanical Exhaust Air 1		2000 CFM
Mechanical Exhaust Air 7		420 CFM
Mechanical Exhaust Air 9		200 CFM
Return Air		
Mechanical Return Air 1		0 CFM
Mechanical Return Air 2		0 CFM
Mechanical Return Air 3		205 CFM
Mechanical Return Air 4		500 CFM
Mechanical Return Air 5		500 CFM
Mechanical Return Air 6		500 CFM
Mechanical Return Air 10		0 CFM
Mechanical Return Air 14		205 CFM
Supply Air		
Mechanical Supply Air 1		4000 CFM
Mechanical Supply Air 2		2400 CFM
Mechanical Supply Air 3		2900 CFM
Mechanical Supply Air 4		3500 CFM
Mechanical Supply Air 8		0 CFM
Mechanical Supply Air 9		2900 CFM
Mechanical Supply Air 10		3900 CFM
Mechanical Supply Air 15		3090 CFM
Mechanical Supply Air 19		2400 CFM

Figure 2–27

Task 1 - Create a Duct System schedule.

1. Open the project **Freel Office-Create-MEP.rvt** found in the *MEP* folder of your class files folder.

2. In the *View* tab>Create panel, expand ▦ (Schedules) and click ▦ (Schedule/Quantities).

3. In the New Schedule dialog box, set the *Filter list* to **Mechanical** and the *Category* to **Duct Systems** and name it **Duct Systems**, as shown in Figure 2–28.

Figure 2–28

4. Click [OK].

5. In the Schedule Properties dialog box, in the *Fields* tab, add the following fields:

   • *System Classification*
   • *System Name*
   • *Comments*
   • *Flow*

6. In the *Sorting/Grouping* tab, sort by **System Classification**. Select **Ascending** and **Header**.

7. Click [OK] to create the schedule and stretch out the columns to be able to read all of the information, as shown in Figure 2–29.

Duct System Schedule			
System Classification	System Name	Comments	Flow
Exhaust Air			
Exhaust Air	Mechanical Exhaust Air 1		2620 CFM
Return Air			
Return Air	Zone 6 Return		500 CFM
Return Air	Zone1 Return		0 CFM
Return Air	Zone 7 Return		205 CFM
Return Air	Zone 9 Return		205 CFM
Return Air	Zone 2 Return		0 CFM
Return Air	Mechanical Return Air 1		0 CFM
Return Air	Mechanical Return Air 2		500 CFM
Return Air	Mechanical Return Air 3		500 CFM
Return Air	Mechanical Return Air 4		0 CFM
Supply Air			
Supply Air	Zone 6 Supply		3200 CFM
Supply Air	Zone 1 Supply		4000 CFM
Supply Air	Zone 7 Supply		3090 CFM
Supply Air	Zone 3 Supply		2900 CFM
Supply Air	Zone 9 Supply		0 CFM
Supply Air	Zone 5 Supply		3900 CFM
Supply Air	Zone 2 Supply		2400 CFM
Supply Air	Mechanical Supply Air 1		0 CFM
Supply Air	Mechanical Supply Air 2		0 CFM
Supply Air	Mechanical Supply Air 3		2900 CFM
Supply Air	Mechanical Supply Air 4		3900 CFM
Supply Air	Mechanical Supply Air 5		2400 CFM

Figure 2–29

8. Right-click on the *System Classification* column and select **Hide Column**. (The System Classification is specified by the Header).

9. Open the **M601- Mechanical Schedules** sheet. Drag and drop the duct system schedule to this sheet. Modify the width of each field as needed.

10. Save the project.

Task 2 - Create a Plumbing Fixture schedule.

1. In the *View* tab>Create panel, expand (Schedules) and click (Schedule/Quantities).

2. In the New Schedule dialog box, set the *Filter list* to **Piping**, set *Category* to **Plumbing Fixtures**, and name it **Plumbing Fixtures**. Click [OK].

3. In the Schedule Properties dialog box, in the *Fields* tab, add the following fields:

- *Family*
- *Type*
- *Manufacturer*
- *Count*

4. In the *Sorting/Grouping* tab, sort by Family, and clear **Itemize every instance**.

5. Click [OK] to create the schedule. Stretch the columns such that all the words are visible, as shown in Figure 2–30.

Plumbing Fixture Schedule			
Family	Type	Manufacturer	Count
Drinking Fountain-Hi-Lo-3D	Drinking Fountain-Hi-Lo-3D		2
Shower Base-Round Corner	36" x 36"		1
Sink Kitchen-Double	42" x 21"		3
Sink Vanity-Round	19" x 19"		8
Toilet-Commercial-Wall-3D	15" Seat Height		6
Urinal-Wall-3D	Urinal-Wall-3D		2

Figure 2–30

6. Open the **P601- Plumbing Schedules** sheet. Drag and drop the schedule to this sheet. Modify the width of each field as needed.

7. Save the project.

Task 3 - Create electrical-related schedules and a sheet.

1. If you have time, create an electrical circuit system schedule using the same process as the duct system schedule and a lighting fixture schedule using the same process as the plumbing fixture schedule. Place these schedules on the E601 - Electrical and Lighting Schedules sheet.

2. Save the project.

Practice 2c

Create Schedules for Structural Projects

Learning Objectives

- Create a structural schedule that includes all types of structural elements.
- Reorganize the schedule content by sorting and grouping.
- Place the schedule on a sheet.

Estimated time for completion: 15 minutes

In this practice you will create a schedule displaying structural elements by category, You will then place it on a sheet and modify it to fit, as shown in Figure 2–31.

Figure 2–31

Task 1 - Create a Structural schedule.

1. Open the project **Axiom-Building-Create-S.rvt** found in the *Structural* folder of your class files folder.

2. In the *View* tab>Create panel, expand (Schedules) and click (Schedule/Quantities).

3. In the New Schedule dialog box, set *Filter list* to **Structure**, set *Category* to **<Multi-Category>**, and name it **Structural Schedule**. Click OK.

4. In the Schedule Properties dialog box, in the *Fields* tab, add the following fields:

   • *Type Mark*
   • *Family and Type*
   • *Count*
   • *Category*

5. Use Move Up and Move Down to change the order of the scheduled fields if needed so they display as shown in Figure 2–32.

Scheduled fields (in order):

Type Mark
Family and Type
Count
Category

Figure 2–32

6. Click OK. The new schedule displays with all of the structural elements in the project in a long list, as shown in part in Figure 2–33.

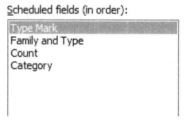

<Structural Schedule>

A	B	C	D
Type Mark	Family and Type	Count	Category
	W-Wide Flange-Colum	1	Structural Columns
	W-Wide Flange-Colum	1	Structural Columns
	W-Wide Flange-Colum	1	Structural Columns
	W-Wide Flange-Colum	1	Structural Columns
	W-Wide Flange-Colum	1	Structural Columns
	W-Wide Flange-Colum	1	Structural Columns
	W-Wide Flange-Colum	1	Structural Columns
	W-Wide Flange-Colum	1	Structural Columns
	W-Wide Flange-Colum	1	Structural Columns
	W-Wide Flange-Colum	1	Structural Columns
	W-Wide Flange-Colum	1	Structural Columns
	W-Wide Flange-Colum	1	Structural Columns
	W-Wide Flange-Colum	1	Structural Columns
	W-Wide Flange-Colum	1	Structural Columns
	W-Wide Flange-Colum	1	Structural Columns
	W-Wide Flange-Colum	1	Structural Columns
	W-Wide Flange-Colum	1	Structural Columns
	W-Wide Flange-Colum	1	Structural Columns
	Wall Foundation: Beari	1	Structural Foundati
	Wall Foundation: Beari	1	Structural Foundati
	Wall Foundation: Beari	1	Structural Foundati

Figure 2–33

7. Save the project.

Task 2 - Add filtering, sorting, and grouping to the schedule.

1. In Properties, in the *Other* category, next to **Sorting/Grouping**, click [Edit...]. The Schedule Properties dialog box opens with the *Sorting/Grouping* tab selected.

2. In the *Sorting/Grouping* tab, sort by **Category**, and select **Header**. Then sort by **Family and Type** with no header. Clear **Itemize every instance**, as shown in Figure 2–34.

Figure 2–34

3. In the Schedule Properties dialog box, in the *Filter* tab, add the Filter: **Category Type does not equal Structural Rebar**, as shown in Figure 2–35.

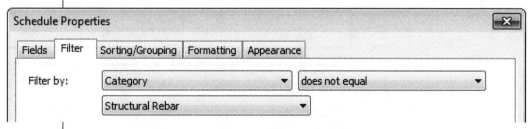

Figure 2–35

4. Click [OK] to create the schedule.

5. Resize the columns to see the information. Right-click on the *Category* column and select **Hide Columns**. The schedule displays as shown in Figure 2–36.

<Structural Schedule>		
A	**B**	**C**
Type Mark	Family and Type	Count
Structural Columns		
P-1	Concrete-Rectangular-Column: 24 x 24	22
	W-Wide Flange-Column: W10X33	1
	W-Wide Flange-Column: W10X49	22
Structural Foundations		
F-2	Footing-Rectangular: 14'x14'x2'-0"	1
F-1	Footing-Rectangular: 36" x 36" x 12"	21
	Foundation Slab: 6" Foundation Slab	1
	Step Footing: Step Footing	4
	Wall Foundation: Bearing Footing - 24" x 12"	6
	Wall Foundation: Bearing Footing - 36" x 12"	4
	Wall Foundation: Retaining Footing - 24" x 12" x 12"	1
Structural Framing		
	HSS-Hollow Structural Section: HSS6X6X.500	9
	K-Series Bar Joist-Rod Web: 16K6	65
	W-Wide Flange: W8X10	6
	W-Wide Flange: W12X26	63
	W-Wide Flange: W14X48	62
	W-Wide Flange: W16X45	1

Figure 2–36

6. Open the **S601- Schedules** sheet. Drag and drop the schedule to this sheet. Modify the width of each field as needed.

7. Save the project.

Task 3 - Optional Schedules

1. If you have time, create schedules that incorporate the information shown in Figure 2–37 and Figure 2–38.

<Structural Foundation Schedule>				
A	**B**	**C**	**D**	**E**
Type Mark	Count	Type	Width	Length
F-1	21	36" x 36" x 12"	3' - 0"	3' - 0"
F-2	1	14'x14'x2'-0"	14' - 0"	14' - 0"
Grand total: 22				

Figure 2–37

- Hint: Create a Structural Column Schedule, change the name and Filter by **Type Mark begins with "P"** so that only the foundation columns display.

- Hint: Filter by **Type Mark begins with "F"** so that only the individual footing foundations display and sort by Type Mark.

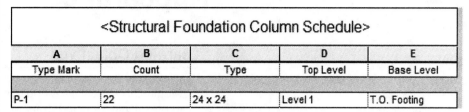

<Structural Foundation Column Schedule>				
A	B	C	D	E
Type Mark	Count	Type	Top Level	Base Level
P-1	22	24 x 24	Level 1	T.O. Footing

Figure 2–38

2. Save the project.

2.3 Modifying Schedule Appearance

 Learning Objectives

- Modify the appearance and content of individual schedule cells, especially the title and header cells.
- Add Image Fields to schedules.

While you assign global appearance settings in the Schedule Properties dialog box, you can also modify the appearance of each cell in a schedule and add other rows and columns. Title and Heading cells can include both text and parameter values and have different text formatting, as shown in Figure 2–39. You can also add images to title cells and to individual rows in a schedule.

<Window Schedule>						
<Toronto Towers>				Project No.	<1234-5678>	
A	B	C	D	E	F	G
Type	Count	Height	Width	Manufacturer	Model	Comments
36 x 36	72	3' - 0"	3' - 0"	Anderson	FX3636	
36" x 48"	84	4' - 0"	3' - 0"	Anderson	FX3648	
Grand total: 156						

Figure 2–39

- These modifications work with all types of schedules.

- Most of these modifications can be accessed in the *Modify Schedule/Quantities* tab (as shown in Figure 2–40), which is available when you are in a schedule view.

Figure 2–40

- Many of these options are also found in the right-click menu.

Parameter Values

Parameter values and options (as shown in Figure 2–41) can be set up by cell. In title cells you can use the **Schedule** and **Project Information** parameters. If you select a header cell the parameters match the type of schedule in which you are working. If you change this you are changing the field as you did in the Schedule Properties dialog box, in the *Field* tab. In number-based data cells you can modify the **Format Unit** or add **Calculated** values (formulas).

Figure 2–41

- Parameter values in titles are displayed in the schedule view with <> at either end of the value. This does not display on the sheet view.

How To: Add Parameters to Schedule Cells

1. Select the cell in which you want to place the parameter.
2. In the Parameters panel, expand the top drop-down list (as shown for Title options in Figure 2–42), and select the type of parameter that you want to use.

Figure 2–42

3. Expand the lower drop-down list and select the parameter that you want to use as shown in Figure 2–43.

   - The list of parameters for Project Information is shown in Figure 2–43. Schedule parameters include **Phase**, **Phase Filter**, and **View Name**.

Figure 2–43

- If you select a data cell you can modify the units of the cell by clicking 📟 (Format Unit) or create a formula in a cell by clicking 𝑓𝑥 (Calculated).

Columns and Rows

The options for Columns and Rows (as shown in Figure 2–44), vary according to the type of cell selected. You can **Insert**, **Delete**, and **Resize** title columns and rows. If you select a header column you can insert, delete, resize, and hide the column.

Figure 2–44

- Be careful about making changes in the Ribbon when you are in a data cell because any changes you make apply to the entire row or column.

How To: Hide a Column

1. Select any cell in the column that you want to hide.
2. In the *Modify Schedule/Quantities* tab>Columns panel, click

   (Hide). Alternatively, if you have selected the header cell, right-click and select **Hide Columns**.
3. The column is hidden.

- If you have hidden any columns and no longer want them

  hidden, you can click (Unhide All) or right-click and select **Unhide All Columns** at any time.

- Hiding columns is typically used when you want to sort or filter and do not want them to display in the final schedule.

- You can also hide columns when you are creating the schedule. In the Schedule Properties dialog box, in the *Formatting* tab, select the Field you want to hide and in the *Field formating* area, select **Hidden field** as shown in Figure 2–45.

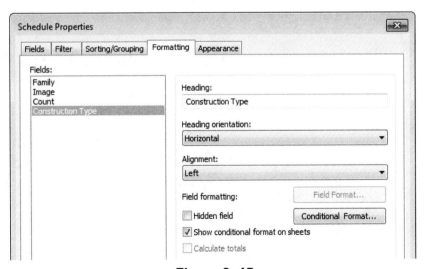

Figure 2–45

How To: Resize a Row or Column

1. Select a cell. If the cell is a title cell you can resize both the row and column
2. In the *Modify Schedule/Quantities* tab>Columns panel, click ⊹]⊹ (Resize) or in the Rows panel, click ⇌ (Resize).
3. In the Resize Column (or Row) dialog box (as shown in Figure 2–46), type a size and click | OK |.

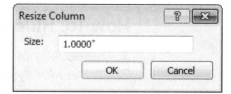

Figure 2–46

4. The column (or row) is resized in the schedule view and on the sheet.

Titles and Headers

The more complex and extensive a schedule, the more it can help to modify the title and header cells, using the commands shown in Figure 2–47. The title cells can be merged or unmerged. You can also insert images and delete the contents of title cells. Header cells can be grouped and ungrouped.

Figure 2–47

How To: Add and Merge Title Cells

1. Click inside a title cell.
2. In the *Modify Schedule/Quantities* tab>Rows panel, expand ⊐⁺⊏ (Insert) and click ⊐⁺⊏ (Above Selected) or ⊐₊⊏ (Below Selected). When inserting below the primary cell it typically comes in matching the number of header cells as shown in Figure 2–48.

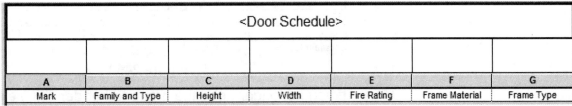

Before

After

Figure 2–48

3. Pick and drag across the cells that you want to merge.

4. Click ⬜ (Merge Unmerge).

5. The cells are now merged together as shown in Figure 2–49.

Figure 2–49

6. Add a parameter, text, or image in the newly merged cell.

- If you no longer want the cells to be merged, select the cell and click ⬜ (Merge Unmerge).

- To insert an image file (such as a .BMP, .JPG, or .PNG) in a title cell, select the title cell and click ⬜ (Insert Image) and select the image from the list.

- Use ⬜ (Clear Cell) to delete the text, image, or parameter used in that cell (Titles only).

How To: Setting up Sub-headers

1. In the Schedule view, drag the cursor over the headers you want to group.

2. In the *Modify Schedule/Quantities* tab>Titles & Headers panel, click ⬜ (Group).

3. A new header area is created above the selected columns. Enter a new name as shown in Figure 2–50.

A	B	C	D	E
		Window Dimensions		
Window Type	Count	Height	Width	Sill Height
36 x 36	72	3' - 0"	3' - 0"	3' - 0"
36" x 48"	84	4' - 0"	3' - 0"	3' - 0"
Grand total: 156				

Figure 2–50

• If you no longer need the grouped header cell, select the grouped cell and click ⬚ (Ungroup).

Appearance

The overall appearance of a schedule, including the text types used in the various cells, is set up in the Schedule Properties. You can also modify individual title and header cells using the options in the Appearance panel as shown in Figure 2–51.

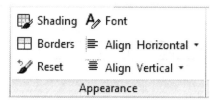

Figure 2–51

(Shading)	Opens the Color dialog box in which you can select a background color for the selected cells.
(Borders)	Opens the Edit Borders dialog box in which you can specify the line style and locations of borders around the selected cells.
(Reset)	Returns the formatting of selected cells to the original specified in the schedule properties.
(Font)	Opens the Edit Font dialog box in which you can specify the **Font**, **Font size**, **Font Style** (**Bold**, **Italic**, or **Underline**) and **Font Color** for the selected cells.
(Align Horizontal)	Aligns the text in the selected cells to the **Left**, **Center**, or **Right** justification.
(Align Vertical)	Aligns the text in the selected cells to the **Top**, **Middle**, or **Bottom** justification.

Adding Image Fields and Images

In addition to adding images in the title cells of a schedule you can assign images to elements and have them display in the schedule on a sheet, as shown in Figure 2–52.

Lighting Fixture Types			
Type Mark	Image	Family	Count
A		Troffer Light - 2x2 Parabolic	17
B		Troffer Light - 2x4 Parabolic	48
C		Pendant Light - Hemisphere	10

Figure 2–52

- Images can be set by instance or by type.

How To: Add Images to Schedules

New
in 2015

1. In the schedule view, open the Schedule Properties dialog box in the *Fields* tab.
2. Add the *Image* (or *Type Image*) field to the scheduled fields, as shown in Figure 2–53.

Figure 2–53

3. Complete the rest of your schedule design and click

.

4. In the schedule view, the *Image* (or *Type Image*) column displays as part of the schedules, as shown in Figure 2–54.

<Lighting Fixture Types>			
A	**B**	**C**	**D**
Type Mark	Image	Family	Count
A	<None>	Troffer Light - 2x2 Parabolic	17
B	<None>	Troffer Light - 2x4 Parabolic	48
C	<None>	Pendant Light - Hemisphere	10

Figure 2–54

5. Assign the appropriate image file to the instances or types.

- Type images for component families (such as light fixtures) are assigned directly in the family file and are read-only in the project. Type images for system families (such as walls) are assigned in the Type Properties.
- Instance images are assigned in Properties for each instance of the element.

6. To display the images, place the schedule on a sheet.

How To: Assign Image Files

1. Navigate to the appropriate place at which to assign the Image or Type Image. (Type Images for component families are assigned using Type Properties in the family file, not the project.)

2. Next to the **Image** or **Type Image** parameter, click ▣ (Browse), as shown in Figure 2–55.

Figure 2–55

3. In the Manage Images dialog box, select the image that you want to use, as shown in Figure 2–56

Figure 2–56

4. Click [OK]

- To add images to the Manage Image dialog box, click
  [Add...] and navigate to the location in which the images are stored.

- You can also delete and reload images as you would reload linked files.

- Image file types include BMP, JPG, JPEG, PNG, and TIF.

Practice 2d

Modify Schedules for Architectural Projects

 Learning Objectives

- Modify the look of the schedule using parameters, and by merging and grouping cells.
- Add images to a schedule.

Estimated time for completion: 15 minutes

In this practice you will modify the appearance of a schedule by adding parameters and text to the title and by merging group headers, as shown in Figure 2–57 (on a sheet). You will also add an image field (column) and assign images to a schedule.

Door Schedule - Level 1							
Clark Hall Performing Arts Building				Project Number: 1234.56			
	Door Size			Frame Information			
Mark	Height	Width	Fire Rating	Frame Type	Frame Material	Finish	Comments

Figure 2–57

Task 1 - Modify the appearance of the schedule.

1. Open the project **Clark-Hall-Schedules-Modify-A.rvt** found in the *Architectural* folder of your class files folder.

2. Open the **Door Schedule-Level 1** view.

3. Select the top title row of the schedule.

4. In the *Modify Schedule/Quantities* tab>Row panel, expand ⌐ᵗᶜ (Insert) and click ⌐ᵤᶜ (Below Selected).

5. Drag the cursor over approximately half of the new heading columns on the left and, in the Titles & Headers panel, click ▦ (Merge Unmerge). The cells are merged as shown in Figure 2–58.

Figure 2–58

6. Select the newly merged cell. In the Parameters panel, expand Category and select **Project Information**. Expand Parameter and select **Project Name**. The name of the project displays in brackets indicating that it is a parameter rather than text, as shown in Figure 2–59.

7. Merge the other cells and add text (**Project Number**) and another parameter (**Project Number**) as shown in Figure 2–59.

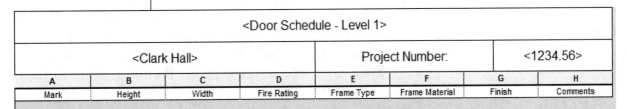

<Door Schedule - Level 1>							
<Clark Hall>				Project Number:		<1234.56>	
A	B	C	D	E	F	G	H
Mark	Height	Width	Fire Rating	Frame Type	Frame Material	Finish	Comments

Figure 2–59

8. In the *Manage* tab>Settings Panel, click ⬚ (Project Information).

9. In the Project Properties dialog box, update the *Project Name* to **Clark Hall Performing Arts Building**. Click [OK].

10. The Project Name updates, as shown in Figure 2–60.

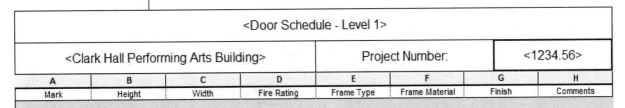

<Door Schedule - Level 1>							
<Clark Hall Performing Arts Building>				Project Number:		<1234.56>	
A	B	C	D	E	F	G	H
Mark	Height	Width	Fire Rating	Frame Type	Frame Material	Finish	Comments

Figure 2–60

11. Drag the cursor over the *Height* and *Width* header cells.

12. In the Titles & Headers panel, click ⬚ (Group).

13. Select the new cell and type **Door Size**.

14. Repeat for Frame Type, Frame Material, and Finish and type **Frame Information** as shown in Figure 2–61.

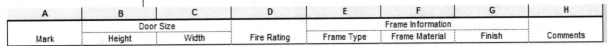

A	B	C	D	E	F	G	H
	Door Size			Frame Information			
Mark	Height	Width	Fire Rating	Frame Type	Frame Material	Finish	Comments

Figure 2–61

15. Save the project.

Task 2 - Modify the Appearance of the Title

1. Select the title cell and, in the *Schedules/Quantities* tab> Appearance panel, click $A\!\!\!/$ (Font).

2. In the Edit Font dialog box, change the *Font size* to **1/4"** and set the *Font style* to **Bold**.

3. Modify the other title and header cells as needed. In the example shown in Figure 2–62, in addition to changing the font appearance, the Project Number text and parameter have been aligned horizontally to be closer to each other and the border between the two of them has been removed.

<Door Schedule - Level 1>							
<Clark Hall Performing Arts Building>				Project Number: <1234.56>			
A	B	C	D	E	F	G	H
	Door Size				Frame Information		
Mark	Height	Width	Fire Rating	Frame Type	Frame Material	Finish	Comments

Figure 2–62

4. Open the **A601-Schedules** view to display the images and adjust it as needed.

5. Save the project.

Task 3 - Add Images to a schedule.

1. Open the **Window Schedule** view.

2. In the Schedule Properties dialog box, in the *Fields* tab add the **Type Mark** and **Image** parameters to the Scheduled Fields above the **Type** parameter. Move the **Count** parameter to the bottom of the list (as shown in Figure 2–63), and click OK .

In this situation the Type Image is only accessible by opening and adjusting the family file. Therefore, you can use the instance Image parameter.

Figure 2–63

3. In the Window Schedule view, select the Image cell for the first type and click [...].

4. In the Manage Images dialog box, click [Add...]

5. In the Import Image dialog box, navigate to the *Architectural>Images* folder, select the two window images, and click [OK].

6. In the Manage Images dialog box, select the image that matches the window row in which you are working.

7. Repeat the process with the other window image. The schedule should look similar to Figure 2–64.

<Window Schedule>					
A	B	C	D	E	F
Type Mark	Image	Type	Manufacturer	Comments	Count
18	Window 36 x 72.png	36" x 72"			3
19	Window 48x48.png	48" x 48"			36
Grand total: 39					

Figure 2–64

8. Open the **Sheets (all)>A601 - Schedules** view. The images should display as shown in Figure 2–65

Figure 2–65

9. If you have time, modify the schedule appearance to match the Door Schedule.

10. Save the project.

Practice 2e

Modify Schedules for MEP Projects

Learning Objectives

- Modify the look of the schedule using parameters and by merging and grouping cells.
- Add images to a schedule.

Estimated time for completion: 15 minutes

In this practice you will modify the appearance of a schedule by adding parameters and text to the title and by merging headers. You will also add an image field (column) and assign images to a schedule, as shown in Figure 2–66 (on a sheet).

Lighting Fixture Types			
Type Mark	Image	Family	Count
A		Troffer Light - 2x2 Parabolic	17
B		Troffer Light - 2x4 Parabolic	48
C		Pendant Light - Hemisphere	10

Figure 2–66

Task 1 - Modify the appearance of the schedule.

1. Open the project **Freel-Office-Modify-MEP.rvt** found in the *MEP* folder of your class files folder.

2. Open the **Plumbing Fixtures** schedule view.

3. Select the top title row of the schedule.

4. In the *Modify Schedule/Quantities* tab>Row panel, expand ⌐ (Insert) and click ⌐ (Below Selected).

5. Drag the cursor over half of the new heading columns on the left. In the Titles & Headers panel, click ▦ (Merge Unmerge). The cells are merged, as shown in Figure 2–67.

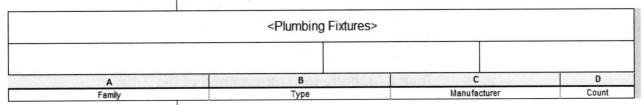

Figure 2–67

6. Select the newly merged cell. In the Parameters panel, expand Category and select **Project Information**. Then expand Parameter and select **Project Name**. The name of the project displays in brackets, indicating that it is a parameter

7. In the other cells and add text (**Project Number:**) and another parameter (**Project Number**) as shown in Figure 2–68.

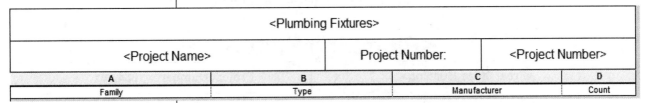

Figure 2–68

8. In the *Manage* tab>Settings Panel, click ▦ (Project Information).

9. In the Project Properties dialog box, update *Project Name* to **Freel Office Building** and *Project Number* to **1234.56.** Click OK . The parameters update as shown in Figure 2–69.

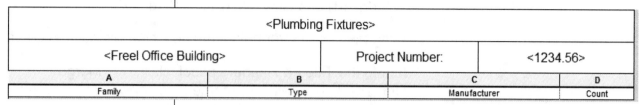

Figure 2–69

10. Save the project.

Task 2 - Modify the Appearance of the Title

1. Select the title cell and, in the Schedules/Quantities tab> Appearance panel click $A_{\mathscr{P}}$ (Font).

2. In the Edit Font dialog box change the *Font size* to **1/4"** and set the *Font style* to **Bold**.

3. Modify the other title and header cells as desired. In the example shown in Figure 2–70, besides changing the font appearance, the Project Number text and parameter have been aligned horizontally so they are closer to each other and the border between the two of them has been removed.

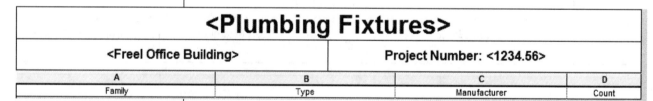

Figure 2–70

4. Open the **E 601 - Electrical and Lighting Schedules** view to display the images and adjust it as needed.

5. Save the project.

Task 3 - Add Images to a schedule.

1. Open the **Lighting Fixture Types** view.

2. In the Schedule Properties dialog box, in the *Fields* tab, add the **Image** parameter to the Scheduled Fields after the **Type** parameter as shown in Figure 2–71, and click [OK].

In this situation the Type Image is only accessible by opening and adjusting the family file. Therefore, you can use the instance Image parameter.

Schedule Properties

Fields | Filter | Sorting/Grouping | Formatting | Appearance

Available fields:

Apparent Load
Assembly Code
Assembly Description
Assembly Name
Ballast Loss

Add -->

<-- Remove

Scheduled fields (in order):

Type Mark
Image
Family
Count

Figure 2–71

3. In the Lighting Fixture Types view, select the Image cell for the first type and click [...].

4. In the Manage Images dialog box, click [Add...].

5. In the Import Image dialog box, navigate to the *MEP>Images* folder. select the three light images. and click [OK].

6. In the Manage Images dialog box, select the image that matches the row in which you are working.

7. Repeat the process with the other lighting fixture images. The schedule should look similar to the one shown in Figure 2–72.

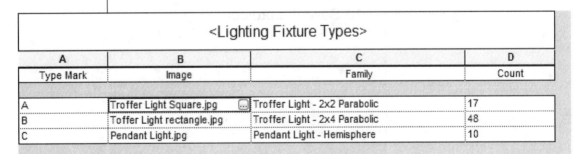

	<Lighting Fixture Types>		
A	**B**	**C**	**D**
Type Mark	Image	Family	Count
A	Troffer Light Square.jpg	Troffer Light - 2x2 Parabolic	17
B	Toffer Light rectangle.jpg	Troffer Light - 2x4 Parabolic	48
C	Pendant Light.jpg	Pendant Light - Hemisphere	10

Figure 2–72

8. Open the **Sheets (all)>E601 - Electrical and Lighting Schedules** view. The images should display as shown in Figure 2–73

Lighting Fixture Types			
Type Mark	Image	Family	Count
A		Troffer Light - 2x2 Parabolic	17
B		Troffer Light - 2x4 Parabolic	48
C		Pendant Light - Hemisphere	10

Figure 2–73

9. If you have time, modify the schedule appearance to match the other schedule.

10. Save the project.

Practice 2f

Modify Schedules for Structural Projects

Learning Objective

- Modify the look of the schedule using parameters, and merging and grouping cells.

Estimated time for completion: 15 minutes

In this practice you will modify the appearance of a schedule by adding parameters and text to the title and by merging cells, as shown in Figure 2–74.

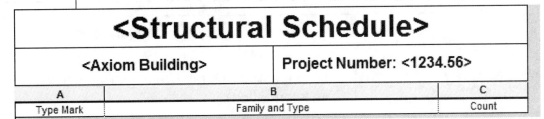

Figure 2–74

Task 1 - Modify the appearance of the schedule.

1. Open the project **Axiom-Building-Modify-S.rvt** found in the *Structural* folder of your class files folder.

2. Open the **Structural Schedule** view.

3. Select the top title row of the schedule.

4. In the *Modify Schedule/Quantities* tab>Row panel, expand ⌐⌐ (Insert) and click ⌐⌐ (Below Selected).

5. If there are more than three new cells, drag the cursor over half of the new heading columns on the left and, in the Titles & Headers panel, click ▦ (Merge Unmerge). The cells are merged as shown in Figure 2–75.

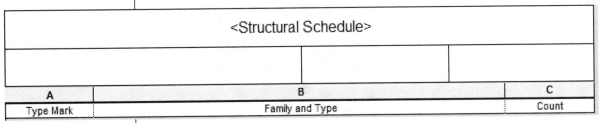

Figure 2–75

6. Select the newly merged cell. In the Parameters panel, expand Category and select **Project Information**. Then expand Parameter and select **Project Name**. The name of the project displays in brackets indicating that it is a parameter rather than text, as shown in Figure 2–76.

7. Add text (**Project Number:**) and another parameter (**Project Number**) as shown in Figure 2–76.

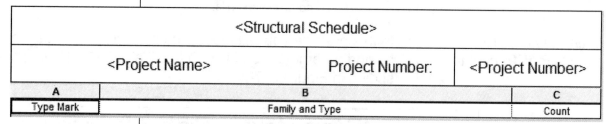

Figure 2–76

8. In the *Manage* tab>Settings Panel, click (Project Information).

9. In the Project Properties dialog box, update *Project Name* to **Axiom Building** and *Project Number* to **1234.56**. Click OK . The project name and number update as shown in Figure 2–77.

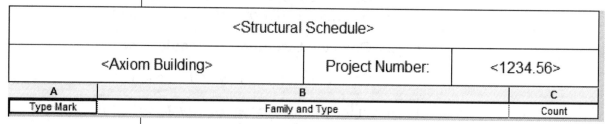

Figure 2–77

10. Save the project.

Task 2 - Modify the appearance of the title.

1. Select the title cell. In the *Schedules/Quantities* tab> Appearance panel, click A (Font).

2. In the Edit Font dialog box, change the *Font size* to **1/4"** and set the *Font style* to **Bold**.

3. Modify the other title and header cells as needed. In the example shown in Figure 2–78, in addition to changing the font appearance, the Project Number text and parameter have been aligned horizontally to be closer to each other and the border between them has been removed.

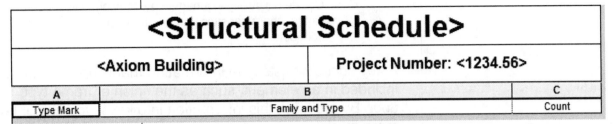

Figure 2–78

4. Modify the other two schedules to match the appearance.

5. Save the project.

2.4 Creating Key Schedules

Learning Objective

- Create a Key Style schedule by defining keys for elements with similar characteristics that automatically fill in the properties in a schedule.

A *key schedule* lists type information that is not automatically included in an element, such as the finish or frame type of a door. By grouping this information into keys, you can enter it more quickly.

Schedule key styles are useful when you have a large number of elements that need to have the same finish information, as shown in Figure 2–79. Fields in key styles are typically controlled by instance rather than by type. Grouping styles together makes it easier to apply this information to large numbers of instances.

\<Room Style Schedule\>					
A	B	C	D	E	F
Key Name	Wall Finish	Floor Finish	Base Finish	Ceiling Finish	Comments
Corridor	Painted	Carpet	Vinyl	Painted	
Executive Office	Wall Paper	Wood	Wood	ACT	
Standard Office	Painted	Carpet	Vinyl	ACT	
Utility	Painted	Vinyl	Vinyl	ACT	

Figure 2–79

How To: Create a Schedule Key Style

1. In the *View* tab>Create panel, expand ▦ (Schedules) and click ▦ (Schedule/Quantities).
2. In the New Schedule dialog box, select a category.
3. Select the **Schedule keys** option and type a *Name* for the key, as shown in Figure 2–80. This adds an **Instance** parameter in the Properties dialog box for the selected category and adds a field to the schedule properties.

Use the Filter list to limit the number of categories with which you can work.

Figure 2–80

4. Click [OK].
5. In the Schedule Properties dialog box, the *Fields* tab displays the new **Key Name** that has already been added to the *Scheduled fields*, as shown in Figure 2–81.
6. Add other fields from the list of *Available fields*, as shown in Figure 2–81.

Figure 2–81

7. Fill out the rest of the tabs as needed and click OK . The new schedule opens with only the fields displayed, as shown in Figure 2–82.

<Room Style Schedule>					
A	B	C	D	E	F
Key Name	Wall Finish	Floor Finish	Base Finish	Ceiling Finish	Comments

Figure 2–82

8. In the *Modify | Schedule/Quantities* tab>Rows panel, expand ⇥ (Insert) and click ⊞ (Data Row) or right-click on the schedule and select **Insert Data Row**. A new row with the default label **1** is displayed, as shown in Figure 2–83. Type a new name for the row.

<Room Style Schedule>					
A	B	C	D	E	F
Key Name	Wall Finish	Floor Finish	Base Finish	Ceiling Finish	Comments
1					

Figure 2–83

9. Continue adding rows and names as shown in Figure 2–84.

<Room Style Schedule>					
A	B	C	D	E	F
Key Name	Wall Finish	Floor Finish	Base Finish	Ceiling Finish	Comments
Corridor					
Executive Office					
Standard Office					
Utility					

Figure 2–84

10. Fill in the values for the rows as shown in Figure 2–85.

<Room Style Schedule>					
A	B	C	D	E	F
Key Name	Wall Finish	Floor Finish	Base Finish	Ceiling Finish	Comments
Corridor	Painted	Carpet	Vinyl	Painted	
Executive Office	Wall Paper	Wood	Wood	ACT	
Standard Office	Painted	Carpet	Vinyl	ACT	
Utility	Painted	Vinyl	Vinyl	ACT	

Figure 2–85

11. To assign the key style, add a column to the schedule (such as the *Room Style* column in a Room Schedule shown in Figure 2–86).

Figure 2–86

You can also modify the properties of various instances in the project as shown in Figure 2–87.

Figure 2–87

2.5 Advanced Schedule Options

 Learning Objectives

- Create additional parameters that are used in projects and shared with other projects.
- Create Calculated Value Fields and Percentage Fields in schedules.
- Apply Conditional formatting to fields in a schedule.
- (Autodesk Revit MEP software only.) Embed a schedule into an existing schedule.

When you are working in a variety of schedules, you might want to include additional parameters, create fields that include formulas, as shown for a rounded area in Figure 2–88. You can also add conditional formatting that adds a background color to cells that meet the condition. For MEP projects you can also create nested schedules.

<Room Schedule>			
A	B	C	D
Number	Name	Area	Floor Area
101	Office	280.49 SF	280 SF
102	Conference	337.38 SF	340 SF
103	Office	199.63 SF	200 SF
104	Office	199.63 SF	200 SF
105	Office	193.17 SF	190 SF
106	Office	243.22 SF	240 SF
107	Work Room	154.77 SF	150 SF
108	Reception	327.48 SF	330 SF
109	Library	404.78 SF	400 SF

Figure 2–88

Creating Project Parameters

Two types of custom parameters can be used in schedules: project parameters and shared parameters.

- Project parameters can be used in schedules, but not in tags.

- Shared parameters can be used in schedules and in tags. They can also be used in other projects and exported to a database.

- Both project and shared parameters can be created wherever parameter options exist. They are also available in the *Manage* tab>Settings panel.

How To: Create a Project Parameter

1. In the Schedule Properties dialog box, in the *Fields* tab, click
   Add Parameter... (or other Project Parameter access).
2. In the Parameter Properties dialog box, select **Project parameter**, as shown in Figure 2–89.

Figure 2–89

3. In the *Parameter Data* area shown in Figure 2–90, Set the value as an **Instance** or a **Type**. and then specify a new *Name* for the parameter and select the *Discipline*, *Group*, and *Type of Parameter* in the drop-down lists. You can also add a custom tooltip.

Enhanced
in 2015

Figure 2–90

- **Instance parameters:** Set for each instance of the associated element. For example, if you create a **Material** parameter when you are creating a furniture schedule, you can assign a different material to each instance of the component.

- **Type parameters:** Modify all instances of a specific type. For example, if you create a **Material** parameter for a furniture component, changing the material for one component changes all of them.

- **Values are aligned per group type:** (Instance Parameters only.) If an element that includes this parameter is part of multiple groups, the value remains the same for all of the groups. Changing the value in one group changes the value in all of the groups.

- Values can vary by group instance: (Instance Parameters only.) If an element that includes this parameter is part of multiple groups, the value can vary according to the group. Changing the value in one group changes the value for all other instances of that group, but does not change the value for instances of other groups that also include the element.

- The *Discipline* can be set to **Common**, **Structural**, **HVAC**, **Electrical**, **Piping**, or **Energy**.

- The *Type of Parameter* specifies how the parameter value is stored, The options available for Discipline impact the types of parameters in the list, as shown in Figure 2–91.

Figure 2–91

Common Parameter Types

Text	A text parameter can host any type of information that consists of both numbers and letters. Examples could be the fabric color or part number of the element.
Integer	Any value that is always represented by a whole number. Examples could be the number of chairs that fit around a conference table or the number of shelves in a bookcase.
Number	Any numeric value: whole, decimal, or fraction. You can use formulas with **Number** parameters.
Length	When you label dimensions, you create **Length** parameters. You can use formulas with **Length** parameters.
Area	Establishes the area of an element. It is numeric and can have formulas applied to it.
Volume	Establishes the volume of an element. It is numeric and can have formulas applied to it.
Angle	Establishes the angle of an element. It is numeric and can have formulas applied to it.
Slope	Displays a slope, as set up in the Field Format.
Currency	Displays the amount in dollars or other currencies, as set up in the Field Format.
Mass Density	Displays the mass per unit volume of material.
URL	Specifies a link to a web site.
Material	Provides a place to assign a material from the list of materials that are set up in the project.
Image	Creates a parameter in which you can add a raster image connected to the family.
Yes/No	Used with instance parameters where you need a **Yes** or **No** answer to a question listed in the name. The default is **Yes**.
<Family Type>	Opens a dialog box where you can select from the list of family types, such as doors, furniture, or tags.

New
in **2015**

The Group parameter under drop-down list lists groups that categorize parameters in the Properties and Family Types dialog boxes, as shown in Figure 2–92.

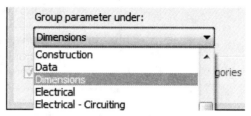

Figure 2–92

You can create a tooltip that displays when you hover the cursor over the new parameter in Properties, as shown in Figure 2–93.

In the Parameter Properties dialog box, click and, in the Edit Tooltip dialog box, type the new description and click

OK .

Figure 2–93

Creating Fields from Formulas

In a variety of schedules, you need to gather numerical information and apply formulas to it for a new parameter. For example, you can include cost and quantity information in a Material Takeoff, as shown in the schedule in Figure 2–94.

<Brick - Material Takeoff>					
A	B	C	D	E	F
Material: Name	Material: Area	Material: Manufacturer	Material: Cost	Total Cost	Total Units of Brick
Masonry - Brick	22160 SF	XYZ Masonry	3.00	$66480	155123
Masonry - Brick: 14	22160 SF			$66480	155123

Figure 2–94

- You can create calculated value fields to add formulas to a schedule, or create a percentage field using values in the schedule.

- Gather the information you need to use to create formulas, including the exact name of any fields, before you start the process of creating the calculated value.

- Formula outcomes can be rounded off.

How To: Create a Calculated Value Field

1. In the Schedule Properties dialog box, in the *Fields* tab, click

   Calculated Value... . The Calculated Value dialog box opens, as shown in Figure 2–95.

A formula has been added for this figure.

Formulas can only reference fields that are included in the schedule.

Figure 2–95

2. Type a *Name* for the new field.
3. Specify **Formula** as the type of field.
4. Select the *Discipline* and *Type* as needed.

5. Type the formula you want to use in the *Formula* field. (The full formula in is (Material: Area / 1 SF) * Material: Cost).) To ensure you get the exact field name, click 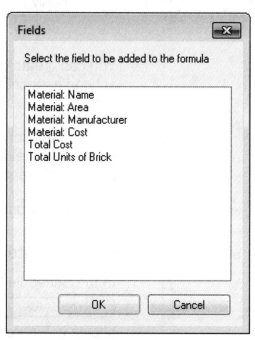 (Browse) to select from a list of fields, as shown in Figure 2–96.

Figure 2–96

6. Click [OK].

Percentage Fields

Percentage fields can be used with area schedules, as shown in Figure 2–97.

<Area Schedule (Rentable)>		
A	B	C
Name	Area	Percent of Total Area
Office	2657 SF	9%
Auditorium	9694 SF	33%
Classrooms	13533 SF	46%
Area	3682 SF	12%

Figure 2–97

How To: Create a Percentage Field

1. In the Schedule Properties dialog box, in the *Fields* tab, click
   Calculated Value... . The Calculated Value dialog box opens, as
   shown in Figure 2–98.

Figure 2–98

2. Type a *Name* for the new field.
3. Specify **Percentage** as the type of field.
4. Select the field you want to take a percentage *Of*.
5. Select the field you want to take a percentage *By*.

   • The default option is **<Grand total>**, which calculates the
     percentage based on the total of the entire schedule.

   • If you have created groups in the *Sorting/Grouping* tab,
     they are also available. For example, if Fields are sorted
     by **Level**.

6. Click OK .

Conditional Formatting

Conditional formatting can be applied to any field where you
need to display some specific information that can easily be seen
at a glance. For example, in Figure 2–99, the *Area* field is
highlighted according to a conditional test for any size over
10000 SF.

*Conditional formatting is
typically used for testing
and does not carry over
when placed on a sheet.*

Area Schedule Over 10000 SF			
A	**B**	**C**	**D**
Number	Name	Area Type	Area
1	Office	Building Common Area	2657 SF
2	Auditorium	Building Common Area	9694 SF
3	Classrooms	Building Common Area	13533 SF
4	Area	Building Common Area	3682 SF

Figure 2–99

How To: Add Conditional Formatting in a schedule

1. Open the schedule you want to work in and select the *Formatting* tab.
2. Select the field to which you want to apply the conditional formatting.
3. Click [Conditional Format...] .
4. In the Conditional Formatting dialog box, select the *Field*, *Test*, and specify a *Value*, as shown in Figure 2–100.

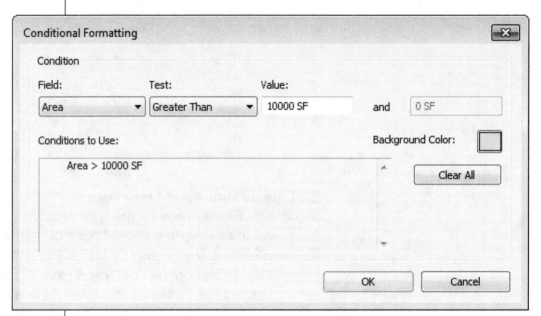

Figure 2–100

5. Click the **Background Color** button and select a color to display in the schedule when the conditions are met.
6. You can select additional fields, test, and values to further refine the conditional statements.

7. When you are finished, click [OK] to close the dialog box and continue working on the Schedule Properties as needed.

Embedded Schedules

When working with Autodesk Revit MEP schedules that need to refer to spaces or rooms, you can use embedded schedules. For example, in Figure 2–101, a space schedule that is displaying the Space **Number** and **Name**, also has an embedded schedule displaying information about the air terminals in each space.

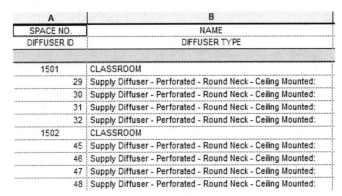

Figure 2–101

How To: Add an embedded schedule

1. Create the base Space or Room schedule.
2. In the Schedule Properties dialog box, select the *Embedded Schedule* tab.
3. Select **Embedded Schedule** and then select a category type from the Category list as shown in Figure 2–102.

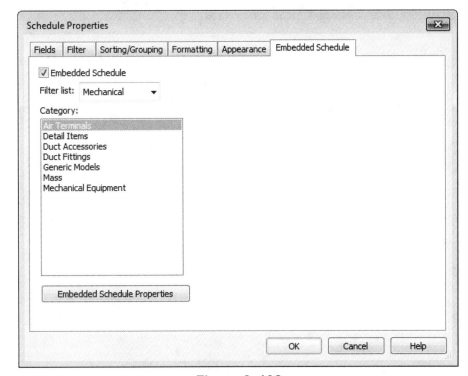

Figure 2–102

4. Click [Embedded Schedule Properties].

5. In the Schedule Properties dialog box, in the *Field* tab, add the necessary fields. The fields display in order directly under the base schedule columns, as shown in Figure 2–103.

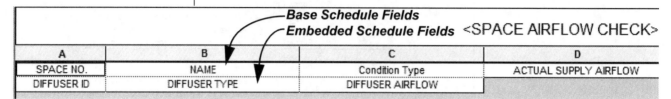

A	B	C	D
SPACE NO.	NAME	Condition Type	ACTUAL SUPPLY AIRFLOW
DIFFUSER ID	DIFFUSER TYPE	DIFFUSER AIRFLOW	

Figure 2–103

6. Add any filters, sorting, and formatting as required.

7. Click [OK] until the schedule displays.

2.6 Creating Material Takeoff Schedules

Learning Objective

- Create material takeoff schedules.

Schedules are powerful features that interact with all parts of an Autodesk Revit project. A special schedule, called a Material Takeoff, gathers information about the materials in a project (such as the area and volume) and user-designated properties (such as the cost or manufacturer). You can also create formulas or percentages based on material properties to include in a schedule using the **Calculated value** option, as shown in Figure 2–104. Custom parameters are also permitted in Material Takeoffs.

Figure 2–104

- Creating material takeoff schedules follows the same procedure as when creating building component schedules, except that it uses a different command. In the *View* tab> Create panel, expand ▦ (Schedules) and click

  ▦ (Material Takeoff) or in the Project Browser, right-click on the Schedule/Quantities node and select **New Material Takeoff**.

- The options for fields include all of the material parameters, as shown in Figure 2–105.

Figure 2–105

How To: Create a Material Takeoff Schedule

1. In the *View* tab>Create panel, expand ▦ (Schedules) and click ▦ (Material Takeoff).

2. In the New Material Takeoff dialog box, use the *Filter list* to limit the categories and then select the *Category* you want to schedule. Enter a *Name* and select the *Phase* you want to include, as shown in Figure 2–106.

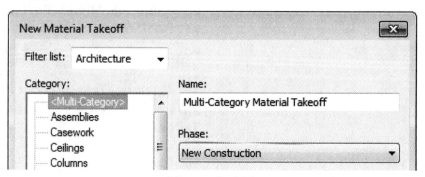

Figure 2–106

3. Click ▢OK▢.

4. In the Material Takeoff Properties dialog box, in the *Fields* tab, select the fields you want to include in the takeoff, as shown in Figure 2–107. Select from the *Available fields* list on the left side and click [Add -->] to move the field to the *Scheduled fields* list on the right.

Figure 2–107

- Click [Add Parameter...] to create a new parameter to be used in the schedule.

- Click [Calculated Value...] to create fields using formulas.

5. Arrange the fields in order using [Move Up] and [Move Down] as needed.

- When you apply materials to faces using (Paint), you can now incorporate that area into schedules using the *Material: As Paint* field. Each instance displays as either **Yes** or **No** in the finished material takeoff schedule.

6. Use the *Filter* tab to limit the elements covered in a schedule, as shown in Figure 2–108. Use the *Sorting/Grouping* tab to arrange the order in which the elements are displayed in the schedule.

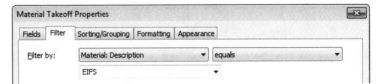

Figure 2–108

7. In the *Formatting* tab, set the format for the individual headers, as shown in Figure 2–109. Here you can also modify numerical information, such as the *Material: Area* and *Material: Volume*. Select the field and the **Calculate totals** option. Click Field Format... if you want to modify the way the numbers are displayed in the schedule.

Figure 2–109

8. By default, the field format uses the project settings. You can clear the **Use project settings** option and modify the options, as shown in Figure 2–110. This is only available for numerical fields.

A numerical value can be assigned a currency. Zeros can be suppressed. Spaces can be suppressed and large numbers can include commas as separators.

Figure 2–110

9. Define the look of the schedule grids and text in the *Appearance* tab and click OK .

Hint: Material Properties

Most material properties used in material takeoff schedules can be set by material. In the *Manage* tab>Settings panel, click

(Materials). In the Material Browser, select the material that you want to modify. In the *Identity* tab, you can add information, such as **Manufacturer** and **Cost** as shown in Figure 2–111.

Figure 2–111

Practice 2g

Create Complex Schedules for Architectural Projects

 Learning Objective

- Create material takeoff schedules.
- (Optional) Create a percentage-based calculated value field for use in a schedule.

Estimated time for completion: 15 minutes

In this practice you will create a material takeoff schedule that includes several calculated value formulas. You will then add it to a sheet, as shown in Figure 2–112, and test it and other material takeoff schedules by modifying the wall type and material properties. As an optional task, you will create a percentage-based field for an area schedule.

Brick - Material Takeoff					
Material: Name	Material: Area	Material: Manufacturer	Material: Cost	Total Cost per SF	Total Units of Brick
Masonry - Brick	2749 SF	XYZ Masonry	3.00	$8250	19242
Masonry - Brick: 11	2749 SF			$8250	19242

Figure 2–112

Task 1 - Create a material takeoff schedule.

1. Open the project **Mall-Addition-A.rvt** found in the *Architecture* folder of your class files folder.

2. In the *View* tab>Create panel, expand ▦ (Schedules) and click 🚚 (Material Takeoff).

3. In the New Material Takeoff dialog box, in the *Filter* list, select **Architecture**, and in the *Category* list, select **Walls**. Name the schedule **Brick – Material Takeoff** and select **New Construction** from the *Phase* list.

4. Click ⬚ OK ⬚.

5. In the *Fields* tab of the Material Takeoff Properties dialog box, add the fields **Material: Name**, **Material: Area**, **Material: Manufacturer**, and **Material: Cost**, as shown in Figure 2–113.

Figure 2–113

*Area and Cost are two different types of parameters. Therefore, in this practice, you need to divide the **Material: Area** parameter by 1 to get the correct result.*

6. Click [Calculated Value...] and set the following parameters, as shown in Figure 2–114. (Make sure you account for the spaces in the field names when typing the formulas. There should be a space after the colon for the software to recognize **Material: Area** as a field.)

- **Name:** Total Cost per SF
- **Discipline: Common**
- *Type:* Number
- **Formula:** (Material: Area / 1SF) * Material: Cost

You can click

[...] *(Browse) to select from a list of fields as you are creating the formula to prevent you from misspelling parameter names.*

Figure 2–114

7. Create another calculated value fields using the following parameters. (There are seven standard bricks in a square foot. The type and size of bricks being used might vary and that can affect the number of bricks.)

- **Name:** Total Units of Brick
- **Discipline:** Common
- **Type:** Number
- **Formula:** (Material: Area / 1) *7

8. In the *Filter* tab, filter the schedule using **Material: Name equals Masonry - Brick**, as shown in Figure 2–115.

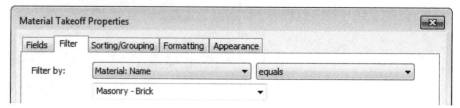

Figure 2–115

9. In the *Sorting/Grouping* tab, sort by **Material: Name** and select **Footer**, as shown in Figure 2–116.

Figure 2–116

10. In the *Formatting* tab, in the *Fields* list, select **Material: Area**, **Total Cost per SF**, and **Total Units of Brick.** In the *Field formatting* area, select the **Calculate totals** option, as shown in Figure 2–117.

Figure 2–117

11. In the *Appearance* tab, modify the grid lines or text fonts as needed and click OK .

Task 2 - Modify the material takeoff schedule.

1. The units for the *Total Cost per SF* and *Total Units of Brick* fields have six decimal places, as shown in Figure 2–118. This is more than required.

<Brick - Material Takeoff>					
A	B	C	D	E	F
Material: Name	Material: Area	Material: Manufact	Material: Cost	Total Cost per SF	Total Units of Brick
Masonry - Brick	192 SF		4.00	769.675167	1346.931543
Masonry - Brick	756 SF		4.00	3023.630924	5291.354117
Masonry - Brick	474 SF		4.00		

Figure 2–118

2. In Properties, next to *Formatting*, click [Edit...]. The Material Takeoff Properties dialog box opens with the *Formatting* tab selected.

3. Select the *Total Cost per SF* field and click [Field Format...].

4. In the Format dialog box, clear the **Use default settings** option. Set the *Units* to **Currency**, *Rounding* to **To the nearest 10** and *Unit symbol* to **$**, as shown in Figure 2–119.

   Click [OK].

Figure 2–119

5. Select the *Total Units of Brick* field and click

.

6. In the Format dialog box, clear the **Use default settings** option. Set the *Units* to **Fixed** and *Rounding* to **0 decimal places**. Click .

7. Click [OK] to close the dialog box.

8. In the schedule view, add a manufacturer's name and change the *Material: Cost* of the Brick to **3.00**. The Total Cost updates, but the Total Units of Brick remains the same.

Task 3 - Test the material takeoff schedule.

1. Open the **A102 – Plan and Schedules** sheet.

2. Zoom in on the existing schedules to one side.

3. Add the new **Brick – Material Takeoff** schedule to the sheet. Use grips to modify the size of the schedule as needed.

4. This schedule is different from other schedules because it includes all the instances of Brick. In the Project Browser, select the **Brick - Material Takeoff** schedule (you do not have to open it to change the properties).

5. In Properties, in the *Other* area, next to Sorting/Grouping, click [Edit...] .

6. In the Material Takeoff Properties dialog box, in the *Sorting/Grouping* tab, clear the **Itemize every instance** option. The schedule updates on the sheet.

7. Open the 3D Views>**Front View**. Arrange the views so that you can see the 3D view and the top two schedules on the sheet, as shown in Figure 2–120.

Figure 2–120

8. In the 3D view, select one of the walls on the tower to the left and change its wall type to **Basic Wall: FCE – Exterior – EIFS on Mtl.Stud**, as shown in Figure 2–121.

Figure 2–121

9. The schedules change to display a smaller amount of the stone used and add to the EIFS schedule that was blank before, as shown in Figure 2–122.

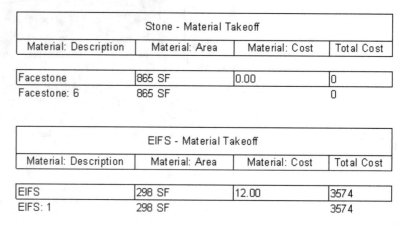

Stone - Material Takeoff			
Material: Description	Material: Area	Material: Cost	Total Cost
Facestone	865 SF	0.00	0
Facestone: 6	865 SF		0

EIFS - Material Takeoff			
Material: Description	Material: Area	Material: Cost	Total Cost
EIFS	298 SF	12.00	3574
EIFS: 1	298 SF		3574

Figure 2–122

10. Double-click on the Stone - Material Takeoff schedule in the sheet to open the related schedule view.

11. Change the *Material: Cost* to **10**.

12. The *Material: Cost* and *Total Cost* fields update on the sheet as well.

13. Modify these fields so that they display as currency.

Task 4 - (Optional) Create a percentage-based Calculated Value field.

---

1. Using (Schedule/Quantities), create a new area schedule (Rentable).

2. Add the fields *Name* and *Area*.

3. Click ⌊ Calculated Value... ⌋ and add the new *Calculated Value* field, as shown in Figure 2–123.

Figure 2–123

4. Click [OK] twice to create the schedule.

5. Open the **A103 – Area Plans** sheet and add the new area schedule to the sheet next to the colored legend, as shown in Figure 2–124.

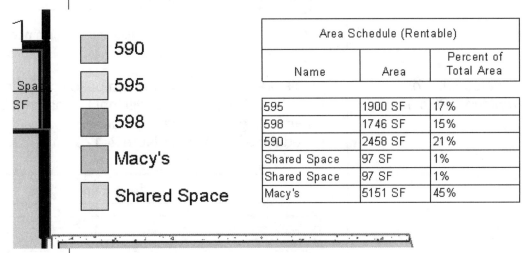

Figure 2–124

6. Save and close the project.

Practice 2h

Create Complex Schedules for MEP Projects

 Learning Objective

- Create a base schedule and add an embedded schedule into it.
- Test the scheduled information using conditional formatting.

Estimated time for completion: 20 minutes

In this practice you will create a base schedule including a Calculated Value and Conditional Formatting. You will then add an embedded schedule to create an Space Air Flow Check schedule, as shown in Figure 2–125.

<Space Air Flow Check>					
A	B	C	D	E	F
Space Number	Name	Condition Type	Actual Supply Airfl	Calculated Supply	Airflow Check
Diffuser ID	Diffuser Type	Diffuser Airflow			
101	Office Area 1	Heated and cooled	0 CFM	2833 CFM	-2833 CFM
102	Office Area 2	Heated and cooled	0 CFM	2546 CFM	-2546 CFM
103	Vestuble 1	Heated and cooled	0 CFM	351 CFM	-351 CFM
104	Foyer 1	Heated and cooled	0 CFM	718 CFM	-718 CFM
105	Conf. Room	Heated and cooled	800 CFM	519 CFM	281 CFM
1	Supply Diffuser	400 CFM			
2	Supply Diffuser	400 CFM			
106	Women's 1	Heated and cooled	500 CFM	203 CFM	297 CFM
13	Supply Diffuser	500 CFM			
107	Mens 1	Heated and cooled	500 CFM	201 CFM	299 CFM
14	Supply Diffuser	500 CFM			
108	Hall 1	Heated and cooled	500 CFM	864 CFM	-364 CFM
8	Supply Diffuser	500 CFM			
109	Mech. Room	Heated and cooled	100 CFM	90 CFM	10 CFM
50	Supply Diffuser	100 CFM			
110	Elec. Room	Heated and cooled	100 CFM	168 CFM	-68 CFM
49	Supply Diffuser	100 CFM			
111	Utility	Heated and cooled	0 CFM	54 CFM	-54 CFM
112	Break Room 1	Heated and cooled	500 CFM	527 CFM	-27 CFM
9	Supply Diffuser	500 CFM			
113	Vestuble 2	Heated and cooled	0 CFM	150 CFM	-150 CFM
114	Stair	Heated and cooled	0 CFM	53 CFM	-53 CFM
115	Elev.	Heated and cooled	0 CFM	25 CFM	-25 CFM
201	Office Space 3	Heated and cooled	0 CFM	7327 CFM	-7327 CFM
202	Office Space 4	Heated and cooled	0 CFM	6196 CFM	-6196 CFM
203	Foyer 2	Heated and cooled	0 CFM	867 CFM	-867 CFM
204	Womens 2	Heated and cooled	0 CFM	203 CFM	-203 CFM
205	Mens 2	Heated and cooled	140 CFM	201 CFM	-61 CFM
37	Supply Diffuser	140 CFM			
206	Hall 2	Heated and cooled	0 CFM	1003 CFM	-1003 CFM
25	Supply Diffuser	500 CFM			
207	Stair	Heated and cooled	0 CFM	238 CFM	-238 CFM
208	Break Room 2	Heated and cooled	410 CFM	497 CFM	-87 CFM
24	Supply Diffuser	205 CFM			
34	Supply Diffuser	205 CFM			
209	Mechanical Ro	Heated and cooled	0 CFM	268 CFM	-268 CFM

Figure 2–125

Task 1 - Create a Base schedule.

1. Open the project **Office-Airflow-MEP.rvt** found in the *MEP* folder of your class files folder.

2. Create a new Schedules/Quantities schedule.

3. In the New Schedule dialog box, filter the list by *Mechanical* if needed, and select **Spaces**. Name the schedule **Space Air Flow Check** and click OK .

4. Add the following fields: **Number**, **Name**, **Condition Type**, **Actual Supply Airflow**, and **Calculated Supply Airflow**, as shown in Figure 2–126.

Figure 2–126

5. While still in the *Fields* tab, click Calculated Value... .

6. In the Calculated Value dialog box, specify the *Name* as **Airflow Check**, *Discipline* as **HVAC**, and *Type* as **Air Flow**.

7. For the Formula, click ... and select **Actual Supply Airflow** and click OK . Type a minus sign (-) and then click ... again and select **Calculated Supply Airflow**. Click OK .

By browsing for the fields, you save time by not misspelling or mis-capitalizing the field names.

8. In the *Sorting/Grouping* tab, sort by **Number**.

9. In the *Formatting* tab, select **Airflow Check** and click Conditional Format... .

10. In the Conditional Formatting dialog box, specify the different fields as shown in Figure 2–127. You can select any color you want.

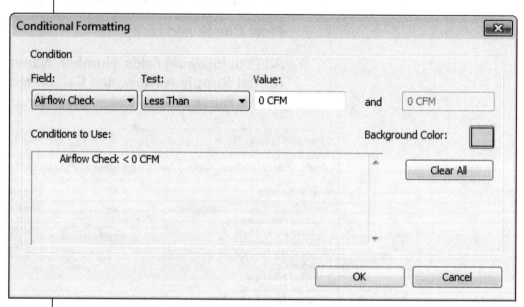

Figure 2–127

11. Click OK to display the schedule (shown in part) up to this point. Expand the columns as shown in Figure 2–128.

		<Space Air Flow Check>			
A	B	C	D	E	F
Number	Name	Condition Type	Actual Supply Airfl	Calculated Supply	Airflow Check
101	Office Area 1	Heated and cooled	0 CFM	2833 CFM	-2833 CFM
102	Office Area 2	Heated and cooled	0 CFM	2546 CFM	-2546 CFM
103	Vestuble 1	Heated and cooled	0 CFM	351 CFM	-351 CFM
104	Foyer 1	Heated and cooled	0 CFM	718 CFM	-718 CFM
105	Conf. Room	Heated and cooled	800 CFM	519 CFM	281 CFM
106	Women's 1	Heated and cooled	500 CFM	203 CFM	297 CFM
107	Mens 1	Heated and cooled	500 CFM	201 CFM	299 CFM
108	Hall 1	Heated and cooled	500 CFM	864 CFM	-364 CFM

Figure 2–128

12. Click inside the **Number** Heading and change it to **Space Number**.

13. Save the project.

Task 2 - Add an embedded schedule.

1. While still in the Space Air Flow Check schedule view, in Properties, beside *Embedded Schedule*, click .

2. In the Schedule Properties dialog box, in the *Embedded Schedule* tab, select **Embedded Schedule**.

3. In the Category list, select **Air Terminals**.

4. Click ⎡ Embedded Schedule Properties ⎤.

5. In the Schedule Properties dialog box, in the *Field* tab, add the following fields:

   - *System Classification*
   - *Mark*
   - *Family and Type*
   - *Flow*

6. In the *Filter* tab, filter by: **System Classification equals Supply Air**.

7. In the *Sorting/Grouping* tab, set *Sort by* as **Mark** and *Then by* as **Family and Type**, as shown in Figure 2–129.

Figure 2–129

8. In the *Formatting* tab, select the *Field* **System Classification** and select **Hidden field**.

9. Select **Mark** and set *Heading* as **Diffuser ID**. Set *Heading orientation* as **Horizontal** and *Alignment* as **Right**.

10. Select **Family and Type** and set *Heading* as **Diffuser Type**. Set *Heading orientation* as **Horizontal** and *Alignment* as **Left**.

11. Select **Flow** and set *Heading* as **Diffuser Airflow**. Set *Heading orientation* as **Horizontal** and *Alignment* as **Left**.

12. Click [OK] until the schedule displays, as shown in part in Figure 2–130.

<Space Air Flow Check>					
A	**B**	**C**	**D**	**E**	**F**
Space Number	Name	Condition Type	Actual Supply Airfl	Calculated Supply	Airflow Check
Diffuser ID	Diffuser Type	Diffuser Airflow			
101	Office Area 1	Heated and cooled	0 CFM	2833 CFM	-2833 CFM
102	Office Area 2	Heated and cooled	0 CFM	2546 CFM	-2546 CFM
103	Vestuble 1	Heated and cooled	0 CFM	351 CFM	-351 CFM
104	Foyer 1	Heated and cooled	0 CFM	718 CFM	-718 CFM
105	Conf. Room	Heated and cooled	800 CFM	519 CFM	281 CFM
1	Supply Diffuser	400 CFM			
2	Supply Diffuser	400 CFM			
106	Women's 1	Heated and cooled	500 CFM	203 CFM	297 CFM
13	Supply Diffuser	500 CFM			

Figure 2–130

13. Save the project.

14. If you have time, work with the project to establish the correct air flow for the various spaces.

Practice 2i

Create Complex Schedules for Structural Projects

Learning Objective

- Create project parameters and modify an existing schedule using them.
- Modify and group headers in a schedule to graphically link the parameter types.

Estimated time for completion: 20 minutes

In this practice you will create project parameters for structural footing types. Then you will add the new parameters to a schedule, add an additional parameter, add headers to the schedule, and fill in the schedule as shown in Figure 2–131.

<Structural Foundation Schedule>

A	B	C	D	E	F	G	H	I	J
		Dimensions			Reinforcement				
					Cover		Bars		
Type	Length	Width	Thickness	Top Cover	Bottom Cover	Major Bars	Minor Bars	Count	Volume
FC3.0		3' - 0"	1' - 0"	0' - 3"	0' - 1 1/2"	#4 @ 1'-0"	#4 @ 1'-0"	4	715.22 CF
FC5.0	139' - 10"	5' - 0"	1' - 0"	0' - 3"	0' - 2"	#4 @ 0'-9"	#4 @ 0'-9"	1	553.47 CF
FS6.0	6' - 0"	6' - 0"	1' - 0"	0' - 3"	0' - 1 1/2"	#4 @ 1'-0"	#4 @ 1'-0"	27	972.00 CF
FS8.0	8' - 0"	8' - 0"	1' - 0"	0' - 3"	0' - 2"	#4 @ 0'-9"	#4 @ 1'-0"	3	192.00 CF
Grand total: 35								35	2432.69 CF

Figure 2–131

Task 1 - Add Project parameters.

1. Open the project **Century-Building-S.rvt** found in the *Structural* folder of your class files folder.

2. In the Project Browser, in the *Schedules/Quantities* area, open the **Structural Foundation Schedule** as shown in Figure 2–132. This schedule is limited to existing parameters and does not include any rebar information. Also, the **Foundation Thickness** parameter is recorded for continuous footing (FC) types but not for spot footings (FS) types.

<Structural Foundation Schedule>

A	B	C	D	E	F
		Dimensions			
Type	Length	Width	Foundation Thickness	Count	Volume
FC3.0		3' - 0"	1' - 0"	4	715.22 CF
FC5.0	139' - 10"	5' - 0"	1' - 0"	1	553.47 CF
FS6.0	6' - 0"	6' - 0"		27	972.00 CF
FS8.0	8' - 0"	8' - 0"		3	192.00 CF
Grand total: 35				35	2432.69 CF

Figure 2–132

3. Open the Structural Plans>**T.O.F.** view.

4. Select one of the spot footings.

5. In Properties, click ⊞ (Edit Type).

6. In the Type Properties dialog box, there are parameters for **Dimensions** and **Identity Data** (as shown in Figure 2–133), but no information about the rebar that typically needs to be included in a foundation schedule.

You can see a **Thickness** *parameter, but this does not link into schedules.*

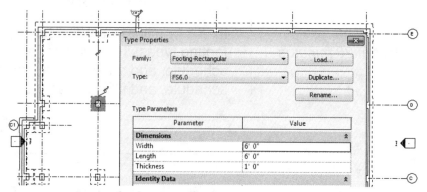

Figure 2–133

7. Click the **Cancel** button to close the dialog box and click in the view to clear the foundation selection.

8. In the *Manage* tab>Settings panel, click ⬚ (Project Parameters).

9. In the Project Parameters dialog box, click ⬜ Add ⬜.

10. In the Parameter Properties dialog box, create a *Project parameter* named **Bottom Cover**. Make it a **Type** parameter and set *Discipline* to **Common**, *Type of Parameter* to **Length**, and *Group parameter under* to **Rebar Set**. In *Categories*, set the *Filter list* to **Structure**, and select **Structural Foundations**, as shown in Figure 2–134.

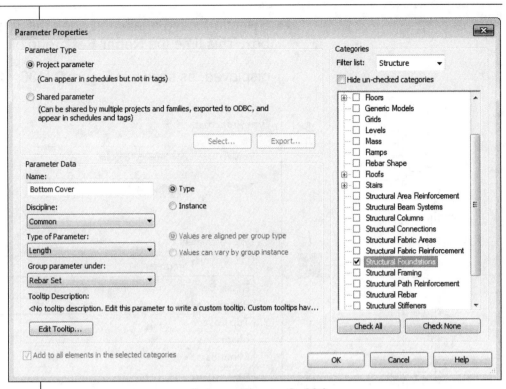

Figure 2–134

11. Click [OK].

12. Create additional Type parameters. Set *Discipline* as **Common** and *Group parameter under* as **Rebar Set** with the following additional information:

Name	Type of Parameter	Categories
Top Cover	Length	Structural Foundations
Major Bars	Text	Structural Foundations and Walls
Minor Bars	Text	Structural Foundations and Walls

13. When you are finished, the four parameters display as shown in Figure 2–135. Click [OK].

Figure 2–135

14. Select a footing again and open the Type Properties dialog box. This time the **Rebar Set** group of parameters is also displayed, as shown in Figure 2–136. Click OK .

Figure 2–136

15. Save the project.

Task 2 - Modify a Foundation schedule.

1. Switch back to the Structural Foundation Schedule.

2. In Properties, in the *Other* area, next to *Fields*, click Edit... .

3. In the Schedule Properties dialog box, in the *Fields* tab, add the following fields: **Top Cover**, **Bottom Cover**, **Major Bars** and **Minor Bars**. Place them in the order shown in Figure 2–137.

Figure 2–137

4. In the *Scheduled fields (in order)* area, select the existing **Foundation Thickness** parameter and click

.

5. In the *Fields* tab, click .

6. In the Parameter Properties dialog box, select **Project parameter**, and enter the *Name* **FS and FC Foundation Thickness**. Set it as a **Type** parameter with *Discipline* set to **Common**, *Type of Parameter* set to **Length**, and *Group* with **Dimensions**.

This parameter is automatically applied to Structural Foundations because that is the type of schedule in which you are working.

7. Click OK .

8. Use Move Up to move it below the existing **Width** parameter.

9. Select it and click Edit... .

10. The full Parameter Properties dialog box opens. Select the Category **Walls** and **Structural Foundations**.

11. Click OK twice to close the dialog boxes.

12. The schedule displays as shown in Figure 2–138.

A	B		C	D	E	F	G	H	I	J
	Dimensions			FS and FC Foundation						
Type	Length		Width		Top Cover	Bottom Cover	Major Bars	Minor Bars	Count	Volume
FC3.0			3' - 0"						4	715.22 CF
FC5.0	139' - 10"		5' - 0"						1	553.47 CF
FS6.0	6' - 0"		6' - 0"						27	972.00 CF
FS8.0	8' - 0"		8' - 0"						3	192.00 CF
Grand total: 35									35	2432.69 CF

<Structural Foundation Schedule>

Figure 2–138

13. Save the project.

Task 3 - Modify and apply headers.

1. Click inside the header for FS and FC Foundation Thickness. Delete **FS and FC Foundation** so it displays as only *Thickness*.

A column cannot be added under an existing header. Therefore, delete the header and then remake it with the correct associations.

2. In the schedule view, select the *Dimensions* header and in the *Modify Schedule/Quantities* tab>Titles & Headers panel, click ⬚ (Ungroup).

3. Press and drag your cursor over the columns from *Length* to *Thickness*.

4. In the Titles & Headers panel, click ⬚ (Group).

5. Type a header name of **Dimensions**.

6. Repeat the process to create a header from *Top Cover* to *Minor Bars* with the name **Reinforcement**.

7. Group *Top Cover* and *Bottom Cover* and name the header **Cover**.

8. Group *Major Bars* and *Minor Bars* and name the header **Bars**. The schedule displays as shown Figure 2–139.

A	B	C	D	E	F	G	H	I	J
	Dimensions				Reinforcement				
				Cover		Bars			
Type	Length	Width	Thickness	Top Cover	Bottom Cover	Major Bars	Minor Bars	Count	Volume
FC3.0		3' - 0"						4	715.22 CF
FC5.0	139' - 10"	5' - 0"						1	553.47 CF
FS6.0	6' - 0"	6' - 0"						27	972.00 CF
FS8.0	8' - 0"	8' - 0"						3	192.00 CF
Grand total: 35								35	2432.69 CF

<Structural Foundation Schedule>

Figure 2–139

9. Set the *Thickness* to **1'-0"** for each of the types.

10. Open the Structural Plans>**T.O.F.** view and select one of the spot footings.

11. In Properties, click (Edit Type). The **FS and FC Foundation Thickness** parameter has been added and set to **1'-0"**. Fill out the rest of the information for the *Cover* and *Bars* (as shown in Figure 2–140) and close the Type Properties dialog box.

Figure 2–140

12. In the Type Properties of each foundation type or in the schedule view, fill out the rest of the information as shown in the schedule in Figure 2–141.

| | | Dimensions | | | Reinforcement | | | | |
| | | | | | Cover | | Bars | | | |
Type	Length	Width	Thickness	Top Cover	Bottom Cover	Major Bars	Minor Bars	Count	Volume
FC3.0		3' - 0"	1' - 0"	0' - 3"	0' - 1 1/2"	#4 @ 1'-0"	#4 @ 1'-0"	4	715.22 CF
FC5.0	139' - 10"	5' - 0"	1' - 0"	0' - 3"	0' - 2"	#4 @ 0'-9"	#4 @ 0'-9"	1	553.47 CF
FS6.0	6' - 0"	6' - 0"	1' - 0"	0' - 3"	0' - 1 1/2"	#4 @ 1'-0"	#4 @ 1'-0"	27	972.00 CF
FS8.0	8' - 0"	8' - 0"	1' - 0"	0' - 3"	0' - 2"	#4 @ 0'-9"	#4 @ 1'-0"	3	192.00 CF
Grand total: 35								35	2432.69 CF

<Structural Foundation Schedule>

Figure 2–141

13. Save the project.

Chapter Review Questions

1. In the Schedule Properties dialog box (shown in Figure 2–142), in which tab do you define the order of the list of elements?

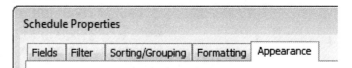

Figure 2–142

   a. *Fields*

   b. *Filter*

   c. *Sorting/Grouping*

   d. *Formatting*

   e. *Appearance*

2. Which type of schedule lists style information that is not automatically included in an element, such as the finish or frame type of a door?

   a. Material Takeoff

   b. Quantities

   c. Key

   d. Building Component

3. When creating *Calculated Value* fields (such as shown in Figure 2–143), the parameters you use must first be added to the list of fields in the schedule.

Figure 2–143

   a. True

   b. False

4. When creating a Material takeoff schedule, where do you modify information about the material, such as the cost or manufacturer, as shown in Figure 2–144? (Select all that apply.)

Stone - Material Takeoff			
Material: Description	Material: Area	Material: Cost	Total Cost
Stone	865 SF	0.00	0
Stone: 6	865 SF		0

EIFS - Material Takeoff			
Material: Description	Material: Area	Material: Cost	Total Cost
EIFS	298 SF	12.00	3574
EIFS: 1	298 SF		3574

Figure 2–144

a. In the Type Properties dialog box.

b. In the schedule, fill out the columns related to the type information.

c. In the Material Editor.

d. In the Material Browser.

5. (Autodesk Revit MEP) Which of the following should be created before you can create an embedded schedule, as shown in Figure 2–145?

A	B
SPACE NO.	NAME
DIFFUSER ID	DIFFUSER TYPE
1501	CLASSROOM
29	Supply Diffuser - Perforated - Round Neck - Ceiling Mounted:
30	Supply Diffuser - Perforated - Round Neck - Ceiling Mounted:
31	Supply Diffuser - Perforated - Round Neck - Ceiling Mounted:
32	Supply Diffuser - Perforated - Round Neck - Ceiling Mounted:
1502	CLASSROOM
45	Supply Diffuser - Perforated - Round Neck - Ceiling Mounted:
46	Supply Diffuser - Perforated - Round Neck - Ceiling Mounted:
47	Supply Diffuser - Perforated - Round Neck - Ceiling Mounted:
48	Supply Diffuser - Perforated - Round Neck - Ceiling Mounted:

Figure 2–145

a. Rooms or Spaces.

b. Elements covered in the schedule.

c. The schedule that you want to embed.

d. A key schedule.

Command Summary

Button	Command	Location
Schedule Types		
NA	Graphical Column Schedule	• **Ribbon:** *View* tab>Create panel> expand Schedules (*Structural Columns only*)
	Material Takeoff Schedule	• **Ribbon:** *View* tab>Create panel> expand Schedules
	Note Block	• **Ribbon:** *View* tab>Create panel> expand Schedules
	Schedule/ Quantities	• **Ribbon:** *View* tab>Create panel> expand Schedules
	Sheet List	• **Ribbon:** *View* tab>Create panel> expand Schedules
	View List	• **Ribbon:** *View* tab>Create panel> expand Schedules
Schedule Appearance		
	Align Horizontal	• **Ribbon:** *Modify Schedule/Quantities* tab>Appearance panel
	Align Vertical	• **Ribbon:** *Modify Schedule/Quantities* tab>Appearance panel
	Borders	• **Ribbon:** *Modify Schedule/Quantities* tab>Appearance panel
	Calculated	• **Ribbon:** *Modify Schedule/Quantities* tab>Parameters panel
	Clear Cell	• **Ribbon:** *Modify Schedule/Quantities* tab>Titles & Headers panel
	Delete (Columns)	• **Ribbon:** *Modify Schedule/Quantities* tab>Columns panel
	Delete (Rows)	• **Ribbon:** *Modify Schedule/Quantities* tab>Rows panel
	Font	• **Ribbon:** *Modify Schedule/Quantities* tab>Appearance panel
	Format Unit	• **Ribbon:** *Modify Schedule/Quantities* tab>Parameters panel
	Group	• **Ribbon:** *Modify Schedule/Quantities* tab>Titles & Headers panel
	Hide (Columns)	• **Ribbon:** *Modify Schedule/Quantities* tab>Columns panel
	Insert (Columns)	• **Ribbon:** *Modify Schedule/Quantities* tab>Columns panel
	Insert (Rows)	• **Ribbon:** *Modify Schedule/Quantities* tab>Rows panel

	Insert Image	• **Ribbon:** *Modify Schedule/Quantities* tab>Titles & Headers panel
	Merge Unmerge	• **Ribbon:** *Modify Schedule/Quantities* tab>Titles & Headers panel
	Reset	• **Ribbon:** *Modify Schedule/Quantities* tab>Appearance panel
	Resize (Columns)	• **Ribbon:** *Modify Schedule/Quantities* tab>Columns panel
	Resize (Rows)	• **Ribbon:** *Modify Schedule/Quantities* tab>Rows panel
	Shading	• **Ribbon:** *Modify Schedule/Quantities* tab>Appearance panel
	Ungroup	• **Ribbon:** *Modify Schedule/Quantities* tab>Titles & Headers panel
	Unhide All (Columns)	• **Ribbon:** *Modify Schedule/Quantities* tab>Columns panel

Chapter 3

Custom System Families

In this chapter you learn how to create wall, roof, and floor types and to create vertically stacked and vertically compound walls. The tools introduced here are used in the Autodesk® Revit® Architecture software and the Autodesk® Revit® Structure software. You also learn how to create system families for the Autodesk® Revit® MEP software, including duct, pipe, conduit, and cable tray families.

This chapter contains the following topics:

- **Creating Wall, Roof, and Floor Types**
- **Vertically Compound Walls**
- **Stacked and Embedded Walls**
- **Creating MEP System Families**

3.1 Creating Wall, Roof, and Floor Types

Autodesk Certification Topics & Objectives

Pro.   User

Elements

* Create compound walls ✓
* Differentiate system and component families ✓

 Learning Objective

* Create compound or layer-based types including walls, roofs, floors, and ceilings.

When you begin a project, you often use the default types supplied with the software for elements (such as walls). Later, you start creating custom standards and need element types in accordance with those standards. This section covers how to create compound or layer-based types, which include walls, roofs, floors, and compound ceilings. These are all considered system families and can be created and modified by creating a new type. For example, when you edit the **Structure** parameter of a wall type, the Edit Assembly dialog box opens, as shown in Figure 3–1, enabling you to modify the elements.

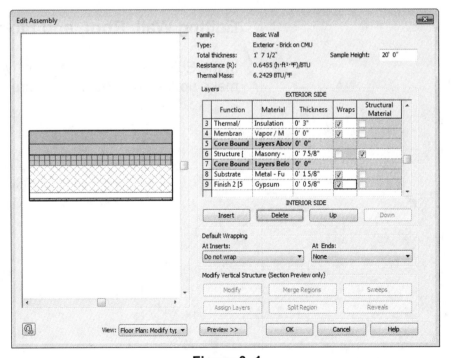

Figure 3–1

- Walls are used as the primary example, but floors, roofs, and compound ceilings follow the same pattern.

- Structural Floors often use profiles for metal decking. Creating this type of floor is covered in the profile families topic.

How To: Create a Compound Wall

1. In the *Architecture* tab>Build panel, or the *Structure* tab> Structure panel, expand ☐ (Wall) and click ☐ (Wall: Architectural), or ☐ (Wall: Structural), or type **WA**.

2. In Properties, select a wall similar to the one you want to create and click ⊞ Edit Type .

3. In the Type Properties dialog box, click Duplicate... .

4. In the Name dialog box, enter a name for the new type and click OK .

5. Next to the **Structure** parameter, click Edit... to edit the structure of the wall. The Edit Assembly dialog box opens. Modify the assembly as needed and click OK to close the Edit Assembly dialog box.

6. Modify any Type Parameters in the Type Properties dialog box. Click OK to close the dialog box.

Editing Wall, Roof, and Floor Assemblies

In the Edit Assembly dialog box, you can define the layers that make up the compound structure, as shown in Figure 3–2.

To better visualize the wall, click << Preview *to open a view of the layers in the structure. You can preview the structure in a plan or section view, and zoom or pan within the preview screen.*

Figure 3–2

Assembly Information

The top of the dialog box lists the *Family* (such as **Basic Wall** or **Floor**), the *Type* that you gave to the new type, and the *Total thickness* (which is the sum of the layers defined in the wall), as shown in Figure 3–3. It also includes *Resistance (R)* and *Thermal Mass* which are automatically calculated from the materials assigned to the layers. You can also set a *Sample Height* for your wall design.

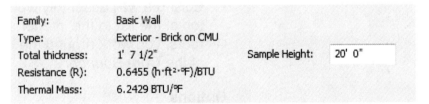

Figure 3–3

Layers

When you specify the layers for the compound element, you assign them a *Function*, *Material*, and *Thickness*, as shown in Figure 3–4.

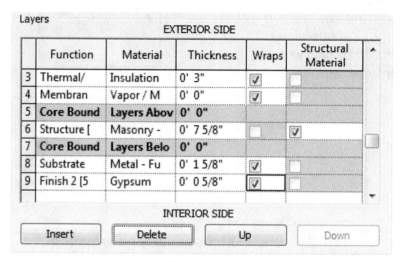

Figure 3–4

- Use the buttons to insert additional layers and to rearrange them in the layer list. You can also delete layers from the list.

- The *Core Boundary* function defines the layers above and below the wrapping; a heavier line is displayed when a plan or section view is cut.

- Editing a wall assembly works from the exterior side at the top of the list to the interior side at the bottom. For floors and roofs, you work around the layers above and below the wrap of the *Core Boundary*.

Options

Function	Select from a set list of functions in the drop-down list with a priority of highest (1) to lowest (5). High priority layers connect before low priority layers.
Structure [1]	The structural support for the wall, floor, or roof.
Substrate [2]	A material that acts as a foundation for another material, such as plywood or gypsum board.
Thermal/ Air Layer [3]	A material that acts as a foundation for another material, such as plywood or gypsum board.
Finish 1 [4]	The exterior finish layer, such as brick for a wall.
Finish 2 [5]	The interior finish layer, such as drywall for a wall.

Membrane Layer	A vapor barrier. Typically, this is set to a zero thickness. Therefore, it does not have a priority code.
Structural (1)	(Floors only) A structural support based on a Deck Profile. You can also specify the Deck Usage with a Bound Layer Above or a Standalone Deck as shown in Figure 3–5.

Figure 3–5

	Select from a list of available materials. You can also create your own materials. Layers clean up if they share the same material. If they do not, a line displays at the join.
Thickness	Set the thickness of the particular layer.

Wall Only Options

Sample Height	Displays the height of a wall in section when you are creating it. It does not impact the height of the wall in the project.
Default Wrapping	Set up how the heavy line style wraps around walls: *at Inserts* (**Do not wrap**, **Interior**, **Exterior**, or **Both**), and *at Ends* (**None**, **Exterior**, or **Interior**). Wrapping is only visible in plan view.
Wraps	Set up individual layers to wrap—select the Wraps option at the end of each layer.

- Wall wrapping can be set in the assembly or in the Type Properties, as shown in Figure 3–6.

Wrapping at Inserts	Do not wrap
Wrapping at Ends	None

Figure 3–6

- Roofs, floors, and structural slabs have an additional **Variable** thickness parameter that relates to sloping for drains.

Practice 3a

Estimated time for completion: 15 minutes

For creating a wall type, it does not matter which command you started with.

Create Compound Wall Types

 Learning Objectives

- Create an exterior wall with two different types of layers on the interior and the exterior.
- Create an interior wall that has the same material on either side of the structural core.

In this practice you will create interior and exterior wall types, and then draw walls using them, as shown in Figure 3–7.

Figure 3–7

Task 1 - Create a Wall type.

1. Start a new project based on the default architectural template and save it as **SW House.rvt**.

2. In the *Architecture* tab>Build panel or *Structure* tab> Structure panel, click ⬭ (Wall).

3. In Properties, click 🗗 Edit Type .

4. In the Type Properties dialog box, click ⬜ Duplicate... ⬜ .

5. In the Name dialog box, type **Exterior – Adobe** and click ⬜ OK ⬜ .

6. Next to the **Structure** parameter, click ⬜ Edit... ⬜ .

7. Next to the **Structure [1]** layer, select the *Material* column and click ⬚ (Browse).

8. Expand the Library panel to display it more clearly and select **AEC Materials>Masonry>Brick, Adobe** as shown in Figure 3–8.

Figure 3–8

9. Double-click on **Brick, Adobe** to add it to the list of materials that are available in the project. **Brick, Adobe** is now selected in the Material Browser. Click [OK] to apply the material.

10. In the Edit Assembly dialog box, in the *Thickness* column, type **1'-0"** and verify that **Structural Material** is selected, as shown in Figure 3–9.

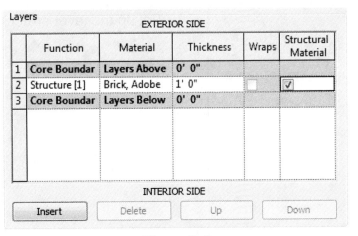

Figure 3–9

*In the Material Browser, type **wood** in the search field to narrow the list of materials.*

11. In the *Layers* area, click [Insert].

12. Set this layer with *Function* set to **Substrate (2)**, *Material* to **Plywood, Sheathing**, *Thickness* to **1 5/8"**. Select **Wraps** but not **Structural Material**, and click [Down] until the new layer is below the Layers Below Wrap as shown in Figure 3–10.

13. Add one more layer on the interior side and set *Function* to **Finish 2**, *Material* to **Cherry**, *Thickness* to **5/8"**. Select **Wraps** but not **Structural Material**, as shown in Figure 3–10.

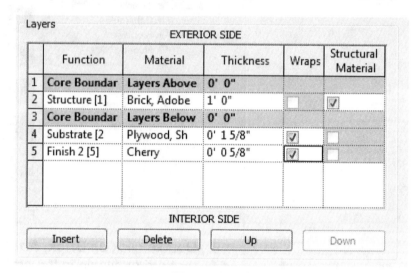

Layers

	Function	Material	Thickness	Wraps	Structural Material
	EXTERIOR SIDE				
1	**Core Boundar**	**Layers Above**	**0' 0"**		
2	Structure [1]	Brick, Adobe	1' 0"	☐	☑
3	**Core Boundar**	**Layers Below**	**0' 0"**		
4	Substrate [2	Plywood, Sh	0' 1 5/8"	☑	☐
5	Finish 2 [5]	Cherry	0' 0 5/8"	☑	☐
	INTERIOR SIDE				

[Insert] [Delete] [Up] [Down]

Figure 3–10

14. Click [OK] to close the Edit Assembly dialog box.

15. Repeat the process to create another new wall type named **Interior – Wood Panel**. In the Type Properties dialog box, change the *Function* to **Interior**.

16. Set up the layer structure as shown in Figure 3–11.

*The **Softwood, Lumber** material is found in the AEC Materials list if it is not in the document list.*

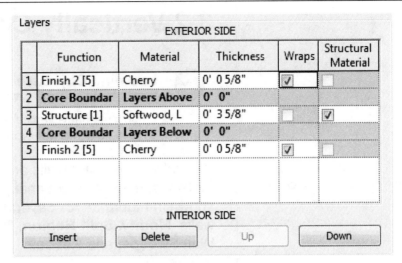

Figure 3–11

17. Click [OK] twice to close the dialog boxes.

Task 2 - Draw walls using the new Wall types.

---

1. Set the *Detail Level* to 🔲 (Medium).

2. Draw the house shown in Figure 3–12.

   - **Exterior: Exterior – Adobe** and *Height* of **10'-0"**
   - **Interior: Interior – Wood Panel** and *Height* of **10'-0"**

*For the Interior walls, set the Location Line to **Finish Face – Interior** or **Finish Face – Exterior** to place the horizontal walls and **Wall Centerline** for the vertical walls.*

Figure 3–12

3. Save the project.

3.2 Vertically Compound Walls

Learning Objective

- Split materials vertically on a wall type and add profiles and reveals to the wall type.

Vertically Compound walls are made of regions of different materials, as well as optional permanent sweeps or reveals, as shown in Figure 3–13. Several options help you create these walls: **Modify**, **Split Region**, **Merge Regions**, **Assign Layers**, **Wall Sweeps**, and **Reveals**.

Figure 3–13

You must be have the *View:* set to **Section: Modify Type Attributes** to work with the **Modify Vertical Structure** tools, as shown in Figure 3–14.

Figure 3–14

How To: Modify the Vertical Structure of a Wall Type

1. Create or edit the wall type you want to work with. In the Type Properties dialog box, click 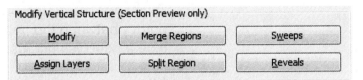 next to the **Structure** parameter to edit the structure of the wall.
2. Create any additional layers that might be needed.
3. In the Edit Assembly dialog box, open the preview and set the *View:* to **Section: Modify Type Attributes**. This activates the *Modify Vertical Structure* tools, as shown in Figure 3–15.

Modify Vertical Structure (Section Preview only)

Modify	Merge Regions	Sweeps
Assign Layers	Split Region	Reveals

Figure 3–15

4. Zoom in as needed to see the various layers.
5. In the Layers list, select the layer you want to work with.
6. Use the various tools that are outlined below.

7. Click [OK] until all of the dialog boxes are closed to save the wall type.

- When making changes to the vertical structure of a wall type it helps to have the *Sample Height* set to the shortest expected height for the wall type so the changes are displayed more clearly.

How To: Split Regions and Assign Layers

1. In the Edit Assembly dialog box, click [Split Region].
2. In the section preview, move your cursor up the wall to the place where you want the region to be cut. Select the wall at that point and a dimension is displayed as shown in Figure 3–16

Figure 3–16

3. In the *Layers* area, highlight the layer that you want to use and click [Assign Layers].

4. In the section view, select the wall part that you want to change and click [Modify].

- You can create as many split regions as needed within one layer.

- To change the dimension, click [Modify] and select the border between the two regions that have been split. Then type a new distance using the temporary dimension.

- You can modify the width of the layer in the section view or in the *Thickness* column in the *Layers* area.

- You can add additional functions as needed. In the example shown in Figure 3–17, two layers have the function **Finish 1**, and each layer has a different material. The *Thickness* is set by the selected layer and cannot be modified.

*Do not select more than you need. There is no **Undo** option in this dialog box.*

Layers

	Function	Material	Thickness	Wraps	
		EXTERIOR SIDE			
1	Finish 1 [4]	Masonry - Bric	0' 3 5/8"	☑	
2	Finish 1 [4]	Masonry - Co	0' 3 5/8"	☑	
3	Thermal/Air L	Misc. Air Layer	0' 3"	☑	
4	Membrane La	Air Barrier - Ai	0' 0"	☑	
5	Substrate [2]	Wood - Sheat	0' 0 3/4"	☑	

Figure 3–17

Merging Regions

To link regions together, click [Merge Regions] and select the line between the layers you want to merge, as shown in Figure 3–18. Watch the arrow cursor. It tells you which way the merge takes place. The tool tip also tells you names of the layers that are being merged. You can only merge layers that are next to each other.

Figure 3–18

- You can merge layers vertically or horizontally. For example, to create the situation shown in Figure 3–18, you need to split the regions horizontally before merging some of the vertical lines.

Wall Sweeps and Reveals

When you split regions, the parts you create cannot have different widths. To create a protrusion or a reveal, add a wall sweep, as shown in Figure 3–19.

Figure 3–19

How To: Add a Sweep

1. In the Edit Assembly dialog box, click [Sweeps] to open the Wall Sweeps dialog box.

2. In the Wall Sweeps dialog box, click [Add]. A default row is added as shown in Figure 3–20.

Wall Sweeps

Wall Sweeps

	Profile	Material	Distance	From	Side	Offset	Flip	Setback	Cuts Wall	Cutt:
1	Default	<By Cate	0' 0"	Ba	Exte	0' 0"	☐	0' 0"	☑	☐

Figure 3–20

3. Select the *Profile* column and select from the list of the existing profiles in the project.

4. Continue setting up the profile by selecting a *Material* and setting the *Distance* from the top or bottom, interior or exterior *Side*, and the *Offset* from that side. If needed, place a check mark in the *Flip* column to flip the profile, as shown in Figure 3–21.

Figure 3–21

5. Click ⌈ **Apply** ⌉ to see the addition before you click ⌈ **OK** ⌉ to finish.

• Reveals work the same way, except that you do not assign a material to a reveal. The whole shape of the reveal profile is visible in the section view, but you only see the cut in the project.

• You can also click ⌈ **Load Profile** ⌉ to add a profile within the Wall Sweeps or Reveals dialog box.

Practice 3b

Estimated time for completion: 15 minutes

Create Vertically Compound Walls

 Learning Objective

- Modify an existing wall type to create a vertically compound wall with two materials and sweeps.

In this practice you will modify a wall type to create a wooden wainscot (**Split Region** and **Assign Layers**) below a chair rail (**Sweep**), as shown in Figure 3–22.

Figure 3–22

Task 1 - Split regions and assign layers in a wall type.

1. Open the project **SW-House-A.rvt** found in the *Architectural* folder of your class files folder.

2. Select one of the **Interior – Wood Panel** walls and in Properties, click 🔲 Edit Type .

3. In the Type Properties dialog box, next to the **Structure** parameter, click [Edit...].

4. In the Edit Assembly dialog box, change the *Sample Height* to **9'-0"**. This sets the correct wall height for the preview.

*The material **Plaster** is located in the AEC Material area of the Material Browser. Add it to the document so that you can select it.*

5. Click << Preview and set the *View:* to **Section: Modify type attributes**.

6. In the *Layers* area, insert an additional finish on both sides of the structure. Set the material to **Plaster**. Do not specify a thickness. Once you apply it to part of the split region, it takes on the appropriate thickness.

7. In the *Modify Vertical Structure* area, click Split Region.

8. In the Section view, move the cursor to a point **3'-6"** above the base, as shown in Figure 3–23. Zoom in to make sure you split the finish layer and not the central structural layer.

Figure 3–23

9. Repeat with the opposite finish layer.

10. Stay zoomed in, close to the place where you made the split.

11. In the *Layers* area, select the **Plaster** layer on the Exterior Side.

12. In the *Modify Vertical Structure* area, click Assign Layers.

13. In the preview, select the top part of the exterior wall where you want the finish applied. Click Modify. The color should change as shown in Figure 3–24.

Figure 3–24

14. Repeat with the other finish and the side of the wall.

15. Click [Modify] to finish the process. The list of layers displays, as shown in Figure 3–25.

Layers

EXTERIOR SIDE

	Function	Material	Thickness	Wraps	Structural Material
1	Finish 2 [5]	Plaster	0' 0 5/8"	✓	
2	Finish 2 [5]	Cherry	0' 0 5/8"	✓	
3	Core Boundary	Layers Above	0' 0"		
4	Structure [1]	Softwood, L	0' 3 5/8"		✓
5	Core Boundary	Layers Below	0' 0"		
6	Finish 2 [5]	Plaster	0' 0 5/8"	✓	
7	Finish 2 [5]	Cherry	0' 0 5/8"	✓	

INTERIOR SIDE

Insert	Delete	Up	Down

Figure 3–25

16. Click [OK] twice to close the dialog boxes.

17. Look at the interior walls in a 3D or section view. Shade the view. You should see the difference above and below the paneling, as shown in Figure 3–26.

Figure 3–26

Task 2 - Add sweeps to the wall type.

1. Edit the structure of the same wall type.

2. In the Edit Assembly dialog box, *Modify Vertical Structure* area, click [Sweeps].

3. In the Wall Sweeps dialog box, click [Load Profile].

4. In Load Family dialog box, navigate to the *Profiles>Finish Carpentry* folder, select **Base 2.rfa** and click <u>Open</u> .

5. In the Wall Sweeps dialog box, click <u>Add</u> and set up two wall sweeps using the following information, as shown in Figure 3–27.

   - **Profile:** Base 2: 3 1/2" x 3/4" (or similar)
   - **Material:** Cherry
   - **Distance:** 3'-6"
   - **From:** Base
   - **Side: Interior** for one sweep and **Exterior** for the other

Wall Sweeps

Wall Sweeps

	Profile	Material	Distance	From	Side	Offset	Flip	Setback	Cuts Wal
1	Base 2 : 3 1/2" x 3/	Cherry	3' 6"	Base	Interior	0' 0"	☐	0' 0"	☑
2	Base 2 : 3 1/2" x 3/	Cherry	3' 6"	Base	Exterior	0' 0"	☐	0' 0"	☑

Figure 3–27

6. Click <u>OK</u> to exit the Wall Sweeps dialog box.

7. In the preview of the Edit Assembly dialog box, you should see the two sweeps, as shown in Figure 3–28 (zoomed in).

Figure 3–28

8. Click <u>OK</u> twice to close the dialog boxes. The entire set of interior walls updates with the new information.

9. Add an additional interior wall using this type so that you can see how it automatically uses the information.

10. If time permits, modify the **Exterior-Adobe** wall so that the inside of that wall matches the interior walls.

11. Save the project.

3.3 Stacked and Embedded Walls

Autodesk Certification Topics & Objectives

Pro.   User

Elements

*   Create a stacked wall   ✓

 Learning Objectives

*   Create a vertically stacked wall type from two or more wall types.
*   Embed walls inside other walls using the **Cut Geometry** command.

A vertically stacked wall is a specific system family that takes two or more existing basic walls and stacks them on top of each other at specific heights, as shown in Figure 3–29. One wall must be variable in height. The basic wall types have to be in place before you create the stacked wall. These walls are created by copying and editing an existing Vertically Stacked Wall type.

Figure 3–29

How To: Create a Vertically Stacked Wall

1. Start the **Wall** command.
2. In Properties, select an existing stacked wall type and click
     Edit Type .
3. In the Type Properties dialog box, click Duplicate... .
4. Type a name for the new stacked wall type and click
     .

5. In the Type Properties dialog box, next to the **Structure** parameter, click [Edit...].

6. In the Edit Assembly dialog box, set the *Offset* for how the walls are stacked, and a *Sample Height* for the preview, as shown in Figure 3–30.

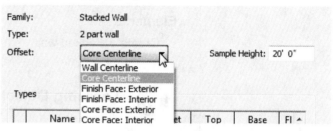

Figure 3–30

7. In the *Name* column, select the basic wall types you want to add to the stacked wall, as shown in Figure 3–31.

	Name	Height	Offset	Top	Base	
1	Exterior - Brick on ▼	Variable	0' 0"	0' 0"	0' 0"	
2	Exterior - CMU on	3' 0"	0' 0"	0' 0"	0' 0"	

Figure 3–31

8. For each wall type, set the appropriate height and location (Up or Down) within the list. One height must be variable. Set the *Offset* of the wall as needed.

9. Click [<< Preview] to see the wall, as shown in Figure 3–32.

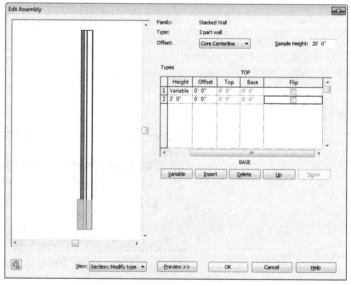

Figure 3–32

10. Click [OK] until all of the dialog boxes are closed.

Hint: Embedding a Wall Inside Another Wall

Another way of creating a compound wall is to embed one wall inside another wall, as shown in Figure 3–33. When you have drawn a host wall, draw another wall on top of, or parallel to it near the host. A warning box opens and recommends that you use **Cut Geometry** to embed the wall in the host wall.

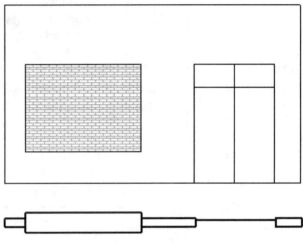

Figure 3–33

1. Add the embedded wall to the host wall.
2. Close the warning box.

3. In the *Modify* tab>Geometry panel, click ⬚ (Cut).
4. Select the host wall.
5. Select the wall that cuts the host wall.

- Embedded walls work similar to windows. You can modify the embedded wall with controls.

- Some curtain wall types are created to be automatically embedded in another wall. The type **Curtain Wall: Storefront** is an example. The Type Parameter *Automatically Embed* is available for all curtain wall types.

- You can separate embedded walls. In the *Modify* tab> Geometry panel, expand ⬚ (Cut) and click ⬚ (Uncut Geometry).

Practice 3c

Estimated time for completion: 10 minutes

Create Stacked and Embedded Walls

 Learning Objectives

- Create a vertically stacked wall type.
- Embed a curtain wall type and a basic wall type into the stacked wall.

In this practice you will create a vertically stacked wall and use it in a project. You will also embed a curtain wall and another wall type into a host wall, as shown in Figure 3–34.

Figure 3–34

Task 1 - Create a stacked wall.

1. Start a new project based on the default template and save it as **Warehouse.rvt**.

2. Start the **Wall** command and select the **Stacked Wall: Exterior – Brick Over CMU w Metal Stud** type.

3. Edit the type and duplicate it to create a new wall type named **Exterior – EIFS over Brick/CMU**.

4. Edit the structure of the new wall.

5. For the top wall, select **Exterior – EIFS on Mtl. Stud**. Leave the *Height* as **Variable** and set the *Offset* to **4"**.

6. For the bottom wall, select **Exterior – Brick on CMU** and set the *Height* to **6'-0"**.

7. Click [OK] to close all of the open dialog boxes.

8. Draw a rectangular building **50'-0" x 30'-0"** using the new wall style.

9. Display the walls in 3D to verify that the Brick/EIFS are displayed on the exterior.

10. Save the project.

Task 2 - Create an embedded wall.

---

1. In the *Floor Plans* area, open the **Level 1** view.

2. On the south face of the building, add a wall using **Curtain Wall: Storefront** at an *Unconnected Height* of **8'-0"**. Place it directly on the center line of the existing wall along only a portion of the wall. It automatically cuts the existing wall.

3. In the *Floor Plans* area, open the **Level 2** view.

4. Add another wall on the same face using **Basic Wall: Exterior – Brick on Mtl. Stud**. This time a warning box opens.

5. Close the warning box.

6. In the *Modify|Place Wall* tab>Geometry panel, click ⟠ (Cut).

7. Select the host wall.

8. Select the wall that cuts the host wall.

9. In the *Elevations* area, open the **South** view.

10. Flip the orientation of the brick insert as needed.

11. Change the size of the embedded wall using the controls, but do not move it down into the lower brick wall.

12. Save the project.

3.4 Creating MEP System Families

 Learning Objectives

- Create Duct and Pipe types using routing preferences.
- Create Cable Tray and Conduit types using Type Properties.

Autodesk Revit MEP comes loaded with a variety of MEP system families for Ducts, Pipes, Cable Trays and Conduits. You can also duplicate and modify these families to create new family types. Ducts (as shown in Figure 3–35), and Pipes are setup using Routing Preferences. Flex Ducts and Flex Pipes as well as Cable Tray and Conduit are set up by defining fittings in the Type Properties.

Figure 3–35

How To: Create Duct Types

*You can also right-click on a type name in the Project Browser and select **Duplicate** before opening the Type Properties.*

1. Start the **Place Duct** command, select one of the existing types, and click 🔲 (Edit Type) or, in the Project Browser, expand **Families>Ducts>Oval, Rectangular** or **Round Duct** and then double-click on one of the existing types as shown in Figure 3–36 to open the Type Properties dialog box.

Figure 3–36

2. In the Type Properties dialog box, click ⌈ Duplicate... ⌋, type a new name in the Name dialog box, and click ⌈ OK ⌋.

3. Next to the **Routing Preferences** parameter, click ⌈ Edit... ⌋.

4. The Routing Preferences dialog box, displays as shown in Figure 3–37.

Figure 3–37

5. Click [Duct Size...] to open the Mechanical Settings dialog box to the Duct Settings so that you can add or remove the typical sizes used in the project.

6. Click [Load Family...] to add any duct fittings that you want to use in the type that are not already loaded in the project.

7. For each of the fittings, expand the drop-down list and select the size that you want use, as shown in Figure 3–38.

Figure 3–38

8. If you want to include more than one option for a fitting, click

    ✚ (Add row) and select the secondary option for the fitting.

    You can also use ↑E (Move row up) or ↓E (Move row down) to specify the order in which the fittings are applied by

    default or click ▬ (Remove Row) to delete the ones you do not need to use.

9. When you have finished assigning fittings, click [OK] to close the Routing Preference dialog box.

10. Fill in the other Parameters for the Type Properties as

    needed and click [OK] to finish the new duct type.

•   Flex ducts do not have routing preferences, the Fitting selection takes place directly in the Type Properties as shown in Figure 3–39.

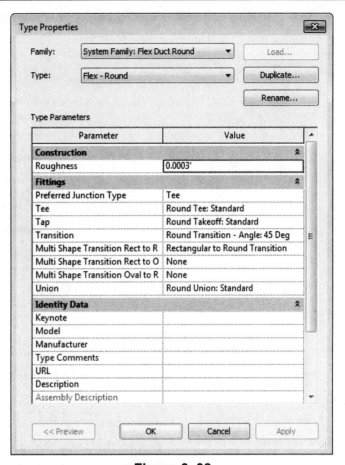

Figure 3–39

How To: Create Pipe Types

*You can also right-click on a type name in the Project Browser and select **Duplicate** before opening the Type Properties.*

1. Start the **Place Pipe** command, select one of the existing types, and click ⊞ (Edit Type) or, in the Project Browser, expand **Families>Pipes>Pipe Types** and double-click on one of the existing types to open the Type Properties dialog box.

2. In the Type Properties dialog box, click ⎟ Duplicate... ⎟, type a new name in the Name dialog box, and click ⎟ OK ⎟.

3. Next to the **Routing Preferences** parameter, click ⎟ Edit... ⎟.

4. The Routing Preferences dialog box opens, as shown in Figure 3–40.

Figure 3–40

5. Click ⌈Segments and Sizes...⌋ to open the Mechanical Settings dialog box to the Pipe Settings. In this dialog box, specify the Segment types and sizes for the various types of pipe as shown in Figure 3–41.

Segment types can be added or removed here.

Figure 3–41

6. Click [Load Family...] to add any pipe fittings that you want to use in the type that have not already been loaded in the project.

7. For the Pipe Segment type and each of the fittings, expand the drop-down list and select the size that you want to use as shown in Figure 3–42.

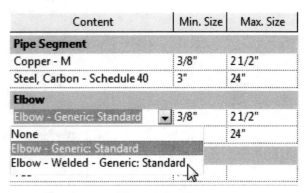

Figure 3–42

8. If you want to include more than one option for a fitting, click

   ✛ (Add row) and select the secondary option for the fitting.

   You can also use ⬆E (Move row up) or ⬇E (Move row down) to specify the order in which the fittings are applied by

   default or ⊟ (Remove Row) to delete the ones you do not need to use.

9. When you have finished assigning fittings, click [OK] to close the Routing Preference dialog box.

10. Fill in the other Parameters for the Type Properties as

    needed and click [OK] to finish the new pipe type.

- Flex pipes do not have routing preferences, the Fitting selection takes place directly in the Type Properties as shown in Figure 3–43.

Figure 3–43

How To: Setup Cable Tray and Conduit Types

1. Start the **Cable Tray** or **Conduit** command, select one of the existing types, and click ⊞ (Edit Type) or, in the Project Browser, expand **Families>Cable Trays** (or Conduits) and double-click on one of the existing types (either with or without fittings, as shown in Figure 3–44) to open the Type Properties dialog box.

Figure 3–44

2. In the Type Properties dialog box, click [Duplicate...], type a new name in the Name dialog box, and click [OK].

3. Select the fittings that you want to use as shown in Figure 3–45.

The fitting families need to be in the project before you get to this point.

Figure 3–45

- For Conduit you first need to specify the Electrical Standard that you are using, as shown in Figure 3–46. Ensure that you also load the correct fittings that match the specific standard as well.

Figure 3–46

4. Fill in the values for any of the Identity Data information you might have and click [OK] to finish.

Chapter Review Questions

1. When creating a compound wall, you assign a Function for each layer. The numbers after the function names is the priority of the layers when they are joined together with other walls, as shown in Figure 3–47. Which of the following function connects first?

Figure 3–47

   a. Membrane Layer

   b. Substrate

   c. Structure

   d. Thermal/Air Layer

   e. Finish

2. How do you create a wall type that has more than one finish material on the vertical plane within the one type, as shown for stone and stucco in Figure 3–48?

Figure 3–48

   a. Create separate wall types for the stone and stucco. Duplicate an existing Stacked Wall type and set the wall types to stone and stucco.

   b. Draw two walls on top of each other and use ⌗ (Join Geometry) to link them.

   c. Duplicate an existing Basic Wall type and use **Split Region** and **Assign Layers** to apply the stone and stucco materials to separate parts of the wall.

   d. Draw the first wall, draw the other wall on top of the first, and use ⌗ (Cut Geometry) to cut the second wall out of the first wall.

3. Which command do you need to use to embed a wall inside another wall?

   a. **Wall Joins**

   b. **Cut Geometry**

   c. **Cope**

   d. **Split Face**

4. (MEP only.) When setting up a new duct or pipe type, which of the following items can be set by type?

   a. System Type

   b. Width and Height

   c. Preferred Junction Type

   d. Justification

5. (MEP only.) When creating a new conduit or cable tray type you need to assign Routing Preferences.

   a. True

   b. False

Command Summary

Button	Command	Location
	Cable Tray	• **Ribbon:** *Systems* tab>Electrical panel • **Shortcut:** CT
	Conduit	• **Ribbon:** *Systems* tab>Electrical panel • **Shortcut:** CN
	Cut Geometry	• **Ribbon:** *Modify* tab>Geometry panel
	Duct	• **Ribbon:** *Systems* tab>HVAC panel • **Shortcut:** DT
	Edit Type	• **Ribbon:** *Modify* tab>Properties panel • **Properties Palette**
	Pipe	• **Ribbon:** *Systems* tab>Plumbing & Piping panel • **Shortcut:** PI
	Uncut Geometry	• **Ribbon:** *Modify* tab>Geometry panel> expand Cut
	Wall: Architectural	• **Ribbon:** *Architecture* tab>Build panel or *Structure* tab>Structure panel>expand Wall • **Shortcut:** WA
	Wall: Structural	• **Ribbon:** *Architecture* tab>Build panel or *Structure* tab>Structure panel>expand Wall • **Shortcut:** WA

Chapter 4

Family Concepts & Techniques

In this chapter you learn how to create families, add parametric dimensions, draw family geometry, create family types, add family parameters, and modify visibility display settings.

This chapter contains the following topics:

- **Introduction to Creating Families**
- **Creating the Parametric Framework**
- **Creating Family Elements**
- **Additional Tools for Families**
- **Creating Family Types**
- **Visibility Display Settings**
- **Overview of Family Creation**

4.1 Introduction to Creating Families

Autodesk Certification Topics & Objectives

Pro.   User

Elements

• Differentiate system and component families   ✓

Families

• Use Family creation procedures   ✓

Learning Objectives

• Understand the different types of families that can be created in the software.
• Understand the difference between Host and Stand-alone families.
• Review the Family Editor interface and work through the general steps for creating a family.

Many families are included in the default installation. These are the main building blocks in the Autodesk® Revit® software. You can also create custom families. Almost every element, from walls to furniture, is a family. Families are model or annotation elements that have been grouped together and set up with dimensions and other parameters, as shown in Figure 4–1. These components can have different sizes and other parameters (such as material) preset so that you can create a list of types in a family. Families are considered *parametric*, meaning they can be changed without having to recreate the elements.

Figure 4–1

- An important source of component families is Autodesk Seek. You can search for families created by manufacturers using the Autodesk Revit software (using the *Insert* tab as shown in Figure 4–2) or directly through your Web Browser at http://seek.autodesk.com.

Figure 4–2

Family Types

The Autodesk Revit software enables you to create several types of families:

- *System Families* (such as walls, roofs, floors, text, and dimensions) have predefined parameters that you can modify. You create new types in these families by modifying existing parameters using Properties.

In-Place families are only available in the project in which you create them.

- *In Place Families* are created in the project and are dependent on the model geometry (e.g., custom gutters, special trim, or built-in columns).

- *Component Families* are defined by drawing elements in the Family Editor. Examples of these families include doors, air handling units, columns, and profiles. They are separate from the project file, but can be inserted into a project. You can create many types in one family using different sizes and materials. The Autodesk Revit software includes family templates for most elements to help you get started. These families are loaded into a project.

Host vs. Stand-alone Families

Families can be *Host-based* or *Stand-alone*. Host-based families include those that are dependent on a host (wall, ceiling, floor, roof, or face). Stand-alone families (such as chairs, some mechanical equipment, and columns) do not need a host. How you create families depends on the way you want to use an element. For example, if you were creating a floor or table lamp, you would create a stand-alone family, as shown in Figure 4–3. You can also create ceiling or wall light fixtures that would be host-based.

Figure 4–3

Family Editor

When you create a family file from a template, the Family Editor automatically loads with the tools you need to create the family elements, as shown in Figure 4–4. Many of the tools used in the project files are available, as well as several family-specific ones.

Figure 4–4

- The family templates supplied with the Autodesk Revit software contain all of the programming needed to create families. All you have to add are the elements.

Preparing to Create Families

As you create families, you should plan ahead by asking a variety of questions, including:

- Is this family going to be used by one project (in-place) or by many projects (component)?

- Do you need different 2D representations in different views? What about 3D elements?

- Is this going to be a host-based or stand-alone family?

- Do you need various sizes of this family component?

- Are you going to post the family on Autodesk Seek?

Overview of Creating a Family

Several steps are needed to create a family, as follows:

1. Start a new family file based on an Autodesk Revit supplied template, or copy and open an existing family that is similar to what you need to create.
2. Create and test the parametric framework. The framework consists of reference planes and dimensions that establish the foundation of the elements that display in the family. An example of a new column family is shown in Figure 4–5.

Figure 4–5

3. Add and associate family elements to the parametric framework. These elements can be 3D or 2D.

4. Create Family Types for different sizes and materials. When you use the family in a project, these types display in the Type List in Properties, as shown in Figure 4–6.

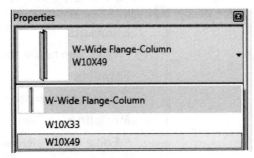

Figure 4–6

5. Set the additional parameters and display settings.

6. Save the family and load it into a project.

4.2 Creating the Parametric Framework

Autodesk Certification Topics & Objectives

	Pro.	User
Elements		
• Work with family Parameters		✓
Families		
• Use Family creation procedures		✓
Modeling		
• Edit a model element's material		✓

Learning Objectives

- Set up Reference Planes and Lines.
- Add dimensions and label (create parameters for) the dimensions.
- Flex the geometry to test all of the parameters and their connections to the reference planes or lines.
- Create non-dimensional parameters and formulas that control parameter values.

Autodesk Revit families can be parametric (i.e., controlled by parameters). These parameters, which include dimensions, as shown in Figure 4–7, and other options (such as materials) are the framework for creating family elements. For example, when you change the *Length* and *Width* of a light fixture, the other parts move with it.

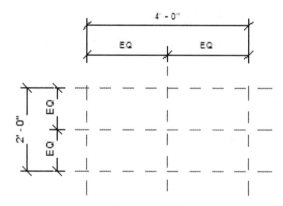

Figure 4–7

There are several steps in creating the parametric framework:

1. Place *reference planes* or *reference lines* at critical locations.
2. *Dimension* the reference planes/lines and *label* some of them so they can be manipulated.
3. *Flex* or test the dimensioned and labeled reference planes/lines to make sure they function as expected.

This is all done before you draw any elements in the family.

Setting up Reference Planes/Lines in Families

Reference planes are the backbone of the geometry. Create as many reference planes as needed before you start creating elements. Reference planes display as dashed green lines, as shown in Figure 4–8.

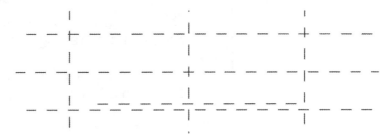

Figure 4–8

How To: Draw Reference Planes

1. In the Family Editor, in the *Create* tab>Datum panel, click

   (Reference Plane).
2. In the *Modify | Place Reference Plane* tab>Draw panel, click

   (Line) or (Pick Lines).
3. Draw or select the lines that define the location of the plane.
4. Draw or select other lines as needed.

5. Click (Modify) to finish the command.

- 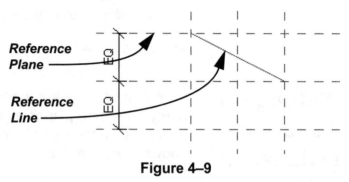 (Reference Lines) are similar to reference planes, but have distinct start and end points. They are most useful for controlling angled dimensions and display as solid green lines, as shown in Figure 4–9.

Figure 4–9

- The number of reference planes/lines you need depends on what you are drawing.

- Reference planes/lines display in plan and elevation views, but not in 3D views.

Reference Plane Options

- By default, the origin of a family is the center of the space where you create the family. In most templates, this is located at the intersection of the existing reference planes. You can also specify your own origin by modifying the properties of two intersecting reference planes to specify that they define the origin, as shown in Figure 4–10.

Figure 4–10

- Reference planes/lines do not display in the project when you insert the family type, but might impact snap and alignment behavior. In Properties, under *Other*, set the **Is Reference** parameter to the plane you want to use, as shown in Figure 4–11. If you do not want a reference plane to be a snap or an alignment, set the **Is Reference** parameter to **Not a Reference**.

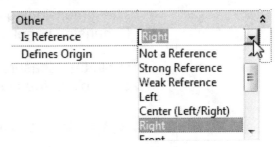

Figure 4–11

- Naming a reference plane enables you to use it to set the work plane when you are ready to add geometry to the family. In Properties, under *Identity Data*, type a *Name*. The name displays in the family file when you select the reference plane, as shown in Figure 4–12.

Figure 4–12

- Reference lines cannot be named.

Adding Dimensions

Add dimensions to reference planes/lines to start the constraining process. For example, you might want to run a string of dimensions and then set the distances to be equal by clicking on the associated **EQ** symbol, as shown in Figure 4–13. This moves the reference planes into place. The other constraining method you can use is to label the dimensions. This creates a parameter that can be modified in the Family Types dialog box.

Figure 4–13

- The dimensioning tools are located in the *Annotate* tab> Dimension panel, as shown in Figure 4–14 or in the *Modify* tab in the Measure panel. (Aligned Dimension) is also available in the Quick Access Toolbar.

Figure 4–14

How To: Label a Dimension

1. Select the dimension you want to label.
2. In Properties or the Options Bar, select an existing label from the list. Alternatively, in the Options Bar, select **<Add parameter...>** to create a new label.

   - If you right-click on a dimension and select **Label**, the label options also display at the dimension, as shown in Figure 4–15.

When naming a parameter, it is good practice to use title case and a short name without abbreviations. Parameters are case sensitive.

Figure 4–15

3. If you are adding a parameter, the Parameter Properties dialog box opens. In the *Parameter Type* area, select the **Family parameter** option, as shown in Figure 4–16.

Shared parameters must be created in your system to be able to use this option.

Figure 4–16

4. In the *Parameter Data* area, specify the *Name*, as shown in Figure 4–17. The *Type of Parameter* is automatically set to **Length** and the *Group parameter under* is set to **Dimensions**, because the parameter is a dimension.

Enhanced
in **2015**

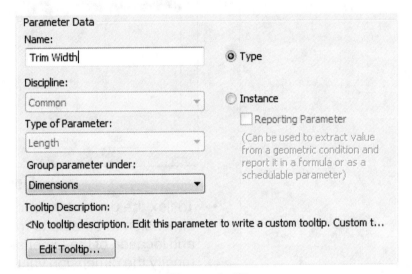

Figure 4–17

5. Select **Type** or **Instance**.
6. Add a tooltip description if needed.

7. Click [OK]. The dimension is labeled and ready to be flexed.

• If you add too many labeled dimensions, the Autodesk Revit software warns that you have over-constrained the sketch. You cannot ignore this warning. The label is not created in this case.

• Creating a parameter by **Type** applies it to all instances of a family when it is inserted into a project. To modify it, you need to change the Type Properties. Creating a parameter by **Instance** applies it to individual instances when inserted into a project. It can be modified directly in Properties.

Flexing Geometry

When you lock a parameter, any associated parameters also lock.

Once you have established dimensions and labeled them, you need to verify that the parameters work correctly with each other. To do this, *flex* the geometry by changing values either directly in the Family Editor or in the Family Types dialog box, as shown in Figure 4–18.

Figure 4–18

- To flex the geometry directly in the Family Editor, select a dimension to be able to modify the witness lines, lock status, and location of the dimension text. Select it twice to be able to modify the dimension value, as shown in Figure 4–19. If there are other dimensions related to this one, they should move as well.

Figure 4–19

- To see all of the values you can flex at one time and to add formulas and non-dimension parameters, you need to work in the Family Types dialog box.

How To: Flex the Geometry in the Family Types Dialog box

1. Move the view to see the elements on one side.
2. In the *Create* or *Modify* tab>Properties panel, click ⊞ (Family Types).
3. Move the dialog box to see the elements you are adjusting.
4. Change the labeled parameters and click [Apply].
5. Do the elements move correctly? Try several modifications.
6. Set the parameters as needed and click [OK] to finish the command.

Adding Formulas to Parameters

You can add formulas to parameters so that they change when a related parameter changes. In the example in Figure 4–20, the *Shelf Height* is defined as the **Height** divided by **4**. When you change the *Shelf Height* or *Height*, the other one updates according to the formula.

Dimensions			⌃
Width	3' 6"	=	
Shelf Height	1' 3"	= Height / 4	
Height	5' 0"	=	

Figure 4–20

You can use several types of formulas with families:

Arithmetic	Basic arithmetic operations in formulas include addition (+), subtraction (-), multiplication (*), division (/), exponentiation, logarithms, and square roots.
Trigonometric	Trigonometric functions include sine, cosine, tangent, arcsine, arccosine, and arctangent.
Conditional	Conditional functions include comparisons in a condition: <, >, =, and Boolean operators with a conditional statement: AND, OR, or NOT. See the Autodesk Revit Help files for more information about creating conditional statements.

- You can enter numbers as integers, decimals, or fractions. Conditional statements can include numeric values, numeric parameter names, or **Yes/No** parameters.

- Formulas are case-sensitive. Therefore, if you have created a dimension label named **Height**, make sure the formula that uses this label also has the H capitalized (e.g., **Height * 2**).

Hint: Formulas in Projects

You can use a formula to specify the length of a wall by typing it in the temporary dimension, as shown in Figure 4–21. Start with an equal sign (e.g., =12 / 3 + 4). The example shown in Figure 4–21 returns the number 8 (interpreted as 8'-0") in the dimension. Formulas also work with numerical values in Properties.

=12/3+4

Figure 4–21

Creating Additional Parameters

In addition to creating parameters for various dimensions in a family, you can add parameters that store other information (such as the material of the element, the wattage of a light fixture, or the reinforcement cover setting in concrete). These parameters can be used in schedules and, if created as Shared Parameters, in Tags.

How To: Create and Organize Parameters

1. In the Family Editor, in the *Create or Modify* tab>Properties panel, click (Family Types).
2. In the Family Types dialog box, in the *Parameters* area, click Add... .
3. In the Parameter Properties dialog box, set up the Parameter Data, as shown in Figure 4–22.

Enhanced
in 2015

Figure 4–22

- The *Discipline* can be set to **Common**, **Structural**, **HVAC**, **Electrical**, **Piping**, or **Energy**. The Type of Parameter list changes according to the discipline.

4. Click OK.

New
in 2015

5. In the Family Types dialog box, use Move Up and

Move Down to organize the parameters or modify the

Sorting Order by clicking Ascending or Descending. This sets the order of the parameters to alphabetical order and removes any changes you might have made otherwise.

- You can delete parameters by clicking Remove.

6. When you have finished creating and organizing parameters, click OK.

Common Parameter Types

Text	A text parameter can host any type of information that consists of both numbers and letters. Examples could be the fabric color or part number of the element.
Integer	Any value that is always represented by a whole number. Examples could be the number of chairs that fit around a conference table or the number of shelves in a bookcase.
Number	Any numeric value: whole, decimal, or fraction. You can use formulas with **Number** parameters.
Length	When you label dimensions, you create **Length** parameters. You can use formulas with **Length** parameters.
Area	Establishes the area of an element. It is numeric and can have formulas applied to it.
Volume	Establishes the volume of an element. It is numeric and can have formulas applied to it.
Angle	Establishes the angle of an element. It is numeric and can have formulas applied to it.
Slope	Displays a slope, as set in the Field Format.
Currency	Displays the amount in dollars or other currencies, as set up in the Field Format.
Mass Density	Displays the mass per unit volume of material.
URL	Specifies a link to a web site.
Material	Provides a place to assign a material from the list of materials that are set up in the project.
Image	Creates a parameter at which you can add a raster image connected to the family.
Yes/No	Used with instance parameters where you need a **Yes** or **No** answer to a question listed in the name. The default is **Yes**.
<Family Type>	Opens a dialog box where you can select from the list of family types, such as doors, furniture, or tags.

New in **2015**

Practice 4a

Setup a Bookcase Family

 Learning Objective

- Add reference planes and dimensions with labels to form the framework of bookcase.

Estimated time for completion: 20 minutes

In this practice you will create a family file based on a template and view the existing reference planes. You will also create reference planes, dimension them, label the dimensions, as shown in Figure 4–23, and use a formula in parameters.

Figure 4–23

Task 1 - Open a family template.

1. Close all open projects.

2. On the Start page, under the *Families* area, select **New**.

3. In the New Family - Select Template dialog box, select the template **Furniture.rft** from the Revit Library and click .

4. In the *View* tab>Windows panel, click ⊟ (Tile) (or type **WT**).

5. The four open views display so you can see each of them. Type **ZA** (the shortcut for **Zoom All to Fit**) to fit the view in all of the windows.

6. Several existing reference planes are included in the file, as well as **Ref.Level**.

7. Save the family in your Architectural class folder as **Barrister Bookcase.rfa**.

Task 2 - Create plan view reference planes.

1. Maximize the **Ref. Level** view.

2. Create four new reference planes, one on each side of the existing planes, as shown in Figure 4–24. Do not worry about the exact location yet.

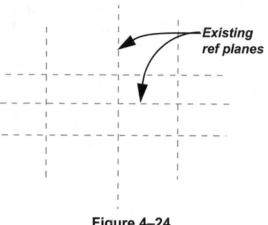

Figure 4–24

3. Add dimensions between each reference plane and across the top and side, as shown in Figure 4–25. Set the interior dimensions to **Equal**.

Figure 4–25

4. Select one of the outside vertical reference planes and change the temporary dimension to **1'-6"**. Repeat with one of the horizontal reference planes and change the temporary dimension to **8"**. The overall width should be 3'-0" and the overall depth should be **1'-4"**.

5. Select the overall horizontal dimension and create a new type parameter label named **Width**. Create a label for the overall vertical dimension named **Depth**. The sketch displays as shown in Figure 4–26.

Your dimensions might vary depending on where you originally placed the reference planes.

Figure 4–26

6. Create one more horizontal reference plane **1"** inside the front reference plane. Dimension and lock it in place, as shown in Figure 4–27.

Figure 4–27

7. Select the new reference plane. In Properties, set the *Name* to **Door Face**.

8. Double-click on the *Width* dimension and change it to **3'-6"**.

9. Double-click on the *Depth* dimension and change it to **1'-1"**.

10. Check if the other reference planes remain in place.

11. Save the family file.

Each of the shelf height dimensions must be separate. Once you have created one shelf height parameter, you can apply the same label to the other dimensions.

Task 3 - Create front view reference planes.

1. Open the Elevations>**Front** view. Create the reference planes and dimensions and label them, as shown in Figure 4–28.

Figure 4–28

2. In the *Modify* (or *Create*) tab>Properties panel, click (Family Types).

3. In the Family Types dialog box, set up a formula for the *Shelf Height*, as shown in Figure 4–29. Lock the **Height** parameter and the **Shelf Height** parameter also locks.

The parameters automatically display in alphabetical order. You can reorganize them as needed.

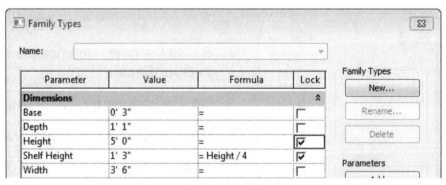

Figure 4–29

4. Move the dialog box to one side and try several different values. Click Apply to apply the changes to the family. Verify that all of the reference planes move together. Click OK.

5. Save the family.

Practice 4b

Setup a Heat Pump Family

 Learning Objectives

- Add reference planes and dimensions with labels to form the framework of the heat pump.
- Add formulas and flex the parameters to test that they work together as expected.

Estimated time for completion: 20 minutes

In this practice you will create a family file based on a template and view the existing reference planes. You will also create

reference planes, dimension them, label the dimensions and use a formula in parameters, as shown in Figure 4–30.

Figure 4–30

Task 1 - Open a family template.

1. Close all open projects.

2. On the Start page, under the *Families* area, click **New**.

3. In the New Family - Select Template dialog box, select the template **Generic Model.rft** from the Revit Library and click Open .

4. In the *View* tab>Windows panel, click ⊟ (Tile) or type **WT**.

5. The four open views display. Type **ZA** (the shortcut for **Zoom All to Fit**) to fit the view in all of the windows.

Changing the units so that they display as inches makes it easier to work with the dimensions.

6. Several existing reference planes are included in the file, as well as **Ref.Level**.

7. Type **UN** to open the Project Units dialog box. Click the button under *Format* for *Length* and change the *Units* to **Fractional inches**.

8. Click [OK] until all of the dialog boxes are closed.

9. In the *Create* tab>Properties panel, click (Family Category and Parameters).

10. In the Family Category and Parameters dialog box, set the *Filter list* to **Mechanical** and select **Mechanical Equipment** as shown in Figure 4–31, and click [OK].

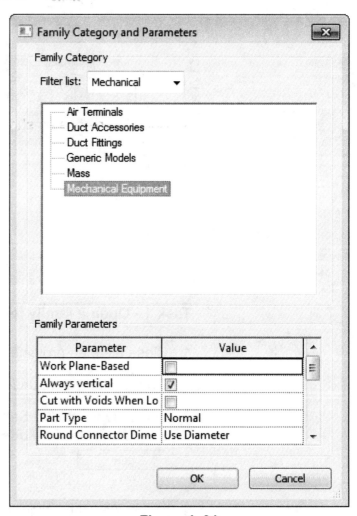

Figure 4–31

11. Save the family in your MEP class folder as **Heat Pump.rfa**.

Task 2 - Create plan view reference planes.

1. Maximize the **Ref. Level** view.

2. Create two new reference planes, above the existing planes, as shown in Figure 4–32. Do not worry about the exact location yet.

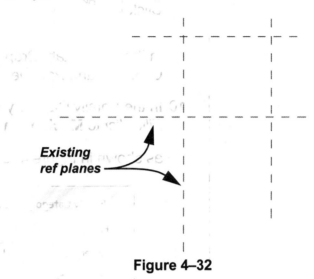

Existing ref planes

Figure 4–32

3. Add dimensions as shown in Figure 4–33.

Your dimensions might vary depending on where you originally placed the reference planes.

43 3/32"

35 7/8"

Figure 4–33

The scale in the graphics have been changed to display the dimensions more clearly.

4. Select the vertical reference plane to the right and change the temporary dimension to **38 7/8"**.

5. Select the top horizontal reference plane and change the temporary dimension to **34 3/4"**.

6. Select the horizontal dimension. In the Options Bar, expand the Label list and select **<Add parameter...>**. In the Parameter Properties dialog box, type the *Name* as **Width** and verify that **Type** is selected. Click [OK].

7. Create a label for the vertical dimension named **Depth** using the same process. The sketch should display as shown in Figure 4–34.

Figure 4–34

8. Add two more reference planes inside the other reference planes. Dimension and label them, as shown in Figure 4–35.

Figure 4–35

These new dimensions are not at the center of the unit but a specific distance from the right side. The exact distance is not required at this time.

9. Open the Elevations>**Front** view.

10. Create the reference planes and dimensions. Label the *Height* dimension, as shown in Figure 4–36, and lock the **1"** and **EQ** dimensions into place. You might need to zoom in to do this.

Figure 4–36

11. In Properties, name the **Top of Unit** and **Top of Base** reference planes, as shown in Figure 4–36.

12. Save the family.

Task 3 - Flex the parameters.

---

1. Remain in elevation view.

2. Select the **Height** parameter and change it to a different height. Verify that the top dimensions moves with the height and the bottom one stays in place.

3. Try a different height to fully check it.

4. Return to the Floor Plans>**Ref. Level** view.

5. In the *Modify* (or *Create*) tab>Properties panel, click 🔳 (Family Types).

6. In the Family Types dialog box, set up a formula for *CenterY* and *CenterX*, as shown in Figure 4–37. Lock one of the center parameters and the related parameters also lock.

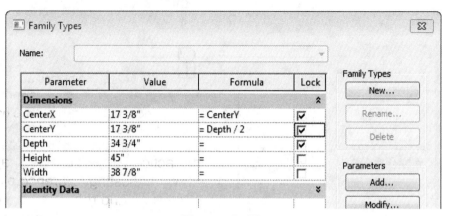

Figure 4–37

7. Move the dialog box to one side and try several different values. Click Apply to apply the changes to the family. Verify that all of the reference planes move together. Click OK.

8. Save the family.

Practice 4c

Setup a Structural Column Family

 Learning Objectives

- Add reference planes and reference lines. Dimension and label them to form the framework of the column.
- Add formulas and flex the parameters to test that they work together as expected.

Estimated time for completion: 20 minutes

In this practice you will create a family file based on a template and view the existing reference planes. You will also create reference lines and reference planes, dimension them, label the dimensions, as shown in Figure 4–38, and use a formula in parameters.

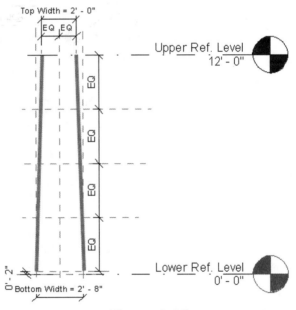

Figure 4–38

Task 1 - Open a family template.

1. Close all open projects.

2. On the Start page, in the *Families* area, select **New**.

3. In the New Family - Select Template dialog box, select the template **Structural Column.rft** from the Revit Library and click Open .

4. Open a 3D view and Elevations>**Front** views.

5. In the *View* tab>Windows panel, click ⊟ (Tile) or type **WT.** The three open views display so you can see each of them.

6. Several existing reference planes are included in the file, as well as **Lower Ref.Level** and **Upper Ref. Level** which set the height of the column once it is used in a project.

7. Save the family in your *Structural* class folder as **Trellis Column.rfa**.

Task 2 - Create reference planes.

1. Maximize the Elevations>**Front** view.

2. Change the *Upper Ref. Level* to **12'-0"**.

3. Draw four new horizontal reference planes between the Lower and Upper Ref. Levels, as shown in Figure 4–39. Do not worry about the exact location yet but the lowest one is close to the Lower Ref. Level and the others are more or less equally spaced in the remaining area.

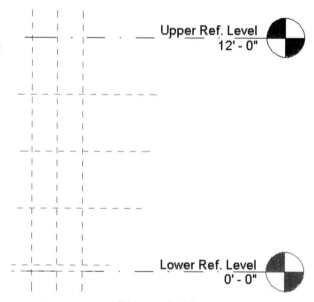

Figure 4–39

4. Dimension the lowest reference plane to the Lower Ref. Level. Set the dimension to **2"** and lock the dimension as shown in Figure 4–40.

Figure 4–40

5. Add a string of dimensions between the evenly spaced reference planes and the lowest reference plane, as shown in Figure 4–41. Set the dimension string to **Equal**.

Figure 4–41

6. Add two short vertical reference planes crossing the Upper Ref. Level.

7. Dimension and set them as equal, as shown in Figure 4–42.

Figure 4–42

8. Add another dimension from side to side of the new short reference planes.

9. Select the dimension.

10. In the Options Bar, expand the *Label* list and select **<Add parameter...>**.

Your dimensions might vary depending on where you originally placed the reference planes.

11. In the Parameter Properties dialog box, name it **Top Width** and click OK . The new parameter displays with the dimension, as shown in Figure 4–43.

Figure 4–43

12. Add another dimension to the overall vertical reference planes below the Lower Ref. Level and label it **Bottom Width**, as shown in Figure 4–44.

13. In the *Create* tab>Datum panel, click (Reference Line).

14. Draw a line between the lower left intersection of the bottom width and lowest reference plane (not the level) and the upper left intersection of the Top Width and Upper Ref. Level. Repeat on the other side. This creates the framework for the taper of the column, as shown in Figure 4–44.

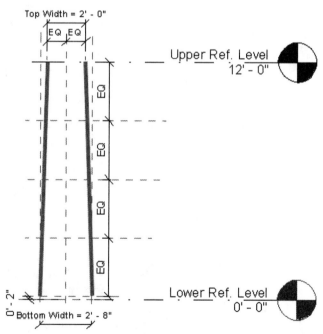

Figure 4–44

15. In the *Modify* (or *Create*) tab>Properties panel, click (Family Types).

16. Set up a formula for the *Top Width*, as shown in Figure 4–45.

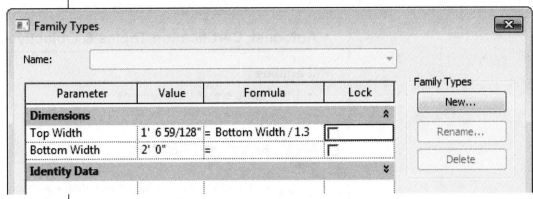

Figure 4–45

17. Move the dialog box to one side and try several different values for the bottom width. Click ⌐ Apply ⌐ to apply the changes to the family. Verify that all of the reference planes and lines move together. Click ⌐ OK ⌐.

18. Save the family.

4.3 Creating Family Elements

Autodesk Certification Topics & Objectives

Pro.　User

Families

* Use Family creation procedures　✓

Learning Objective

* Create solid/void forms including extrusions, blends, revolves, sweeps, and swept blends.

When you have built the parametric framework, the next step in creating families is to add the actual geometry to the family file, as shown in Figure 4–46. You can use a variety of 2D and 3D drawing tools. You can also add controls, openings, and components, such as the sink shown in the countertop in Figure 4–46. These elements can be aligned and locked to reference planes and other geometry.

Figure 4–46

The actual components in a family can include both 2D and 3D elements. 3D elements are either solids or voids. 2D elements include model lines, symbolic lines, text, and model text. All of these tools are located in the Family Editor.

Creating 3D Elements

There are five methods of creating solid forms, as shown in Figure 4–47.

Figure 4–47

Void forms use the same methods, but must be placed inside solid forms to create a subtracted area.

Each method uses a sketched 2D profile as the basis of the 3D shape.

- **Extrusion** pushes the profile out in one direction.

- **Blend** links two profiles together.

- **Revolve** rotates the profile around an axis.

- **Sweep** extends a profile along a path.

- **Swept Blend** connects two different profiles along a path.

How To: Create Solid Extrusions

Extrusions are the simplest elements to create. All you need to do is draw a closed profile using Autodesk Revit sketch tools and assign a depth for the extrusion, as shown in Figure 4–48.

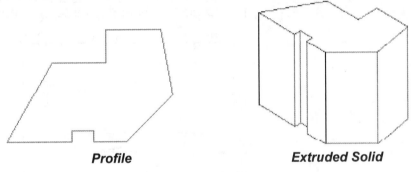

Profile   *Extruded Solid*

Figure 4–48

1. In the *Create* tab>Forms panel, click ⬜ (Extrusion).
2. In the Options Bar, set the *Depth* for the extrusion, as shown in Figure 4–49.

Figure 4–49

- A positive value for the depth extrudes up or toward you depending on the work plane. A negative value extrudes down or away from you.

3. In the *Modify | Create Extrusion* tab>Draw panel, use the sketch tools to create the profile for the extrusion. You can add dimensions and reference planes as needed to create the profile.

4. In the Mode panel, click ✓ (Finish Edit Mode) to create the extrusion.

*By default, **Start** is at the work plane and **End** is at the depth.*

5. In the *Modify | Extrusion* tab, make changes to the extrusion as needed.
6. In Properties, you can adjust the *Extrusion Start* and *Extrusion End*, the *Visibility* and *Visibility Graphics Overrides*, and *Material*. You can also change it from a **Solid** to a **Void** or vice versa, and place it in the *Subcategory* of **Hidden Lines**.
7. Press <Esc> or click in empty space to finish the command.

• In the *Create* tab>Work Plane panel, click ⬚ (Set) to select the plane on which you want to draw a profile (e.g., on top of another extrusion).

How To: Create Solid Blends

Blends are defined by two profiles: one for the base (bottom) and one for the top. The two profiles are connected by the solid element. If the base and top do not have the same number of corners, adjust the vertex connection, as shown in Figure 4–50.

Figure 4–50

1. In the *Create* tab>Forms panel, click ⬔ (Blend).
2. In the *Modify | Create Blend Base Boundary* tab>Draw panel, use the sketch tools to draw the base profile.
3. In the Mode panel, click ⬔ (Edit Top).
4. In the Options Bar, set the *Depth* for the top.
5. Draw the top profile using the sketch tools.
6. If the intersections are complex, click ⬔ (Edit Vertices) and make sure all of the connections work correctly.
7. Click ✓ (Finish Edit Mode) to create the blend.
8. The *Modify | Blend* tab displays, where you can edit the base or the top. You also have access to the Properties of the blend.
9. Press <Esc> or click in empty space to finish the command.

If the entire blended element is not displayed in plan view, select the View name in the Project Browser, and then in Properties, modify the View Range Cut Plane.

- When you click (Edit Vertices), open blue dots are displayed on the dotted lines. These lines are suggested connections. Select the dot to toggle the connection on or off, and repeat with other corners to obtain the required connections. Use the tools in the *Edit Vertices* tab>Vertex Connect panel, as shown in Figure 4–51, to modify the vertices.

Figure 4–51

How To: Create Solid Revolves

A revolved solid form requires a profile and an axis around which it is revolved, as shown in Figure 4–52. The profile often needs to be sketched in a work plane perpendicular to the *ground*. Before sketching the profile, create a reference plane that you can use for the work plane. For example, if you are creating a dome, create two intersecting reference planes at the center of the dome and name them. Then, when you start the revolution, you can select one reference plane for your work plane and the other for your axis.

You can name a reference plane in Properties.

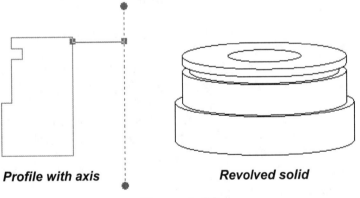

Profile with axis   **Revolved solid**

Figure 4–52

1. In the *Create* tab>Forms panel, click (Revolve).
2. In the *Modify | Create Revolve* tab>Work Plane panel, click

    (Set). In the Work Plane dialog box, select the plane on which you want to draw the profile. A prompt warns you if you need to change views to draw in that work plane.

The axis can be an edge of the profile or some distance away if there is an opening.

3. In the Draw panel, click ◰ (Boundary Line) and draw the profile.

4. In the Draw panel, click ◔ (Axis Line) and draw or select the axis about which the profile will rotate.

5. Click ✓ (Finish Edit Mode) to create the solid.

6. The *Modify | Revolve* tab displays, where you can edit the revolve. You can also change the Properties (such as the *End Angle* and *Start Angle*).

7. Press <Esc> or click in empty space to finish the command.

How To: Create Solid Sweeps

A sweep is similar to an extrusion. However, instead of only extruding in one direction, it follows a path that can have multiple segments, as shown in Figure 4–53. You define the path first and then create the profile on the path.

Figure 4–53

1. In the *Create* tab>Forms panel, click ◳ (Sweep).

2. In the *Modify | Sweep* tab>Sweep panel, click ∠⟩ (Sketch Path) or ◳ (Pick Path). Draw or select the path you want the sweep to follow.

3. Click ✓ (Finish Edit Mode).

4. In the Sweep panel, select a profile from the list or click ◳ (Select Profile), and then click ◳ (Edit Profile) to sketch a profile.

Click ◰ (Load Profile) to load additional profiles into the family file for use with the sweep.

   • The Go To View dialog box opens if you need to change views to draw the profile. Select the view in which you want to draw the profile and click ⬚Open View⬚.

The profile plane is automatically drawn on the first line of the path. It is the red dot with the green line through it, as shown in a 3D view in Figure 4–54. The red dot is the place where the profile and path intersect.

5. Draw the profile for the sweep on the profile plane, as shown in Figure 4–54.

Figure 4–54

6. Click ✓ (Finish Edit Mode) twice to complete the process.
7. The *Modify | Sweep* tab displays, where you can edit the sweep. In Properties, you can change several options of the profile along with the other standard options.
8. Press <Esc> or click in empty space to finish the command.

How To: Create Solid Swept Blends

Swept blends consist of a path and two profiles, as shown in Figure 4–55. The profiles can have different shapes. The path must be one segment, which can be a line, an arc, or a spline.

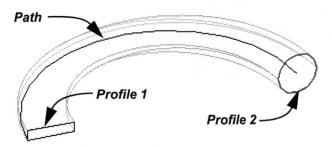

Figure 4–55

1. In the *Create* tab>Forms panel, click (Swept Blend).
2. In the *Modify | Swept Blend* tab>Swept Blend panel, click

   (Sketch Path) or (Pick Path). Draw or select the path you want the swept blend to follow. You can only have one segment in the path.

3. Click ✓ (Finish Edit Mode).

4. In the Swept Blend panel, click (Select Profile 1).
5. Select a profile from the list or create a new profile using

   (Edit Profile).

6. Click (Select Profile 2) and repeat the process. It does not need to be the same size or shape as the first profile.

7. In the Swept Blend panel, click (Edit Vertices) and align the vertices. This controls the twist of the swept blend.

8. Click (Finish Edit Mode).

9. In the *Modify | Swept Blend* tab, make any changes as needed.

10. In Properties, set any options as needed.

11. Press <Esc> or click in empty space to finish the command.

4.4 Additional Tools for Families

Autodesk Certification Topics & Objectives

Pro.   User

Families
- Use Family creation procedures   ✓

Modeling
- Edit room-aware families   ✓

 Learning Objectives

- Align and lock elements to reference planes.
- Add controls that can be used to flip or mirror geometry.
- (Autodesk Revit MEP only) Add connectors to attach other Autodesk Revit MEP elements to the family.
- Add openings in host elements.
- Add Model and Symbolic lines to 2D views in the family.

A critical tool for establishing geometrical location is to align and lock elements to reference planes so that they move as expected. You use the **Align** command to do this. Family-specific functions include adding *controls* to flip and mirror the family, making a family room-aware by establishing the room calculation point, applying connectors for MEP families and creating openings in a host, such as a wall or ceiling. You can also include 2D lines, text, and other components.

Aligning and Locking

As you draw elements in families, it is important to lock and align them to reference planes so that they can be moved parametrically. The padlock symbol displays when you snap to reference planes while drawing, as shown in Figure 4–56. Select the padlock to lock the element to the reference plane.

Figure 4–56

You can also use the **Align** command to align and lock 2D elements to reference planes and 3D elements to each other so that they move together.

How To: Align and Lock Elements in Families

1. In the *Modify* tab>Modify panel, click ⬒ (Align).
2. Select the reference plane or other element to align to.
3. Select the element to align.
4. Select the padlock symbol to lock it.
5. Continue aligning elements as needed.

6. Click ↖ (Modify) or press <Esc> to finish the command.

• Both aligning and locking elements are critical when you are creating families.

Hint: Locking Sketches to Reference Planes

It is important to lock sketches to reference planes rather than other elements in a family. If you lock the sketch to other family members, it might not flex correctly. To verify that you have the right intersection, press <Tab> until the appropriate elements are highlighted, and then snap in the required location, as shown in Figure 4–57.

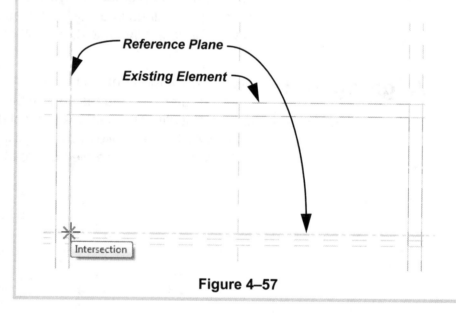

Figure 4–57

Adding Controls

You can place control arrows to flip or mirror geometry in the family, as shown in Figure 4–58. The controls also display on doors and other elements. Some family templates already include controls and you can add others.

Figure 4–58

How To: Add Controls

1. In the *Create* tab>Control panel, click ⊹ (Control).
2. In the *Modify | Place Control* tab>Control Type panel, click

   ⬆ (Single Vertical), ⬅ (Single Horizontal), ⬍ (Double Vertical), or ⬌ (Double Horizontal).
3. Click on the screen to place the control in the view.

4. Click ⬉ (Modify) or press <Esc> to finish the command.

Setting Room Calculation Points

Occasionally some families, such as lighting fixtures, specialty equipment, casework, furniture, etc., are placed so that the default center of the element is not in the room where it needs to be counted, as shown in Figure 4–59. You can change by modifying the Room Calculation Point. This makes the family a room-aware family.

<Furniture Schedule>			
A	B	C	D
Family and Type	Room: Number	Room: Name	Count
Sofa-Pensi	101	Lobby	1
Sofa-Pensi	102	Seating	1
Grand total: 2			

Before room calculation point

<Furniture Schedule>			
A	B	C	D
Family and Type	Room: Number	Room: Name	Count
Sofa-Pensi	102	Seating	2
Grand total: 2			

After room calculation

Figure 4–59

- Room Calculation Points must be set in the family.

How To: Set the Room Calculation Points

1. Open the Family file.
2. In Properties select Room Calculation Point as shown in on the left in Figure 4–60
3. Move the room calculation point to where it needs to be as shown on the right in Figure 4–60.

Figure 4–60

4. Save and load (or reload) the family file into the project.

Adding Connectors

In the Autodesk Revit MEP software, there is an additional option for creating connectors for the various systems. For example, you can create a duct connector to an air terminal where the duct element attaches to the air terminal, as shown in Figure 4–61.

Figure 4–61

These tools are found on the *Create* tab>Connectors panel, as shown in Figure 4–62.

Figure 4–62

How To: Add a Connector

1. In the *Create* tab>Connectors panel, select the type of connector you want to use.
2. In the Options Bar, specify the type of connector (if applicable), as shown for an electrical connector in Figure 4–63.

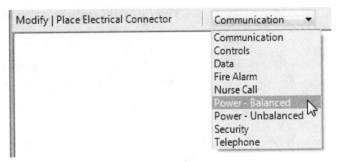

Figure 4–63

3. In the *Modify | Place Connector* tab>Placement panel, click (Face) or (Work Plane).
4. Select a face or workplane that matches the location and direction of the connector.
5. Select the connector and make any adjustments needed in Properties.

Adding Openings

The **Opening** command enables you to sketch an opening in a host element. You need to have started the family using one of the host-based templates.

How To: Add an Opening to a Host Element

1. In the *Create* tab>Model panel, click (Opening).
2. In the *Modify | Create Opening Boundary* tab>Draw panel, use the sketch tools to create the opening. Use reference planes and dimensions as needed.
3. Click (Finish Edit Mode).

4. In the *Modify | Opening Cut* tab, make changes as needed.
5. In the Options Bar, select when you want the cut to display transparently—in **3D** and/or in **Elevation**—as shown in Figure 4–64.

Figure 4–64

6. Press <Esc> or click in empty space to finish the command.

Adding Lines

In some cases, you need to draw 2D elements to describe the elements in a family. In the *Create* tab>Model panel, you can use 🝿 (Model Lines) and in the *Annotate* tab>Detail panel, you can use 🝿 (Symbolic Lines). Model Lines are visible in 2D and 3D views. Symbolic Lines are only visible in views parallel to the view in which they were drawn.

For example, you could use Model Lines to draw door hardware that is not three-dimensional. But you would use Symbolic Lines to draw the door swing (as shown in Figure 4–65), so that it does not display in 3D views.

Figure 4–65

- Use the standard sketch tools in the Draw panel to draw Model and Symbolic Lines.

- Lines are often used to display the model elements in plan and elevation views at the Coarse (and sometimes Medium) Detail Level.

- You can create entire families made up of Model and Symbolic lines if they are only going to be used in a plan view. For example, create a 2D family for a hospital bed, as shown in Figure 4–66, and use it in a large hospital layout where most of the instances do not need to be full 3D.

Figure 4–66

2D families can still be robust in the number and types of parameters they hold for use in schedules and quantity takeoffs.

Text Tools

You can add text to families the same way you add text to projects. In the *Create* tab>Model panel, you can use

(Model Text). Model Text is the real-world size of the text on the elements (such as a name painted on a door). In the

Annotate tab>Text panel, you can use **A** (Text). Text takes on the scale of the view and is typically used in Annotation families.

Adding Components

You can add components to families in the same way you add them to projects. For components that display in all views, use Model Components; in the *Create* tab>Model panel, click

(Component). For components that only display in the current view, use Detail Components; in the *Annotate* tab>Detail

panel, click (Detail Component).

- Adding a component to a family produces a nested family. In most cases, you want to do this with elements that are used multiple times in other families also, such as hardware shown in Figure 4–67.

Figure 4–67

- Nesting families increase the file size and slows down performance.

Practice 4d

Create Family Geometry for the Bookcase

 Learning Objectives

- Create elements for the base, frame, shelves, and the back of a bookcase.
- Align and lock the elements to reference planes.
- (Optional) Add a component, a glass door for the shelves, and use it repeatedly in the family.

Estimated time for completion: 30 minutes

In this practice you will create extruded solids for the base, frame, shelves, and back of a bookcase, and lock them in place with dimensions. You will also load components for the shelf doors and align and lock them in place, as shown in Figure 4–68.

Figure 4–68

Task 1 - Create a base for the bookcase.

1. Open the project /Architectural/**Barrister-Bookcase-1-A.rfa** from your class folder.

2. Open the Floor Plans>**Ref. Level** view.

3. In the *Create* tab>Forms panel, click ⬜ (Extrusion). In the Options Bar, set the *Depth* to **4"**.

4. In the *Modify | Create Extrusion* tab>Draw panel, use the sketch tools to draw a rectangle across the outside intersections of the reference planes. Lock all four lines to the reference planes, as shown in Figure 4–69.

Figure 4–69

5. Click (Finish Edit Mode).

6. Press <Esc> or click in empty space to finish the command.

7. Open the Elevations>**Front** view.

8. In the *Modify* tab>Modify panel, click (Align). Align the top of the extrusion to the *Base* reference plane and lock it. Align and lock the bottom of the base to the *Ref Level* reference plane.

Task 2 - Create the frame and shelves for the bookcase.

---

1. In the *Create* tab>Work Plane panel, click (Set).

2. In the Work Plane dialog box, set the *Name* to **Reference Plane : Door Face** and click OK .

3. Draw four reference planes inside the existing reference planes. Dimension and label them as shown in Figure 4–70.

Figure 4–70

4. Flex the *Height* and *Width* of the overall bookcase to verify that the new **Frame Width** parameters move as expected.

5. Start the **Extrusion** command. In the Options Bar, set the *Depth* to **1'-0"**.

6. Draw and lock two rectangular sketches to the reference planes (as shown in Figure 4–71), and finish the extrusion.

Figure 4–71

7. Draw two reference planes on either side of the shelf height reference plane. Dimension and label them as shown in Figure 4–72. Repeat with the other two shelf height locations.

Figure 4–72

- To make the labels more readable, change the scale to **1"=1'-0"**. You can also create an additional dimension style with the *Read Convention* set to **Horizontal** and use it for the **Shelf** parameters, as shown in Figure 4–72.

8. Open the Family Types dialog box and use [Move Up] and [Move Down] to move the *Height*, *Width*, and *Depth* to the top of the parameters list.

9. Flex the *Height* and *Width* of the overall bookcase to verify the new **Shelf Width** parameters move as expected. Finish the flexing with the *Height* set to **5'-0"** and the *Width* to **3'-0"**.

10. Start the **Extrusion** command again. In the Options Bar, verify that the *Depth* is set to **1'-0"**.

11. Draw the sketch around each shelf, as shown in Figure 4–73. Lock the sketch to the reference planes and finish the extrusion.

Figure 4–73

12. Click ✓ (Finish Edit Mode) and click in empty space to finish the command.

Task 3 - Create the back of the bookcase.

1. Open the Floor Plans>**Ref. Level** view.

2. Align and lock the back of the frame and shelf extrusions to the back reference plane.

3. Add another reference plane **1/4"** from the back of the bookcase. Dimension and lock it in place, as shown in Figure 4–74.

Create a label if you want to change the size of the back.

Figure 4–74

4. Start the **Extrusion** command again. Set the *Depth* to **2'-6"**. (This is less than the bookcase height. You will adjust it later.)

5. Draw a rectangular sketch across the back and lock it to the reference planes.

6. Click ✓ (Finish Edit Mode) and click in empty space to finish the command.

7. Open the Elevations>**Back** view. Switch the Visual Style to ⬛ (Hidden Line), if needed.

8. Align and lock the top of the back panel with the top reference plane. Select the top reference plane first, and then select the top of the panel to align with it, as shown in Figure 4–75.

Figure 4–75

9. Switch to a 3D view. The base, frame, shelves, and back are all separate elements.

10. In the *Modify* tab>Geometry panel, click (Join) and join the four elements. The bookcase should display as shown in Figure 4–76.

Figure 4–76

11. Save the family.

Task 4 - Add door components (optional).

---

1. Open the Floor Plans>**Ref. Level** view.

2. In the *Insert* tab>Load from Library panel, click (Load Family).

3. In the Load Family dialog box, in the *Architectural* folder of your class folder, select **Shelf-Door-Glass-A.rfa** and click [Open].

4. In the *Create* tab>Model panel, click (Component).

5. Place a copy of the door in the view aligned to the **Center L/R** reference plane, as shown in Figure 4–77. The width might not match the bookcase width.

Figure 4–77

6. Use (Align) to lock the center of the bookcase with the center reference plane, as shown in Figure 4–78.

This step keeps the knobs in a logical place in relationship to the width of the door.

Figure 4–78

7. Use (Align) to line up the back of the door with the **Door Face** reference plane and lock it, as shown in Figure 4–79.

Select the Door Face reference plane first when you are aligning.

Figure 4–79

8. Click (Modify) and select the door.

9. In Properties, scroll down until the **Door width** and **Door Height** parameters display. Click at the end of the row and associate the **Door width** with the *Width*, and the **Door Height** with the *Shelf Height*, as shown in Figure 4–80. The parameters in Properties gray out and an equal sign displays in the button.

Figure 4–80

The door should now fit within the shelf, as shown in Figure 4–81.

Figure 4–81

10. Change the *Width* and *Depth* dimensions to flex the model and verify that it works correctly.

11. Open the Elevations>**Front** view and set the Visual Style to (Hidden Line). The door needs to be aligned vertically.

12. Align the top, as shown in Figure 4–82, and bottom of the door with the shelf height reference planes for the bottom shelf. Lock them in place.

Figure 4–82

13. Copy the door to the other shelves.

14. Align and lock into place the top and bottom of each copied door, as shown in Figure 4–83.

Figure 4–83

15. Change the *Height* dimension to flex the model and check the door alignments.

16. Open the Elevations>**Left** view and align the back of the top three doors faces with the **Door Face** reference plane.

17. Switch to a 3D view, as shown in Figure 4–84.

Figure 4–84

18. Use Family Types to flex the model again to make sure everything is working together.

19. Save the family.

Practice 4e

Create Family Geometry for the Heat Pump

 Learning Objectives

- Create extrusions and blends for the components of the heat pump.
- Add a void extrusion to cut out a portion of the main element.
- Add extrusions and place connectors on them for pipe and electrical connections.

Estimated time for completion: 30 minutes.

In this practice you will create extruded solids for the base, cabinet, and fan unit of a heat pump. You will create a void extrusion and add circular extrusions for connectors, as shown in Figure 4–85. Finally, you will place connectors in the appropriate locations on the main unit.

Figure 4–85

Task 1 - Create the main cabinet of a heat pump.

1. Open the project /MEP/**Heat-Pump-1-MEP.rfa** from your class folder.

2. Open the Floor Plans>**Ref. Level** view.

3. In the *Create* tab>Work Plane panel, click 🗔 (Set).

4. In the Work Plane dialog box, set *Name* as **Reference Plane : Top of Base** and click OK .

5. In the *Create* tab>Forms panel, click (Extrusion). In the Options Bar, set the *Depth* to **30"**.

6. Draw a rectangle using the intersections of the reference planes and lock them as shown in Figure 4–86.

Figure 4–86

7. Add a **3" x 3"** chamfer at each corner of the unit and clean them up using (Trim).

8. You will dimension the chamfers. To dimension, make sure to select the end point of the line and the reference plane, as shown in Figure 4–87. Select each dimension and lock it in place.

Figure 4–87

9. Click (Finish Edit Mode) and click in empty space to finish the command.

10. Open the Elevations>**Front** view. Align and lock the top of the unit extrusion to the **Top of Unit** reference plane.

11. Open a 3D view to look at the unit as shown in Figure 4–88.

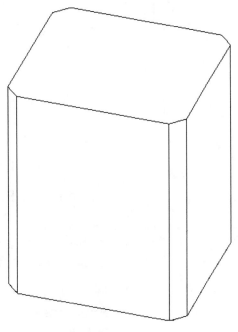

Figure 4–88

12. Save the family.

Task 2 - Create the top and base of the heat pump.

---

1. Return to the Floor Plans>**Ref. Level** view.

2. Set the Work Plane to the **Top of Unit** reference plane.

3. In the *Create* tab>Forms panel, click ⬢ (Blend).

4. In the Options Bar, set the *Depth* to **1/2"** and the *Offset* to **1"**.

5. In the *Modify | Create Blend Base Boundary* tab>Draw panel, click ⬚ (Pick Lines).

6. Select the lines all around the unit making sure the new lines are inside the unit lines.

7. Click ⬟ (Edit Top).

8. In the *Modify | Create Blend Base Boundary* tab>Draw panel, click ⬚ (Pick Lines).

9. In the Options Bar, set the *Offset* to **1/2"**.

10. Pick inside the lines for the Blend base you just created. The lines should look similar to the detail shown in Figure 4–89.

Figure 4–89

11. Click (Finish Edit Mode).

12. Set the Work Plane to **Level: Ref. Level**.

13. In the *Create* tab>Forms panel, click (Extrusion). In the Options Bar, set the *Depth* to **1"**.

14. In the *Modify | Create Extrusion* tab>Draw panel, use the **Pick Lines** tool to draw a boundary at **1/2"** inside the unit outlines.

15. Click (Finish Edit Mode).

16. Press <Esc> or click in empty space to finish the command.

17. Open the Elevations>**Front** view.

18. In the *Modify* tab>Modify panel, click (Align) and align the top of the extrusion to the *Top of Base* reference plane and lock it, as shown in Figure 4–90.

Figure 4–90

19. Open the Family Types dialog box and use Move Up and Move Down to reorder the parameters so the *Height*, *Width*, and *Depth* are at the top.

20. Flex the dimensions to check that everything is working as expected.

21. Save the family.

Task 3 - Add the fan.

1. Return to the Floor Plans>**Ref. Level** view.

2. Set the Work Plane to the **Top of Unit** reference plane.

3. Start the **Extrusion** command and in the Options Bar, set the *Depth* to **1"**.

4. Draw a circle from the intersection of the CenterX and CenterY reference planes with a radius close to the outside, as shown in Figure 4–91. The exact dimension does not matter for this step.

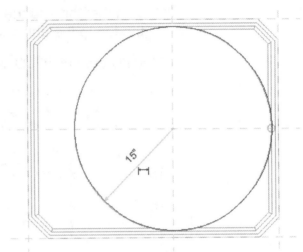

Figure 4–91

5. Dimension the radius of the circle and create a new Label based on the dimension named **Radius of Fan**.

6. Open the Family Types dialog box and move the **Radius of Fan** parameter below all of the others.

7. Next to **Radius of Fan**, in the *Formula* area, type **Depth / 2 - 1"**.

8. Click [Apply].

9. To flex the element, change the Depth and click [Apply]. When it works as expected, click [OK].

10. Click ✓ (Finish Edit Mode).

11. Open the Elevations>**Front** view. Align and lock the top of the fan to the top reference level, as shown in Figure 4–92.

Figure 4–92

12. In the *Modify* tab>Geometry panel, click (Join).

13. Join the unit and the beveled extrusion together. Then join the fan to the unit and the base to the unit.

14. View the unit in 3D, as shown in Figure 4–93.

Figure 4–93

15. Save the family.

Task 4 - Add a void.

1. Open the 3D, Ref. Level, and Front views and tile them so that all three are visible on the screen.

2. In the Front elevation view, add a ref plane to the lower left corner of the unit. Dimension it to **4 1/4"** and in Properties, name it **Bottom of Void,** as shown in Figure 4–94.

Lock the base to the Top of Base ref plane, if you have not locked it already.

Figure 4–94

3. In the Ref. Level view, in the *Create* tab>Forms panel, expand (Void Forms) and click (Void Extrusion).

4. In the *Modify | Create Void Extrusion* tab>Work Plan panel, click (Set).

5. In the Work Plane dialog box, select the *Name* **Reference Plane: Bottom of Void** and click OK .

6. Draw the sketch as shown in Figure 4–95.

Figure 4–95

7. In Properties, set the *Extrusion End* to **9"**.

8. Click ✓ (Finish Edit Mode) and click in empty space to release the selection.

9. Rotate the 3D view so you can see the new void, as shown in Figure 4–96.

Figure 4–96

10. Save the project.

Task 5 - Add Connector extrusions.

1. Working in various views and work planes, add the extrusions as shown in Figure 4–97 and Figure 4–98. These extrusion are the faces for the connectors. Therefore, they need to be on the face where the related system elements need to attach.

   • Set all extrusion heights to **1/4"**.
   • Add any reference lines or dimensions required to get the extrusions into the correct locations.

Void Detail - Elevation Left   Void Detail - Elevation Front

Figure 4–97

Overall Elevation Front

Figure 4–98

Task 6 - Add connectors.

1. Open the 3D view and modify the view to display the corner of the unit where the connectors need to be applied.

2. In the *Create* tab> Connectors panel, click ⚡ (Electrical Connector).

3. In the Options Bar, select **Power-Balanced**.

4. Select the face of the top circular extrusion.

5. Click (Modify) and select the new connector.

6. In Properties, in the *Identity Data* area, in the *Connector Description*, type **Electric Power Supply**.

7. Continue adding the other connectors as shown in Figure 4–99. For the Pipe Connectors, before selecting the location, in Properties, set the *Round Connector Dimension* to **Use Radius**.

Pipe Connector:
Other
Connector Description:
Gas Line

Pipe Connector:
Other
Connector Description:
Liquid Line

Electrical Connector:
Power-Balanced
Connector Description:
Electric Power Supply

Electrical Connector:
Power-Balanced
Connector Description:
Low Voltage

Figure 4–99

8. Save the project.

Task 7 - Create and assign new parameters for piping connectors.

---

1. In the Properties panel, click (Family Types).

2. In the Family Types dialog box, in the *Parameters* area, click Add... . In the Parameter Properties dialog box, create a **Family parameter** and set the *Parameter Data* as shown in Figure 4–100. Click OK .

Figure 4–100

*The **Radius** parameters are going to be linked to existing **Radius** parameters in the connectors. The Autodesk Revit MEP software reads this and sets the correct diameter for the connector in the family when it is inserted into a project.*

3. Add another parameter named **Liquid Line Service Valve** using the same information.

4. Create two parameters named **Gas Line Radius** and **Liquid Line Radius**. Use the same Discipline and Type of Parameter but set *Group parameter under* as **Dimensions**.

5. In the Family Types dialog box, assign the *Value* for **Gas Line Service Valve** as **7/8"** and for **Liquid Line Service Valve** as **3/8"**.

6. For **Gas Line Radius,** in *Formula*, type **Gas Line Service Valve / 2**. For **Liquid Line Radius,** in *Formula*, type **Liquid Line Service Valve / 2**.

7. Move the two radius parameters to the end of the Dimensions section.

8. Click [OK].

9. Select the Gas Line connector.

10. In Properties, in the *Dimensions* area, in the **Radius** parameter, click ⬛ to open the Associate Family Parameter dialog box.

11. Select **Gas Line Radius** as shown in Figure 4–101 and click OK .

Figure 4–101

12. Repeat the process for the Liquid Line connector and associate the **Liquid Line Radius** to it.

13. When it is finished the connectors should be sized accordingly in the family, as shown in Figure 4–102.

Select the connector and click the Flip control if the Z-axis is pointing into the heat pump.

Figure 4–102

14. Save the family.

Practice 4f

Create Family Geometry for the Structural Column

 Learning Objectives

- Create extrusions for the base and framework of the column. Align and lock them to reference lines and planes.
- (Optional) Add dimensions and labels for bars that make up the framework.

Estimated time for completion: 20-30 minutes.

In this practice you will create extruded solids for the base and open framework of the column. You will lock them in place with the **Align** tool. You will also test the geometry by modifying the height and widths of the columns. The final version is shown in Figure 4–103. If you have time, you can add additional flexibility with more parameters.

Figure 4–103

Task 1 - Create a base for the column.

1. Open the project /Structural/**Trellis-Column-1-S.rfa** from your class folder.

2. Open the Floor Plans>**Lower Ref. Level** view.

3. Draw four reference planes to the outside of the existing reference planes. Dimension and lock them at 2", as shown in Figure 4–104.

Figure 4–104

4. In the *Create* tab>Forms panel, click (Extrusion). In the Options Bar, set *Depth* as **2"**.

5. In the *Modify | Create Extrusion* tab>Draw panel, use the sketch tools to draw a rectangle across the outside intersections of the reference planes. Lock all four lines to the reference planes, as shown in Figure 4–105.

Figure 4–105

6. Click (Finish Edit Mode).

7. Press <Esc> or click in empty space to finish the command.

8. Open the Elevations>**Front** view.

9. In the *Modify* tab>Modify panel, click (Align). Align the top of the extrusion to the lower reference plane and lock it, as shown in Figure 4–106.

Figure 4–106

10. Save the family.

Task 2 - Create the open work frame for the column.

---

1. In the *Create* tab>Work Plane panel, click (Set).

2. In the Work Plane dialog box, set *Name* as **Reference Plane : Front**, as shown in Figure 4–107, and click OK .

All of these reference planes were added and named in the family template file.

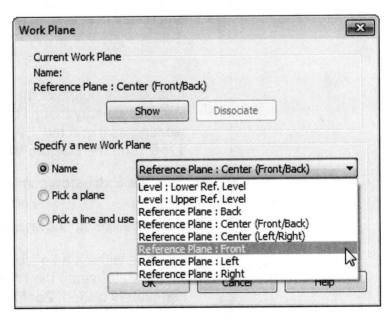

Figure 4–107

3. In the *Create* tab>Datum panel, click (Reference Line).

4. Draw four angled reference lines as shown in Figure 4–108. Make sure you are snapping to the intersections of the horizontal reference planes and the reference lines that establish the taper.

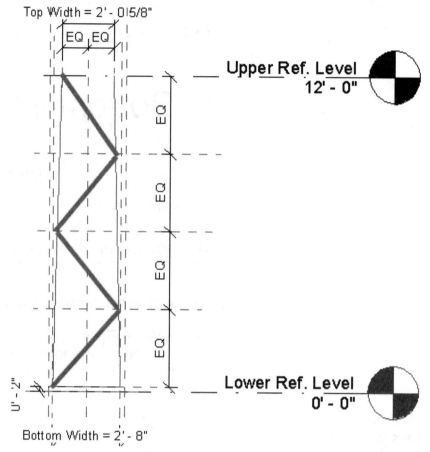

Figure 4–108

5. Change the height of the Upper Ref. Level and the Bottom Width and verify that all of the reference planes and lines are working as expected. End with the **Upper Ref. Level** set to **12'-0"** and the **Bottom Width** set to **2'-8**.

6. Start the **Extrusion** command.

7. Draw the sketch shown in Figure 4–109. Use 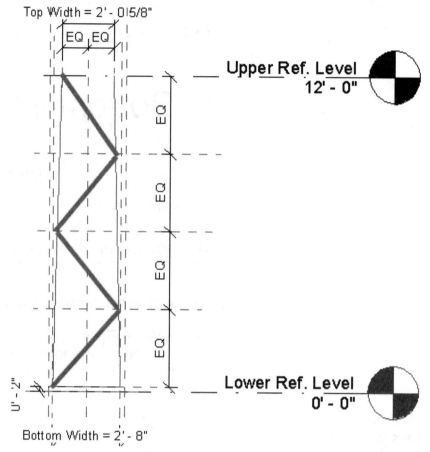 (Pick Lines) with and without an offset, (Split Element), and (Trim Element) to create the lines. Make sure the sketch is completely closed. Zoom in to make adjustments.

   • All dimensions are **2"**.

Figure 4–109

8. Click (Finish Edit Mode) and click in empty space to clear the extrusion selection.

9. Open the Floor Plans>**Lower Ref. Level** view.

10. Align and lock the extrusion to the Front and Back Reference planes as shown in Figure 4–110.

Figure 4–110

11. Open the 3D Views>**View 1** view.

12. In the View Control Bar, set the Visual Style to (Shaded).

13. Rotate the view so you can see the open framework.

14. Save the family.

Task 3 - Dimension the framework for flexing. (Optional)

1. Open the Elevations>**Front** view.

2. Open the Family Types dialog box and move it so you can see the column.

3. In the Family Types dialog box, change the **Top Width** *Formula* to **Bottom Width /1.5** and click ⌐Apply¬ .

4. You can see how the connections of the open framework deform, as shown in the detail in Figure 4–111.

Figure 4–111

5. Close the dialog box and undo the change.

6. Verify that the **Upper Ref. Level** is set as **12'-0"**.

7. Select the extrusion. In the *Modify | Extrusion* tab>Mode panel, click   (Edit Extrusion).

8. Dimension each part of the framework, as shown in part in Figure 4–112. The dimensions around the outside of the framework are dimensioned to a reference line but the ones that are offset on both sides of the reference line are not. Therefore, you have to add 1" dimension to the reference line for the constraints to be satisfied.

It is important to work with the exact sizes when you create the extrusion, otherwise the angled lines are not exactly parallel and you cannot dimension them.

Figure 4–112

9. Open the Family Types dialog box and change the formula again. Does everything work as expected? If not, click the **Cancel** button to close the dialog box and fix the dimensions.

10. Click ✓ (Finish Edit Mode).

11. View the family in 3D.

12. Save the project.

Task 4 - Create parameters for changing the size of the framework components. (Optional)

---

1. Open the Elevations>**Front** view and edit the extrusion.

2. Select one of **1"** dimensions.

3. In the Options Bar, expand the Label list and select **<Add parameter...>**.

4. In the Parameter Properties, set the *Name* as **Bar Halfwidth**.

5. Select all of the other 1" dimensions (hold down <Ctrl>), expand the *Label* list and select **Bar Halfwidth**.

6. Select one of the 2" dimensions associated with the 1" dimensions.

7. Create a label with the name **Bar Width** and apply it to all the related 2" dimensions.

8. Open the Family Types dialog box. For the **Bar Width** parameter, apply the formula **Bar Halfwidth * 2**.

9. Enter different values for **Bar Width** or **Bar Halfwidth** and apply them to test the family.

10. In the Family Types dialog box, in the *Parameters* area, click Add .

11. In the Parameters Properties, create a **Family** parameter named **Side Bar** with the *Discipline* set to **Common**, *Type of Parameter* set to **Length**, and *Group parameter under* set to **Dimensions**.

12. Repeat the process creating two more parameters named **Horizontal Bar Halfwidth** and **Horizontal Bar**.

13. Use Move Up and Move Down to reorder the Parameters so that **Bottom Width**, **Side Bar**, and **Bar Halfwidth** (the ones you typically change) are at the top.

14. Set the formulas and values as shown in Figure 4–113. Doing so forces the dimensions to work together.

Figure 4–113

15. Click   OK   .

The sketch is filled with text that might not be readable. You can change the scale of the view to see the parameters better.

16. Apply the new parameters to the appropriate dimensions, as shown in Figure 4–114.

Figure 4–114

17. Change some of the dimensions either directly in the sketch or through the Family Types dialog box to flex the design.

18. Finish the sketch.

19. Open the 3D view and the Family Types dialog box and flex the model.

20. Save the family.

4.5 Creating Family Types

Autodesk Certification Topics & Objectives

Pro.   User

Elements

• Create a new family type   ✓

Families

• Use Family creation procedures   ✓

Learning Objectives

• Create Family Types using parameters.
• Import and export Family Types for use in other projects.

An important aspect of Family Types is that it helps you *flex* or test the parametric dimensions you set up, as well as helps you create formulas for parameters. A further use for Family Types is the ability to create preset sizes for insertion into a project. When you select the related command, the types display in the Type Selector, as shown in Figure 4–115 for a desk component.

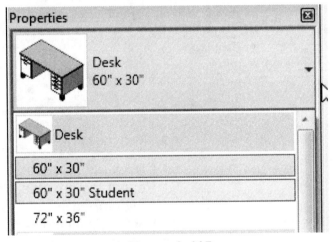

Figure 4–115

How To: Create Family Types

1. In the *Create* or *Modify* tab>Properties panel, click

   (Family Types).

2. In the Family Types dialog box, in the *Family Types* area,

   click .

3. In the Name dialog box, type a name for the Family Type, as shown in Figure 4–116. Select a name that is useful for the entire set of types, typically a size. The name of the family always precedes the name of the type. Therefore, you do not need to re-enter that information.

Figure 4–116

4. In the Family Types dialog box, set the *Value(s)* for that size, as shown in Figure 4–117.

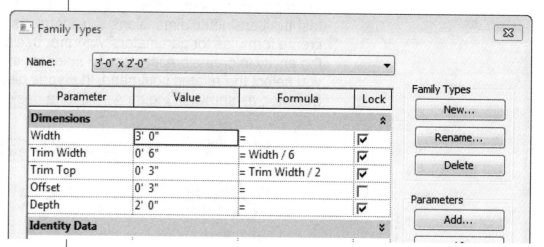

Figure 4–117

5. Click [Apply].
6. Repeat the process. You can create as many different types as you need.
7. Verify that all of the types are functioning correctly.

8. Click [OK] to finish the command.
9. Save the family.
10. Load the family into a project and test the new types you have created.

- Click [Rename...] and [Delete] as needed to modify the list.

- To edit a type, select the type name, change the value(s), and click [Apply].

Hint: Loading Families into Projects

You can load a family into one or more projects.

1. In the Family Editor panel, click ⬆ (Load into Project). The panel is displayed in all of the Family Editor tabs.
2. If only one project is open, the family is automatically loaded into it. If you have more than one project open, the Load into Projects dialog box opens. Select the project(s) to load into, as shown in Figure 4–118.

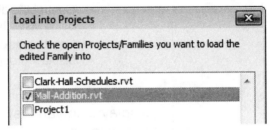

Figure 4–118

Hint: Modifying Families while in a Project

You can modify families by selecting and opening them within a project.

1. Select an instance of the family. In the *Modify* contextual tab>Mode panel, click ✏ (Edit Family).
2. Make any required changes to the family.
3. Save the family file.
4. Click ⬆ (Load into Project) to update the family in the project in which you were working.

• Family Types can be exported to a text file and then imported into a related family. This can save you time when creating different versions of the same basic category.

  • In the Application Menu, expand ▣ (Export), scroll down and click ▤ (Family Types). In the Export As dialog box, select a location and name. Click ⬚Save⬚.

  • In the *Insert* tab>Import panel, click ▤ (Import Family Types). In the Import Family Types dialog box, select the appropriate text file, and click ⬚Open⬚.

4.6 Visibility Display Settings

Autodesk Certification Topics & Objectives

Pro.   User

Families

- Use Family creation procedures   ✓

 Learning Objectives

- Control the display of elements in views at various detail levels using visibility settings.
- Create masking regions to block elements that would otherwise display through a family.

You can make families more versatile by controlling what is displayed in various views and at different detail levels. For example, you can set the Coarse view to display only 2D symbolic lines while the Fine detail view displays the full 3D model, as shown in Figure 4–119. To do this, change the visibility of the elements. You can also add Masking Regions to elements in a family to obscure other elements.

Fine detail level   *Coarse detail level*

Figure 4–119

How To: Control the Display of Elements

1. Select the elements that you want to modify.

2. In the *Modify* contextual tab>Mode panel, click (Visibility Settings).

3. In the Family Element Visibility Settings dialog box, specify the views and detail level in which you want the elements to display, as shown in Figure 4–120.

Figure 4–120

4. Click [OK].

*   All elements typically display in 3D views. You can select how they display in plan and elevation views. The plan is cut at the cut plane specified by the *View Range*.

*   Some elements, such as furniture, cannot be cut in plan view.

*   The *Detail Levels* control whether or not the element displays at various scales. If you clear the checkmark from a level, the lines defining the element turn gray in the family file. They do not display at that detail level when inserted into the project file.

Creating Masking Regions

A masking region obscures other elements in a project. They can be placed in a family or project. For example, in the Desk family shown in Figure 4–121, a chair placed under the desk is masked but the lamp on top of the desk is not.

Figure 4–121

How To: Create Masking Regions

1. Open a plan or elevation view.

2. In the *Annotate tab*>Detail panel, click (Masking Region).
3. In the *Modify | Create Masking Region Boundary* tab>Line Style panel, select the line type you want to use for the boundary of the region.
4. In the Draw panel, select the tools to sketch the region. You can also use most of the Modify options as you draw.

5. Click (Finish Edit Mode) and click in empty space to finish the command.

Practice 4g

Create Family Types for the Bookcase

Learning Objectives

- Add a **Material** parameter and associate it with the bookcase components.
- Create family types of different sizes.
- Create symbolic lines and modify the visibility settings so that they display in 2D plan views at the Coarse and Medium detail levels.

In this practice you will create an additional parameter and apply Family Types to a bookcase, as shown in Figure 4–122. You will also draw symbolic lines to display in plan views at the Coarse and Medium detail levels.

Estimated time for completion: 15 minutes

Figure 4–122

Task 1 - Add a Material parameter.

1. Open the project /Architectural/**Barrister-Bookcase-2-A.rfa** from your class folder.

2. In the *Create* tab>Properties panel, click ⊞ (Family Types).

3. In the Family Types dialog box, in the *Parameters* area, click

   [Add] .

*Setting the type as an **Instance** makes modifying this parameter in the project file easier.*

4. Create a **Family parameter** and set the *Parameter Data* as shown in Figure 4–123. Click [OK].

Figure 4–123

5. In the Family Types dialog box, leave the **Material** parameter set to **<By category>**, as shown in Figure 4–124, and click [OK] to close the dialog box.

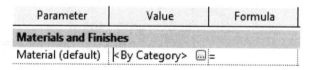

Figure 4–124

6. In the 3D view, select all of the bookcase components, except the doors.

7. In Properties, a new instance parameter labeled **Material** displays under *Materials and Finishes*.

8. In the *Material* row, click , as shown in Figure 4–125.

Figure 4–125

9. In the Associate Family Parameter dialog box, select the **Material** parameter, as shown in Figure 4–126, and click OK .

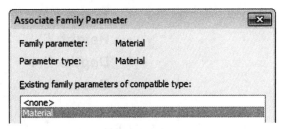

Figure 4–126

• The Material is now marked with the **=** sign, as shown in Figure 4–127.

Figure 4–127

10. Select the bookcase doors.

11. In Properties, click 🔲 (Edit Type).

12. In the Type Propertied dialog box, in the *Other* area, click the button next to the **Door Material** parameter and set it to **Material**.

13. Click OK .

14. Save the family.

Task 2 - Create Family Types.

1. In the *Create* or *Modify* tab>Properties panel, click ⊞ (Family Types).

2. In the Family Types dialog box, in the *Family Types* area, click | New... | .

3. In the Name dialog box, type **3'-0" x 5'-0"** and click | OK | .

4. In the *Dimensions* area, verify or set the following values for the parameters:

   - **Width:** 3'-0"
   - **Height:** 5'-0"
   - **Depth:** 1'-1"
   - **Base:** 4"

5. Click | Apply | . The bookcase should resize to the new sizes.

6. Repeat these steps for the following sizes:

   - **3'-0" x 6'-0"**
   - **3'-6" x 5'-0"**
   - **3'-6" x 6'-0"**

7. In the Family Types dialog box, test each of the new named types.

8. Click | OK | .

9. Save the family.

Task 3 - Use the family in a project.

1. Start a new project and save it as **Furniture Sample.rvt**.

2. In the *View* tab>Windows panel, expand ⬚ (Switch Windows). Select one of the Barrister-Bookcase views.

3. In the Family Editor panel, click ⬚ (Load into Project).

4. If **Furniture Sample.rvt** is the only project open, the family file is automatically loaded into that project.

5. If you have more than one project open, the Load into Projects dialog box opens, as shown in Figure 4–128. Select the project you want to load and click [OK]. Switch to the **Furniture Sample.rvt** project.

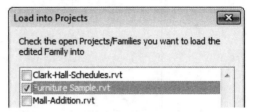

Figure 4–128

6. The **Component** command is automatically started with the Barristers Bookcase family selected.

7. Place one of each type in the project.

8. Create a 3D view to see the differences.

9. In the View Status Bar, set the *Visual Style* to ⬚ (Consistent Colors).

10. Select a bookcase. In Properties, in the *Materials and Finishes* area, next to the **Material** parameter, click [...].

11. In the Material Browser, select a material and click [OK] to apply it to the bookcase. (Several materials starting with the word **Bookcase** are available for you to use.)

12. Repeat with the other bookcases using different materials.

13. Save the project.

Task 4 - Change the visibility settings in a family.

---

1. In the file **Furniture Sample.rvt**, open the Floor Plans> **Level 1** view.

2. Zoom in on one of the bookcases. You can see the knobs on the doors as well as all of the various planes of the doors and base, as shown in Figure 4–129.

Figure 4–129

3. In the View Status Bar, set the *Detail Level* to (Medium) and then to (Fine). You should not see any difference.

4. Double-click on the bookcase to open the family file.

5. Open the Floor Plans>**Ref. Level** view.

6. In the *Annotate* tab>Detail panel, click (Symbolic Line).

7. Draw a rectangle around the outside of the bookcase and lock it to the reference planes, as shown in Figure 4–130.

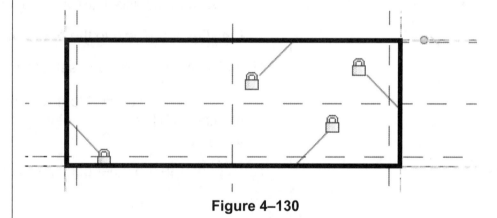

Figure 4–130

8. In the *Modify | Lines* tab>Visibility panel, click (Visibility Settings).

9. In the Family Element Visibility Settings dialog box, in the *Detail Levels* area, select **Coarse** and **Medium** but clear **Fine**, as shown in Figure 4–131. Click OK .

Figure 4–131

10. Open the 3D Views>**View 1** view and set the *Visual Style* to ☐ (Hidden.Line).

11. Select the bookcase elements (but not the doors) and click ☐ (Visibility Settings).

12. In the Family Element Visibility Settings dialog box, in the *Detail Levels* area, clear **Coarse** and **Medium** and select **Fine** as shown in Figure 4–132, and click ☐ OK ☐.

This has to be done in two steps because the doors are a different element (a nested family) from the rest of the elements.

Figure 4–132

13. Select the door elements and repeat the last steps.

14. Save the family.

Task 5 - Reload and test the family.

1. In the bookcase family file, click ⬆ (Load into Project) and reload the bookcase into the **Furniture Sample.rvt** project.

2. In the Family Already Exists dialog box, select **Overwrite the existing version**.

3. In plan view, zoom in on one the bookcases. Set the Detail Level to ☐ (Coarse) if it is not already set. Only the symbolic lines are displayed, as shown on the left in Figure 4–133.

Coarse/Medium Detail Level   *Fine Detail Level*

Figure 4–133

4. Change the visibility to ▣ (Medium) and then ▨ (Fine). Only the symbolic lines display at the Medium detail level, but at the Fine detail level, all of the components of the family display, as shown on the right in Figure 4–133.

5. Save and close the project and the family.

Practice 4h

Create Family Types for the Heat Pump

 Learning Objectives

- Create family types of different sizes.
- Test the family in a project including drawing pipe from the pipe connectors.

Estimated time for completion: 20 minutes.

In this practice you will create and apply Family Types of different sizes to a heat pump and test piping connectors, as shown in Figure 4–134.

Figure 4–134

Task 1 - Create Family Types.

1. Open the project /MEP/**Heat-Pump-2-MEP.rfa** from your class folder.

2. In the *Create* tab>Properties panel, click (Family Types).

3. In the Family Types dialog box, in the *Family Types* area, click New... .

4. In the Name dialog box, type **HP060C** as the name.

5. Set the value for the parameters as follows:

- **Width:** 38 7/8"
- **Height:** 44 3/4"
- **Depth:** 34 3/4"

6. Click [Apply]. The family resizes to match the new information.

7. Create the other models as follows:

Model	Width	Height	Depth
HP048C	38 7/8"	37"	34 3/4"
HP030C	32 7/8"	32 3/4"	28 3/4"
HP024C	32 7/8"	28 5/8"	28 3/4"

8. In the Family Types dialog box, test the family types by selecting the *Name* and clicking [Apply] after each selection.

9. Click [OK].

10. Save the family.

Task 2 - Use the family in a project.

1. Start a new project and save it as **Heat Pump Sample.rvt**.

2. Switch back to one of the Heat Pump family views.

3. In the Family Editor panel, click (Load into Project).

4. If **Heat Pump Sample.rvt** is the only project open, the family file is automatically loaded into that project.

5. If you have more than one project open, the Load into Projects dialog box opens, as shown in Figure 4–135. Select the project you want to load and click [OK].

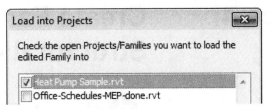

Figure 4–135

6. The **Component** command is automatically started with the new family selected.

7. Place one of each type in the project.

8. Create a 3D view to see the differences, as shown in Figure 4–136.

Figure 4–136

9. Open a floor plan view.

10. Using the Gas Line Service Valve and Liquid Line Service Valve piping connectors, draw some sample pipes off the unit to verify that the pipe diameters are correct, as shown in Figure 4–137.

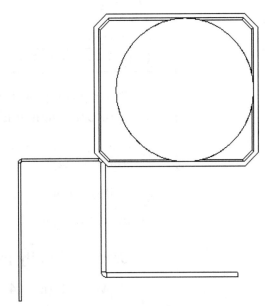

Figure 4–137

11. Save the project.

Practice 4i

Create Family Types for the Structural Column

 Learning Objectives

- Add a **Material** parameter and associate it with the family components.
- Create family types of different sizes.
- Use the family in a project with different sizes and materials.

Estimated time for completion: 15 minutes

In this practice you will create and apply Family Types for the column. You will add the column family to a project, test the columns by modifying levels, and adjusting instance parameters including the **Material** parameter, as shown in Figure 4–138.

Figure 4–138

Task 1 - Add a Material parameter.

1. Open the family **/Structural/Trellis-Column-2-S.rfa** from your class files folder.

2. In the *Create* tab>Properties panel, click ▦ (Family Types).

3. In the Family Types dialog box, in the *Parameters* area, click Add .

4. Create a **Family parameter** and set the *Parameter Data* as shown in Figure 4–139. Click OK .

*Setting the type as an **Instance** makes modifying this parameter in the project file easier.*

Figure 4–139

5. In the Family Types dialog box, verify that **Material** parameter is set to **<By category>**, as shown in Figure 4–140. Click OK to close the dialog box.

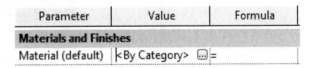

Parameter	Value	Formula
Materials and Finishes		
Material (default)	<By Category> ⊡	=

Figure 4–140

6. In the 3D view, select the column extrusion.

7. In Properties, in *Materials and Finishes* area, a new instance parameter labeled **Material** displays.

8. In the *Material* row, click ⬜, as shown in Figure 4–141.

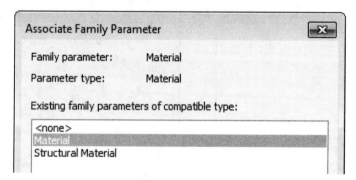

Figure 4–141

9. In the Associate Family Parameter dialog box, select

   Material, as shown in Figure 4–142, and click [OK].

Figure 4–142

- The Material is now marked with the = sign, as shown in Figure 4–143.

Materials and Finishes		
Material	<By Category>	

Figure 4–143

10. Repeat this process and select the base extrusion.

11. Save the family.

Task 2 - Create Family Types.

---

1. In the *Create* or *Modify* tab>Properties panel, click

   🔳 (Family Types).

2. In the Family Types dialog box, in the *Family Types* area, click [New...].

3. In the Name dialog box, set the name as **Over 12'-0"** and click [OK].

4. In the *Dimensions* area, set the formula for the Top *Width* as **Bottom Width / 1.3**, the *Side Bar* as **3"**, and the *Bar Width* as **2"**.

5. Click [Apply]. The column should resize to the new sizes.

6. Create another new Family Type with the name **Under 12'-0"**.

7. In the *Dimensions* area, set the formula for the Top *Width* as **Bottom Width / 1.5**, the *Side Bar* as **2"**, and the *Bar Width* as **1"**.

8. Add other types if required.

9. Click [OK].

10. Save the family.

Task 3 - Use the family in a project.

---

1. Open the project /Structural/**Column-Sample-S.rvt** from your class folder.

2. Open the Structural Plans>**Level 2** view.

3. In the *View* tab>Windows panel, expand (Switch Windows). Select one of the Trellis column views.

4. In the Family Editor panel, click (Load into Project).

5. If **Column-Sample-S.rvt** is the only project open, the family file is automatically loaded into that project. If you have more than one project open, the Load into Projects dialog box opens. Select the project you want to load and click [OK].

6. Switch to the **Column-Sample-S.rvt** project.

7. The **Structural Column** command is automatically started with the Trellis Column family selected. Verify that

    (Vertical Column) is selected.

8. Place one of each type in the project using the default information.

9. Open the Elevations>**South** view.

Change the Top Level first, so that the column does not go in the wrong direction.

10. Select the shorter column. In Properties, set the *Top Level* to **Level 2,** the *Top Offset* to (negative) **-6",** and the *Base Level* to **Level 1** with no *Base Offset*.

11. Select the taller column. In Properties, set the *Top Level* to **Level 3**, the *Top Offset* to (negative) **-6"**, and the *Base Level* to **Level 1** with no *Base Offset*, as shown in Figure 4–144.

Level 3
20' - 6"

Level 2
10' - 0"

Level 1
0' - 0"

Figure 4–144

12. Change the height of the levels to see how the look of the column changes.

13. Save the project.

Task 4 - Modify the material of the columns.

1. Make a copy of each column.

2. In the View Status Bar, set the *Visual Style* to (Consistent Colors).

*You are using colors here to distinguish the use of the **Material** instance parameter. Select a column. In Properties, in the Materials and Finishes area, next to the **Material** parameter, click* [...].

3. In the Material Browser, select a material and click [OK] to apply it to the bookcase. (Several materials of different colors starting with the words **Metal - Paint Finish** are available for you to use.)

4. Repeat with the other columns using different materials.

5. Save the project.

4.7 Overview of Family Creation

Autodesk Certification Topics & Objectives

Pro.   User

Families

• Use Family creation procedures   ✓

 Learning Objectives

• Review the process of creating families.
• Specify folder locations for the family libraries.
• Save families from a project into a library folder.

Many families are complex and time-consuming in creation, but they all have the same basic process.

You can also start with an existing family file, save it to a new name, and modify it.

1. In the Application Menu, click (New) and select **Family**.
2. In the New Family - Select Template dialog box, select the template you want to use and click ⌈ Open ⌋.
3. Set the parametric framework by adding reference planes/lines in plan and elevation views. This step in working with parametric families is very important.
4. Label and dimension the reference planes/lines to help you to control the movement of the elements and create parameters.

Flexing a model means changing its dimensions to test the parametric features.

5. Flex the model to make sure the parameters change as expected.
6. Use the Forms tools, as shown in Figure 4–145, to draw the elements and Symbolic Lines for elements in 2D views.

Figure 4–145

7. Lock the elements to the reference planes/lines.
8. Flex the elements again by changing the parameters to make sure they are working.
9. Create family types with different parameters as needed.
10. Set display settings for individual components in various views.
11. Save the family.

12. Click (Load into Project) to test the family in a project.

Locating Custom Family Files

When you create custom family files, you should save them to a location shared by the entire company, similar to the Autodesk Revit library. For easy access, set the custom library as the primary or secondary library available when you load a family, as shown in Figure 4–146.

Figure 4–146

How To: Specify the File Location for Custom Libraries

1. In the Application Menu, click Options .
2. In the Options dialog box, select the *File Locations* tab.
3. Click Places... .

4. In the Places dialog box, click ➕ (Add Value). A new *Library Name* is added to the list. Specify the name and path for the library, as shown in Figure 4–147.

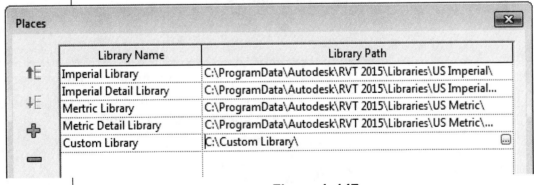

Library Name	Library Path
Imperial Library	C:\ProgramData\Autodesk\RVT 2015\Libraries\US Imperial\
Imperial Detail Library	C:\ProgramData\Autodesk\RVT 2015\Libraries\US Imperial...
Mertric Library	C:\ProgramData\Autodesk\RVT 2015\Libraries\US Metric\
Metric Detail Library	C:\ProgramData\Autodesk\RVT 2015\Libraries\US Metric\...
Custom Library	C:\Custom Library\

Figure 4–147

5. Click ⬆E (Move Rows Up) and ⬇E (Move Rows Down) to reorder the list of library names. The top name is the default library that is open when you click [Load...].

6. Click [OK] twice to close the dialog boxes.

How To: Save a Family Used in a Project to a Library

1. In the Application Menu, expand 📝 (Save As), expand 📚 (Library), and click 📖 (Family).

2. In the Save Family dialog box, as shown in Figure 4–148, select the folder where you want to place the family, select the Family to save from the drop-down list, and specify a *File name*.

Figure 4–148

- The existing family name is used as the default, but you can specify a different name.

- The list of families to select from (as shown in Figure 4–149), includes all the families in the project.

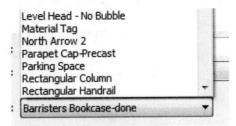

Figure 4–149

- You can also select **<All Families>**.

3. Click Save.

Chapter Review Questions

1. In which of the following views do the Reference planes, as shown in Figure 4–150, display? (Select all that apply.)

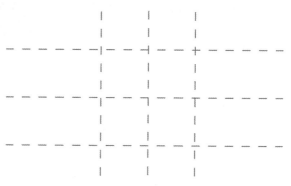

Figure 4–150

   a. Plan

   b. Elevation

   c. 3D

   d. Section

2. Which of the following is created when you label a dimension?

   a. Family

   b. Type

   c. Parameter

   d. Value

3. Which of the following commands, shown in Figure 4–151, require profiles instead of sketches? (Select all that apply.)

Figure 4–151

   a. **Extrusion**

   b. **Blend**

   c. **Revolve**

   d. **Sweep**

   e. **Swept Blend**

4. Which of the following commands creates the element shown in Figure 4–152?

Figure 4–152

   a. **Extrusion**

   b. **Blend**

   c. **Revolve**

   d. **Sweep**

   e. **Swept Blend**

5. In which dialog box do you specify sizes for component types?

   a. Family Editor

   b. Family Types

   c. Family Categories

   d. Family Properties

6. For the elements in a family to display differently at Coarse and Fine detail levels, as shown in Figure 4–153, you must draw everything in 2D.

Figure 4–153

   a. True

   b. False

Command Summary

Button	Command	Location
Forms		
	Blend	• **Ribbon**: *Create* tab>Forms panel
	Extrusion	• **Ribbon**: *Create* tab>Forms panel
	Revolve	• **Ribbon**: *Create* tab>Forms panel
	Sweep	• **Ribbon**: *Create* tab>Forms panel
	Swept Blend	• **Ribbon**: *Create* tab>Forms panel
	Void Forms	• **Ribbon**: *Create* tab>Forms panel
Connectors		
	Cable Tray Connector	• **Ribbon**: *Create* tab>Connectors panel> expand Connector
	Conduit Connector	• **Ribbon**: *Create* tab>Connectors panel> expand Connector
	Duct Connector	• **Ribbon**: *Create* tab>Connectors panel> expand Connector
	Electrical Connector	• **Ribbon**: *Create* tab>Connectors panel> expand Connector
	Pipe Connector	• **Ribbon**: *Create* tab>Connectors panel> expand Connector
Other Tools		
	Align	• **Ribbon**: *Modify* tab>Modify panel
	Component	• **Ribbon**: *Create* tab>Model panel
	Control	• **Ribbon**: *Create* tab>Control panel
	Detail Component	• **Ribbon**: *Annotate tab*>Detail panel
	Family Types	• **Ribbon**: *Create* or *Modify* tab> Properties panel
	Masking Region	• **Ribbon**: *Annotate tab*>Detail panel
	Model Line	• **Ribbon**: *Create* tab>Model panel
	Model Text	• **Ribbon**: *Create* tab>Model panel

	Opening	• **Ribbon:** *Create* tab>Model panel
	Symbolic Lines	• **Ribbon:** *Annotate* tab>Detail panel
A	**Text**	• **Ribbon:** *Annotate* tab>Text panel
	Visibility Settings	• **Ribbon:** Various contextual tabs> Mode panel

Reference and Work Plane

	Reference Lines	• **Ribbon:** *Create tab*>Datum panel
	Reference Plane	• **Ribbon:** *Create* tab>Datum panel
	Set	• **Ribbon:** *Create* tab>Work Plane panel
	Show	• **Ribbon:** *Create* tab>Work Plane panel

Chapter 5

Creating Specific Families

In this chapter you learn how to create in-place families, profiles, and annotation families. You also learn how to use shared parameters in tags and schedules.

This chapter contains the following topics:

- **Creating In-Place Families**
- **Creating Profiles**
- **Creating Annotation Families**
- **Working with Shared Parameters**

5.1 Creating In-Place Families

Learning Objective

- Create in-place families directly in a project.

In-place families use standard family tools to create elements that are specific to the project in which you create them. These might include built-in furniture, sloped walls, as shown in Figure 5–1, custom door or window openings, and roofs.

Figure 5–1

In-place family elements become the actual element you specify, such as a wall, door, roof, column, ceiling fixture, or floor.

- If the element is a host element, such as a wall, you can add elements to it, such as doors or windows.

- Elements, such as in-place doors and windows, can be copied and moved within their host.

- In-place family elements can be aligned and locked to project elements so they move together.

- Make sure reference planes are drawn in the family. If you tie an in-place family to an external reference plane and if the reference plane is deleted, you lose the family.

- In-place families are rarely used in the Autodesk® Revit® MEP software.

How To: Create an In-Place Family

1. In a project, in the *Architecture* tab>Build panel, or *Structure* tab>Model panel, or *Systems* tab>Model panel, expand (Component) and click (Model In-Place).

2. The Family Category and Parameters dialog box opens, as shown in Figure 5–2. You can filter the list to display only the disciplines needed.

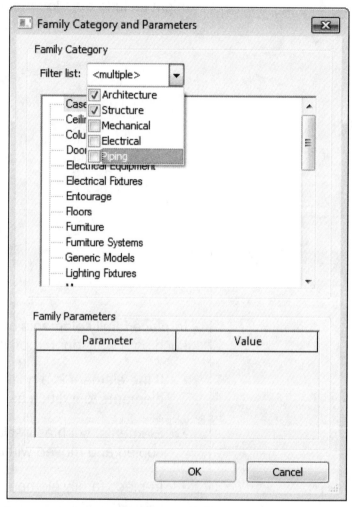

Figure 5–2

3. Select a *Family Category* and click OK. In the Name dialog box, enter a name for the new family.

4. The Family Editor tabs display in the Ribbon. Use the tools as needed to create the elements you want to have in the family.

5. In the In-Place Editor panel, click (Finish Model) to create the in-place element.

5.2 Creating Profiles

Learning Objective

- Create 2D profiles that are used to create 3D wall sweeps, reveals, railings, nosings, and other elements.

Profiles are 2D elements that are used in a variety of commands to create 3D elements. For example, you need a profile to create wall sweeps (as shown in the Base profile in Figure 5–3) and reveals, gutters, fascias, and floor slab edges. They are also used in families for railings, stair nosings, and solid sweeps.

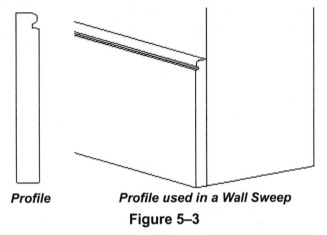

Profile   *Profile used in a Wall Sweep*

Figure 5–3

Several profile templates are supplied with the Autodesk® Revit® software: **Profile**, **Profile-Hosted**, **Profile-Mullion** (Autodesk® Revit® Architecture only), **Profile-Rail**, **Profile-Reveal**, and **Profile-Stair Nosing**. These are created with existing reference planes to help you place the elements correctly on the host element.

- All profiles must be closed shapes.

- Profile families can include detail components.

Practice 5a

In-Place Families and Profiles - Door Opening

 Learning Objectives

- Create an in-place door family and opening.
- Add trim for the in-place door family using a sweep based on a 2D profile.

Estimated time for completion: 15 minutes

In this practice you will create a door in-place family and add an odd-shaped opening. Using a Sweep, you will add a profile for door trim, as shown in Figure 5–4.

Figure 5–4

Task 1 - Create an in-place door family.

1. Start a new project based on the default architectural template.

2. Open the Floor Plans>**Level 1** view and draw a **10'-0"** high wall in the project.

3. In the *Architecture* tab>Build panel, expand ⬚ (Component) and click ⬚ (Model In-Place).

4. In the Family Category and Parameters dialog box, Set the *Filter list* to **Architecture** and then set the *Family Category* to **Doors** and click ⬚ OK ⬚.

5. Name the in-place family **Odd Shaped Opening**.

6. The Family Editor tools display in the Ribbon. In the *Create* tab>Datum panel, click (Ref Plane) and draw a reference plane along the center of the wall.

7. Select the reference plane and, in Properties, set the *Name* to **Center of Wall**. The plane displays as shown in Figure 5–5. Click in empty space to release the selection of the reference plane.

The reference plane is used to specify the work plane. It does not impact the shape of the wall.

Figure 5–5

8. Switch to the Elevations>**South** view and zoom in on the wall.

9. In the *Create* tab>Model panel, click (Opening).

10. If you have more than one wall in the project you are prompted to select a host for the opening. Click OK and select the wall.

11. Draw an opening similar to that shown in Figure 5–6.

The exact design does not matter; make sure it is at least 3'-0" wide and at least 6'-8" tall at its lowest point. The sketch must be closed.

Figure 5–6

12. Click (Finish Edit Mode) but do not finish the model.

Task 2 - Add a sweep for the trim and sketch a profile.

1. In the *Create* tab>Work Plane panel, click (Set).

2. In the Work Plane dialog box, set the *Name* to **Reference Plane : Center of Wall** and click OK.

3. In the *Create* tab>Forms panel, click (Sweep).

4. In the *Modify | Sweep* tab>Sweep panel, click ✍ (Sketch Path).

5. Draw a path around the edge of the opening. Do not close this sketch.

   • Click ⬚ (Pick Lines) and, in the Options Bar, select **Lock**. This locks the sketch to the existing geometry so the sketch updates if the opening is modified, .

6. Click ✓ (Finish Edit Mode).

7. In the *Modify | Sweep* tab>Sweep panel, click ▱ (Edit Profile).

8. In the Go To View dialog box, select **Floor Plan: Level 1** and click ⌷ Open View .

9. Zoom in on the red dot. Draw the profile shown in Figure 5–7. The profile must be closed. You do not need to add the dimensions.

Figure 5–7

10. Click ✓ (Finish Edit Mode) to finish the profile.

11. Click ✓ (Finish Edit Mode) again to finish the sweep.

12. Click ✓ (Finish Model).

13. View the new cased opening in several views.

14. Move the opening. You can see that the opening works just like a door.

15. Save the project as **Sample Opening.rvt**.

Drawing the profile within the in-place model keeps the size of the trim directly connected to the selected wall and opening.

Practice 5b

In-Place Families and Profiles-Concrete Corbeling

 Learning Objectives

- Create a 2D profile and use it in an in-place family to create a concrete corbel.
- Join the corbeling to the wall.

Estimated time for completion: 15 minutes

In this practice you will draw a profile of a corbel and then use it within an in-place family to create a sweep, as shown in Figure 5–8.

Walls : Wall Corbelling : Wall Corbelling

Figure 5–8

Corbel: A stepped bracket, designed to support a weight. It projects from a wall and is created from a building material, such as concrete, stone, or wood.

Task 1 - Create the profile.

1. Create a new family based on the **Profile-Hosted.rft** template found in the Autodesk Revit Library.

2. Save the family to your class folder as **Corbel.rfa**.

3. Draw the four reference planes as shown in Figure 5–9.

Figure 5–9

4. In the *Create* tab>Detail panel, click ⌐ (Line). Draw the profile shown in Figure 5–10.

The Family Editor does not display as many Ribbon tabs or panels because fewer commands are needed to create a 2D profile.

Figure 5–10

5. Save the family.

Task 2 - Add a new wall sweep using the profile.

---

1. Open the project /Structural/**Concrete-Structure-S.rvt** found in your class files folder.

2. Open the Structural Plans>**Level 1** view.

3. In the *Structure* tab>Model panel, expand (Component) and click (Model In-Place).

4. In the Family Category and Parameters dialog box, set the *Filter list* to **Structure** only, select **Walls**, and click OK .

5. In the Name dialog box, type **Wall Corbelling** and click OK .

6. In the In-Place Editor, in the *Create* tab>Forms panel, click (Sweep).

7. In the *Modify | Sweep* tab>Sweep panel, click (Sketch Path).

8. Use the Draw tools to sketch the lines shown in Figure 5–11.

Figure 5–11

9. Click (Finish Edit Mode).

10. In the *Modify | Sweep* tab>Sweep panel, click (Load Profile).

11. In the Load Family dialog box, navigate to the class files folder where you saved the profile created in the previous task. Select it and click Open .

12. In the Sweep panel, click (Select Profile).

13. In the *Profile* list, select **Corbel**.

14. In the Quick Access Toolbar, click (Default 3D View).

15. Zoom in on the profile location, it is facing into the wall as shown in Figure 5–12.

Figure 5–12

16. In the Options Bar, click Flip .

17. In the Options Bar or using the temporary dimension, lower the corbel (negative) **-6"** in the Y-direction, as shown in Figure 5–13.

Figure 5–13

18. Click (Finish Edit Mode).

19. With the new Corbel sweep still selected, in Properties, in the *Materials and Finishes* area, next to Material, click

 (Browse).

20. In the Materials Browser, select **Concrete - Cast-in-Place Concrete** and click OK .

21. In the *Modify* tab>In-Place Editor panel, click (Finish Model).

Task 3 - Join the corbel to the wall.

1. Open the Structural Plans>**Level 1** view.

2. Draw a Wall Section across the wall and corbel, as shown in Figure 5–14.

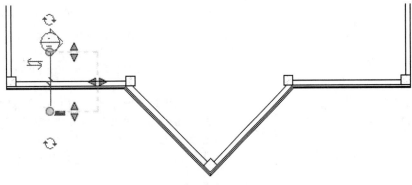

Figure 5–14

3. Open the section. You can see that the wall and corbel are still considered separate entities, as shown on the left in Figure 5–15.

4. In the *Modify* tab>Geometry panel, click (Join). Select the wall and then the corbel. It becomes part of the existing wall, as shown on the right in Figure 5–15.

Figure 5–15

5. Save the project.

Practice 5c

Use a Profile to Create a Structural Floor Type

Learning Objectives

- Create a profile to use in defining a composite metal deck.
- Load the profile into a project and create a new structural floor type using the profile.
- Test the new floor and change the span direction.

Estimated time for completion: 20 minutes

In this practice you will create a profile for a composite metal deck and save it to a library. You will then load the profile into a project, use it to create a new Metal Deck Floor type, as shown in Figure 5–16, and test the new floor type.

Figure 5–16

Task 1 - Create a composite Metal Deck profile.

1. Create a new family based on the **Profile.rft** template found in the Autodesk Revit Library.

2. Save the family to your class folder as **Composite-Metal-Deck.rfa**.

3. Type **UN** to open the Project Units dialog box.

4. Next to *Length Units*, select the **Format** button.

5. In the Format dialog box, change the units to **Fractional inches**. (This makes the dimensions in the family read in inches only so that it is easier to create the profile.)

6. Click [OK] twice to close the dialog boxes.

7. Set the *Scale* to **3" = 1'-0"**.

8. In the *Create* tab>Datum panel, click (Reference Plane).

9. Add reference planes as shown in Figure 5–17. They help you draw the elements (the dimensions are shown for reference only).

Figure 5–17

10. In the *Create* tab>Detail panel, click (Line). In the Options Bar, verify that the **Chain** option is selected.

11. Sketch the profile as shown in Figure 5–18.

Figure 5–18

12. Click (Modify) or press <Esc> when the profile is complete.

13. In the *Create* tab>Properties panel, click (Family Types).

14. In the Family Types dialog box, in the *Family Types* area, click New... .

15. In the Name dialog box, name it **3"**, and click OK .

16. Click OK again to close the dialog box.

17. Save the family without closing the file.

Task 2 - Load the composite Metal Deck profile.

---

1. Start a new project based on the default Structural template.

2. In the Quick Access Toolbar or *View* tab>Windows panel, expand (Switch Windows), and select **Composite-Metal-Deck.rfa** or press <Ctrl>+<Tab> to toggle back to the family file.

If more than one project is open, select the new one from the list that displays.

3. In the Family Editor panel, click (Load into Project) to insert the family into the new project. You should be in the Structural Plans>**Level 2** view of the new project.

4. In the *Structure* tab>Structure panel, click (Floor: Structural).

5. in the Type Selector, verify that **Floor: 3"LW Concrete on 2" Metal Deck** is selected.

6. In the *Modify | Create Floor Boundary* tab>Draw panel, use the **Line** or **Rectangle** tool to draw a slab of any type or size. Set the *Span Direction* to **Horizontal**.

7. Click (Finish Edit Mode).

8. In the Quick Access Toolbar or *View* tab>Create panel, click

   (Section) and place a section vertically through the slab from north to south.

9. Open the new section view and change the *Scale* to **3/4"=1'-0"** and the *Detail Level* to **Fine**. You might need to adjust the crop region and/or zoom in on the slab section. It should look similar to the one shown in Figure 5–19.

Figure 5–19

10. Select the slab.

11. In Properties, click (Edit Type).

12. In the Type Properties dialog box, click Duplicate... .

13. In the Name dialog box, type **6" Concrete on 3" Comp Metal Deck** as shown in Figure 5–20, and click OK .

Figure 5–20

14. In the Type Properties dialog box, next to the **Structure** parameter, click [Edit...].

15. Modify the **Structure [1], Concrete, Lightweight - 4 ksi** layer to a *Thickness* of **6"**, as shown in Figure 5–21.

Layers

	Function	Material	Thickness	Wraps	Structural Material	Variable
1	Core Boundary	Layers Above Wrap	0' 0"			
2	Structure [1]	Concrete, Lightweig	0' 6"	☐	☑	☐
3	Structural Dec	Metal Deck	0' 0"	☐	☐	☐
4	Core Boundary	Layers Below Wrap	0' 0"			

Figure 5–21

16. For the **Structural Deck** layer, select **Composite-Metal-Deck: 3"** in the Deck Profile drop-down list, as shown in Figure 5–22.

Structural Deck Properties

Deck Profile
Composite-Metal-Deck : 3" ▼
Composite-Metal-Deck : 3"
Form Deck_Composite : 1 1/2" x 6"
Form Deck_Composite : 2" x 6"
Form Deck_Composite : 3" x 8"

Deck Usage
Bound Layer Above ▼

Figure 5–22

17. Click [OK] to close all of the dialog boxes. The section should display the metal deck profile that was previously created, as shown in Figure 5–23.

Figure 5–23

Task 3 - Change the Flute Direction of a comp metal deck.

1. Return to the **Level 2** structural plan view.

2. Select the **Span Direction Symbol**. Note that the **Direction Symbol** extends to the edges of the slab. The closed arrowheads represent the flute direction and the open arrowheads represent the extents of the slab in the perpendicular direction.

3. Start the **Rotate** command and rotate the span direction 90 degrees.

4. Return to the section view. The orientation of the composite metal deck has changed as shown in Figure 5–24.

Figure 5–24

5. Save the project as **New Floor.rvt** and close the project.

6. Save and close the file **Composite-Metal-Deck.rfa**.

5.3 Creating Annotation Families

 Learning Objective

• Create 2D annotation symbol families using drawing tools, filled regions, text, and labels.

Annotation symbols are 2D elements that can be inserted into views or sheets to give additional information about a project. You can modify symbols that are supplied with the Autodesk Revit software to fit your company standards. You can also create new symbols using a variety of templates, as shown in Figure 5–25.

Annotation templates in Autodesk Revit

Figure 5–25

The drawing tools for annotation families include the standard line sketching tools, filled region, text, and label. You can also add existing symbols to the family.

• Most annotation symbols do not have family types. They are designed to change size according to the view scale.

• Some annotation family templates include notes to help you create the symbol. Delete them before using the family.

Hint: Modifying Labels

When you add labels, the length of the boundary box impacts the way the text word-wraps. For example, the Viewport: Title w Line tag that comes with the default metric template does not have enough room for a long title, as shown in Figure 5–26.

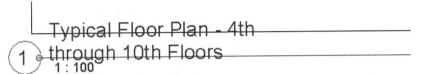

Figure 5–26

To modify it, open the related family file (in this case **M_View Title.rfa**) and stretch the length of the label boundary as shown in Figure 5–27.

Figure 5–27

Save the annotation family and reload it into the project. The length of the title expands to fit the longer title as shown in Figure 5–28.

Figure 5–28

Practice 5d

Estimated time for completion: 10 minutes.

Create Annotation Families - Arrow Symbol - All Disciplines

 Learning Objective

- Create an arrowhead annotation symbol that includes a filled region and test it in a project to see the size change automatically with the scale change.

In this practice you will create an annotation symbol and apply it to a project, as shown in Figure 5–29.

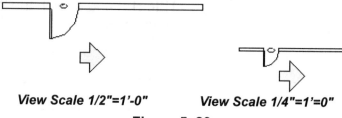

View Scale 1/2"=1'-0"   *View Scale 1/4"=1'=0"*

Figure 5–29

Task 1 - Create an annotation symbol.

1. Create a new annotation symbol family based on the **Generic Annotation.rft** template found in the Autodesk Revit Library in the *Annotations* folder.

2. Save the family to your class folder as **Arrow.rfa**.

3. Draw the arrow as shown in Figure 5–30. The dimensions are for reference only; do not add them to the sketch.

Figure 5–30

4. In the *Create* tab>Detail panel, click (Filled Region). Add a filled region to the arrow, as shown in Figure 5–31. You can use the default solid pattern or create a new pattern if time permits.

Figure 5–31

5. Delete the notes and save the family.

Task 2 - Add the symbol to a project.

---

1. Open a project file.

2. In the *Insert* tab>Load from Library panel, click (Load Family) and select the new file **Arrow.rfa** found in your class files folder.

3. In the *Annotate* tab>Symbol panel, click (Symbol).

4. Select the **Arrow** type.

5. Add some other full-scale elements near the arrow.

6. Change the *View Scale*, as shown in Figure 5–32. The arrow should resize according to the new view scale.

View Scale 1/2"=1'-0"   *View Scale 1/4"=1'=0"*

Figure 5–32

7. Close the project. You do not need to save it.

5.4 Working with Shared Parameters

 Learning Objectives

- Create shared parameters that can be used in both tags and schedules in multiple projects.
- Add shared parameters to a project.

The Autodesk Revit software includes many parameters used in families and schedules. You can work with several types of parameters, including *Family parameters* (specific to a family that constrain or flex geometry and assign attributes, such as material), *Project parameters* (that can be assigned to schedules), and *Shared parameters* (that can be referenced in multiple locations, projects, families, tags, and schedules, and shared between projects).

- Create shared parameters for custom information that needs to be displayed in both tags and schedules, used in multiple projects or families, or exported to ODBC to be put in a database.

- Shared parameters can be created wherever there is an option to create a parameter, as shown in Figure 5–33.

If you are creating a family to post to Autodesk Seek, use the Revit Master Shared Parameters file included in the Revit Model Content Style Guide available on the Autodesk Seek website.

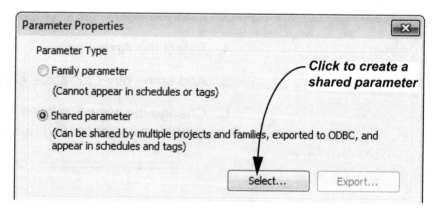

Figure 5–33

- Other ways you can create them include using the *Fields* tab in the Schedule Properties dialog box, using the Family Types dialog box (when you have a family file open), and in the *Manage* tab>Settings panel, clicking (Shared Parameters).

- If you are creating shared parameters in a family file, do it only for elements that constrain or flex the geometry and are used in a schedule.

How To: Create a Shared Parameter

1. Start the process of adding a parameter in Project Parameters, schedules, or family types.
2. Set the *Parameter Type* to **Shared parameter** in the Parameter Properties dialog box, as shown in Figure 5–34.

Figure 5–34

3. Click ⌈ Select... ⌋.
4. If no shared parameter file has been specified, an alert box opens. Click ⌈ Yes ⌋ to select a shared parameter file.
5. In the Edit Shared Parameters dialog box, as shown in Figure 5–35, click ⌈ Create... ⌋ to create a shared parameter file or ⌈ Browse... ⌋ to select an existing one.

Figure 5–35

Shared parameters are stored in a text file that should be placed in a network location available to everyone. This ensures consistency between projects and team members by maintaining naming standards and limiting typical typing errors with spaces and case sensitivity.

6. Creating groups for related parameters makes working with numerous names much easier. In the *Groups* area, click 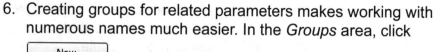 to create a new parameter group.

7. In the New Parameter Group dialog box, as shown in Figure 5–36, type a new name and click [OK].

Only one shared parameter file can be active in a project at a time. Therefore, create one main file with multiple groups instead of creating many files.

Figure 5–36

8. In the Edit Shared Parameters dialog box, in the *Parameters* area, click [New] to create a new shared parameter.

9. In the Parameter Properties dialog box, type a *Name* for the parameter, and set the *Discipline* (**Common**, **Structural**, or **Electrical**) and *Type of Parameter* in the drop-down lists. You can also add a Tooltip. The dialog box is shown in Figure 5–37.

Enhanced in **2015**

Figure 5–37

10. Click [OK].

11. When you have finished creating the shared parameters, click [OK] to close the Edit Shared Parameters dialog box. Then continue with the other steps needed to add the parameter to the project, family, or schedule.

- Other options in the Edit Shared Parameters dialog box include:

    - Properties... : Displays the contents of the Parameter Properties. You cannot modify them.

    - Move... : Moves a parameter from one parameter group to another.

    - Delete : Deletes a parameter. Be careful about using this because it could impact the current project and any other projects that use the parameter.

Project Parameters

Project parameters are created per project in the Parameter Properties dialog box, as shown in Figure 5–38. Each parameter is assigned to one or more categories. Use the *Filter list* to specify the discipline to limit the number of items available.

Figure 5–38

- If you want a parameter to be used in a schedule, such as the manufacturer of a desk family, it can be a project parameter.

- If you want to use a parameter in a tag and a schedule, create a shared parameter.

How To: Add a Shared Project Parameter to a Project

1. In the *Manage* tab>Settings panel, click 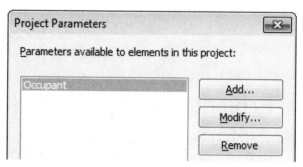 (Project Parameters).
2. In the Project Parameters dialog box, as shown in Figure 5–39, click ⌐ Add ⌐.

Figure 5–39

3. In the Parameter Properties dialog box, select the **Shared parameter** option and click ⌐ Select... ⌐.
4. In the Shared Parameters dialog box, set the *Parameter group* and *Parameters* that you want to add to the project, as shown in Figure 5–40. Click ⌐ OK ⌐.

Figure 5–40

- If the parameter you want to use does not exist, click ⌐ Edit... ⌐ to create a new shared parameter.

5. In the Parameter Properties dialog box, in the *Categories* area, select the categories to which you want the parameter to apply, as shown in Figure 5–41.

Use the Filter List to limit the number of categories available.

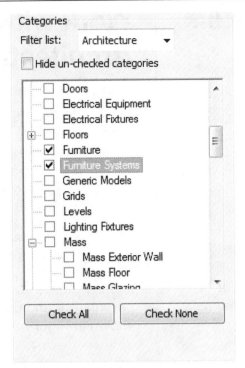

Figure 5–41

6. In the *Parameter Data* area, the Name, Discipline, and Type of Parameter drop-down lists are grayed out, while the shared parameter you just selected is displayed. Select from the Group parameter under drop-down list (this is where it displays in the Element Properties dialog box) and select the **Instance** or **Type** option, as shown in Figure 5–42. Add a Tooltip Description if needed.

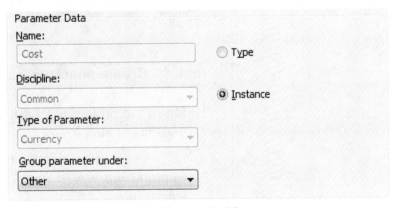

Figure 5–42

7. Click [OK] twice to add the parameter to the project.

Practice 5e

Work with Shared Parameters - Architectural

 Learning Objectives

- Create shared parameters in a project.
- Create an annotation tag family and link the shared parameters into the tag.
- Add the shared parameters to a family and insert them into the project along with the associated tags.
- Create a schedule using the shared parameters including the project, tag, and family.

Estimated time for completion: 20 minutes

In this practice you will create shared parameters through project parameters and use them in a family, tag, and schedule, as shown in Figure 5–43.

Figure 5–43

Task 1 - Create shared parameters.

1. Open the project /Architectural/**Office-Layout-A.rvt** found in your class files folder.

2. In the *Manage* tab>Settings panel, click 🔲 (Project Parameters).

3. In the Project Parameters dialog box, click ⬚ Add ⬚.

4. In the Parameter Properties dialog box, select the **Shared parameter** option and click ⬚ Select... ⬚.

5. If there is no existing shared parameter file, an alert box displays prompting you to select a shared parameter file. Click [Yes]. If the Shared Parameters dialog box opens, click [Edit...].

6. In the Edit Shared Parameters dialog box, click [Create...].

7. Open the class directory and save the new file as **Office-Parameters.txt**.

8. In the *Groups* area, click [New]. Type the name **Office Information** and click [OK]. This becomes the current group, as shown in Figure 5–44.

Figure 5–44

9. In the *Parameters* area, click [New] and create three new shared parameters using the following information:

Name	Discipline	Type of Parameter
Extension	Common	Integer
Employee	Common	Text
Department	Common	Text

10. Click OK .

11. In the Shared Parameters dialog box, as shown in Figure 5–45, select **Department** and click OK .

Figure 5–45

12. In the Parameter Properties dialog box, in the *Parameter Data* area, group the parameter under **Other** and make it an **Instance** parameter. In the *Categories* list, select **Furniture** and **Furniture Systems**, as shown in Figure 5–46.

Figure 5–46

13. Click OK . **Department** is added to the shared parameters in the project.

14. Repeat the process for **Employee** and **Extension**.

15. Click [OK] to finish creating the project parameters.

16. Save the project.

Task 2 - Create a tag with shared parameters.

1. Create a new family based on the **Generic Tag.rft** template found in the *Annotation* folder of Autodesk Revit Library.

2. Save the family to your class folder as **Office-Information.rfa**.

3. Zoom in, read the information in red, and delete the note.

4. In the *Modify* tab>Properties panel, click ⬚ (Family Category and Parameters).

5. In the Family Category and Parameters dialog box, set the *Family Category* to **Furniture Systems Tags**, as shown in Figure 5–47. Click [OK].

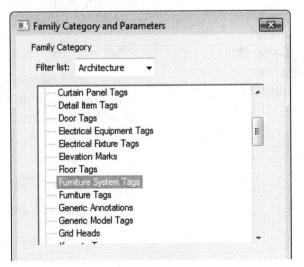

Figure 5–47

6. In the *Create* tab>Detail panel, click (Line). Draw a box, starting at the crossing of the two reference lines, as shown in Figure 5–48. Do not add the dimensions; they are for reference only.

Figure 5–48

7. In the *Create* tab>Text panel, click ▣**A** (Label).

8. Use the default type, **Label: 3/32"**.

9. Click inside the box you just created.

10. In the Edit Label dialog box, which includes a list of the multi-category parameters supplied with the Autodesk Revit software, click ⬚ (Add Parameter).

In the Parameter Properties dialog box, you can only create shared parameters.

11. Click Select... .

12. The shared parameters you created earlier should be available by default in the Shared Parameters dialog box. Select **Extension**, as shown in Figure 5–49, and click OK .

Figure 5–49

13. Click OK until you reach the Edit Label dialog box.

14. Select **Extension** and click ⬛ (Add parameter(s) to label). Click ⬛ OK ⬛ to insert the label into the family.

15. Click ⬐ (Modify) and select the new label. Resize the outline of the text box to fit inside the box. Move the label so that it is centered in the box, as shown in Figure 5–50.

Figure 5–50

16. Save the family and load it into the project **Office-Layout-A.rvt**.

Task 3 - Add shared parameters to a Furniture Systems family.

---

1. Continue working in the project **Office-Layout-A.rvt**.

2. In the *Architecture* tab>Build panel, click ⬛ (Component).

3. In the *Modify | Place Component* tab>Mode panel, click ⬛ (Load Family).

4. Load the family /Architectural/**Work-Station-Cubicle-A.rfa** found in your class files folder.

5. Place a workstation in one of the rooms in the wing to the left of the main building.

6. Click ⬐ (Modify) and select the new workstation.

7. In the *Modify | Furniture Systems* tab>Mode panel, click ⬛ (Edit Family).

8. In the Properties panel, click ⬛ (Family Types).

9. In the Family Types dialog box, in the *Parameters* area, click
   Add .

10. Select the **Shared Parameter** option and click Select... .

11. The shared parameters you created earlier are also available in this family file. Add each of the parameters from the *Office-Information* category into the family as an Instance parameter in the *Other* category.

12. In the Family Types dialog box, set the *Extension (default)* to **1234**, as shown in Figure 5–51. The other values can be left blank.

Other			☆
Department (default)		=	
Employee (default)		=	
Extension (default)	1234	=	⌐

Figure 5–51

13. Click OK .

14. Save the family file and load it into the **Office-Layout-A.rvt** project. Overwrite the existing version and its parameter values.

15. Add several other cubicles in various offices.

Task 4 - Add tags and create a schedule.

1. In the *Annotate* tab>Tag panel, click (Tag by Category).

2. Select the workstations and tag each of them. The default **1234** extension number should display on each tag, as shown in Figure 5–52.

Figure 5–52

3. Select a workstation. In Properties, the **Extension**, **Employee**, and **Department** parameters should be available in the *Other* category, as shown in Figure 5–53.

Figure 5–53

4. Change the *Extension*, and add an *Employee* name and *Department*.

5. Repeat with several other workstations.

6. In the *View* tab>Create panel, expand ▦ (Schedules) and click ▦ (Schedule/Quantities).

7. In the New Schedule dialog box, create a new Furniture Systems schedule and set the *Phase* is set to **Phase 1**, as shown in Figure 5–54.

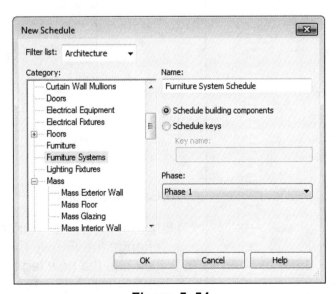

Figure 5–54

8. In the *Fields* tab, add the **Family and Type** parameter and then add **Extension**, **Employee**, and **Department**, as shown in Figure 5–55.

Figure 5–55

9. At this point, you can modify the other schedule properties as needed. Click [OK] when you are finished. The schedule should display the information you entered in the workstation's properties. Change the name of the schedule to **Office Information** and **Hide** the *Family and Type* column, as shown in Figure 5–56.

<Office Information>		
A	**B**	**C**
Employee	Extension	Department
Ronda	1234	Sales
Pual	1235	Engineering
Anne-Marie	1236	Sales
Kareen	1237	Marketing
Martha	1238	Engineering
Jen	1239	Enginering

Figure 5–56

10. Save the project.

11. If you have time, you can copy the Office Information tag and change the *Family Category* to **Furniture Tags**. Then you can use the new tag to tag the desks in the project. Furniture and Furniture Systems are different categories and cannot use the same tag.

Practice 5f

Work with Shared Parameters - MEP

Learning Objectives

- Create a schedule that uses shared parameters.
- Add the shared parameters to a family file and note the impact on the schedule.

Estimated time for completion: 20 minutes

In this practice you will create a mechanical equipment schedule and add shared parameters to the project through the schedule. You will then modify and add the shared parameters in a family file and update the family in the project. The shared parameters then populate the schedule, as shown in Figure 5–57.

Mechanical Equipment Schedule						
Mark	Type	Dimensions			Gas Line Diameter	Liquid Line Diameter
		Height	Width	Depth		
1	HPD60C	44 3/4"	38 7/8"	34 3/4"	1"	1/2"
2	HPD60C	44 3/4"	38 7/8"	34 3/4"	1"	1/2"
3	HPD60C	44 3/4"	38 7/8"	34 3/4"	1"	1/2"
4	HPD60C	44 3/4"	38 7/8"	34 3/4"	1"	1/2"

Figure 5–57

Task 1 - Create a schedule and add shared parameters.

1. Open the project /MEP/**Townhouse-Complex-MEP.rvt** found in your class files folder. Four heat pumps have been added to serve the townhouses.

2. In the *View* tab>Create panel, expand ▦ (Schedules) and click ▦ (Schedule/Quantities).

3. In the New Schedule dialog box, set the *Filter list* to **Mechanical**, select the *Category* of **Mechanical Equipment**, and click [OK].

4. In the Schedule Properties dialog box, in the *Fields* tab, select the following fields: **Mark** and **Type**. The rest of the parameters need to be shared parameters.

5. Click [Add Parameter...].

6. In the Parameter Properties dialog box, select **Shared parameter** and click [Select...].

7. If there is no existing shared parameter file, an alert box displays prompting you to select a shared parameter file. Click [Yes]. If the Shared Parameters dialog box opens, click [Edit...].

8. In the Edit Shared Parameters dialog box, click [Create...].

9. Open the class files folder and save the new file as **Townhouse-Parameters.txt**.

10. In the *Groups* area, click [New]. Set the name as **Heat Pump Information** and click [OK]. This becomes the current group, as shown in Figure 5–58.

Figure 5–58

11. In the *Parameters* area, click [New] and create three new shared parameters using the following information:

Name	Discipline	Type of Parameter
Height	Common	Length
Width	Common	Length
Depth	Common	Length
Gas Line Diameter	Common	Length
Liquid Line Diameter	Common	Length

12. Click [OK].

13. In the Shared Parameters dialog box, select **Height** as shown in Figure 5–59, and click [OK].

Figure 5–59

14. In the Parameter Properties dialog box, in the *Parameter Data* area, group the parameter under **Dimensions**, as shown in Figure 5–60.

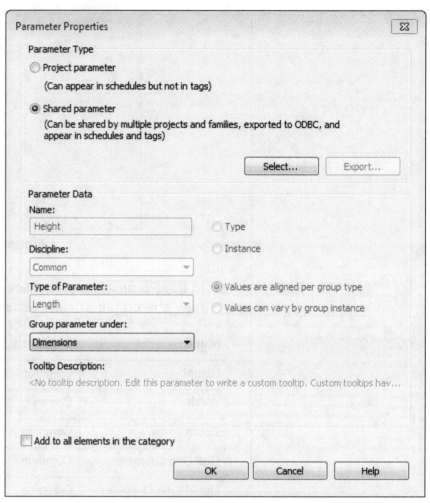

Figure 5–60

15. Click [OK]. Height is added to the scheduled fields.

16. Click [Add Parameter...] again.

17. In the Parameter Properties dialog box, select **Shared parameter** and click [Select...].

18. This time you do not have to create a shared parameter file, as the files created in the previous steps are available. Select **Width** and click [OK] to apply the parameter to the scheduled fields.

19. Repeat the process and add the rest of the new shared parameters as shown in Figure 5–61.

Figure 5–61

20. Click [OK]. The Mechanical Equipment Schedule displays but only includes values for the **Mark** and **Type**, as shown in Figure 5–62. The shared parameters are not yet identified in the Heat Pump family.

<Mechanical Equipment Schedule>						
A	B	C	D	E	F	G
Mark	Type	Height	Width	Depth	Gas Line Diameter	Liquid Line Diamete
1	HP060C					
2	HP060C					
3	HP060C					
4	HP060C					

Figure 5–62

21. Save the project.

Task 2 - Add shared parameters to a family.

1. Open the Mechanical>HVAC>Floor Plans>**Ground-Mech** view and select one of the heat pumps.

2. In the *Modify | Mechanical Equipment* tab>Mode panel, click 📝 (Edit Family). The family file opens in the Family Editor.

3. In the Properties panel, click 🏷 (Family Types).

4. In the Family Types dialog box several of the parameters that already exist in the family are displayed, as shown in Figure 5–63, but they are not connected as shared parameters.

Figure 5–63

5. Select the **Width** parameter and in the *Parameters* area, click Modify... .

6. In the Parameter properties dialog box, select the **Shared Parameter** option and click Select... .

7. The shared parameters you created earlier are also available in this family file, as shown in Figure 5–64.

Figure 5–64

8. Select **Width** and click OK twice. The existing parameter is now connected with the shared parameter.

9. Repeat the process with the **Height** and **Depth** parameters.

10. The information stored in the Heat Pump family for the Liquid Line and Gas Line are set to a radius, because it is required by the connectors. Therefore, you have to add Parameters and formulas for the diameters.

11. In the *Parameters* area, click Add .

12. In the Parameter Properties dialog box, select **Shared parameter** and click Select... .

13. In the Shared Parameters dialog box, select **Gas Line Diameter** and click OK .

14. Set it as a **Type** parameter and group it with the **Dimensions** group. Click OK .

15. Repeat the process for **Liquid Line Diameter**.

16. Set the following formulas for the two diameter parameters, as shown in Figure 5–65.

- Gas Line Diameter = **Gas Line Radius * 2**
- Liquid Line Diameter = **Liquid Line Radius * 2**

Figure 5–65

17. Click [OK] to close the Family Types dialog box.

18. Save the family.

___

Task 3 - Load the family and modify the schedule.

1. In the *Create* tab>Family Editor panel, click (Load into Project).

2. Overwrite the existing version and its parameter values.

3. Open the Mechanical Equipment Schedule. The values for the parameters are now included. Add headers for the dimensions, as shown in Figure 5–66.

<Mechanical Equipment Schedule>						
A	B	C	D	E	F	G
		Overall Dimensions			Pipe Dimensions	
Mark	Type	Height	Width	Depth	Gas Line Diameter	Liquid Line Diamete
1	HP060C	3' - 8 3/4"	3' - 2 7/8"	2' - 10 3/4"	0' - 1"	0' - 0 1/2"
2	HP060C	3' - 8 3/4"	3' - 2 7/8"	2' - 10 3/4"	0' - 1"	0' - 0 1/2"
3	HP060C	3' - 8 3/4"	3' - 2 7/8"	2' - 10 3/4"	0' - 1"	0' - 0 1/2"
4	HP060C	3' - 8 3/4"	3' - 2 7/8"	2' - 10 3/4"	0' - 1"	0' - 0 1/2"

Figure 5–66

4. Typically the values for these parameters should only be in inches. To fix this, in Properties next to **Formatting** parameter, click `Edit...`.

5. The Schedule Properties dialog box opens with the *Formatting* tab selected.

6. In the *Fields* area, select **Height** and click `Field Format...`.

7. Clear **Use project settings** and change the *Units* to **Fractional inches**. Click `OK`.

8. Repeat this for the rest of the length based parameters so that they display in inches and not in feet and inches.

9. Click `OK` to close the dialog box. The schedule updates as shown in Figure 5–67.

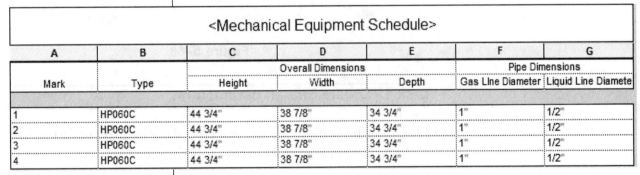

<Mechanical Equipment Schedule>						
A	B	C	D	E	F	G
		Overall Dimensions			Pipe Dimensions	
Mark	Type	Height	Width	Depth	Gas Line Diameter	Liquid Line Diamete
1	HP060C	44 3/4"	38 7/8"	34 3/4"	1"	1/2"
2	HP060C	44 3/4"	38 7/8"	34 3/4"	1"	1/2"
3	HP060C	44 3/4"	38 7/8"	34 3/4"	1"	1/2"
4	HP060C	44 3/4"	38 7/8"	34 3/4"	1"	1/2"

Figure 5–67

10. Save the project.

Practice 5g

Work with Shared Parameters-Structural

Learning Objectives

- Create shared parameters in a project.
- Use the shared parameters in a family, associated tag, and a schedule.

Estimated time for completion: 20 minutes

In this practice you will create shared parameters through project parameters and use them in family, tag, and schedule, as shown in Figure 5–68. The context here is a public plaza with columns, some free-standing and some supporting canopies and roofs. Each column will have custom brackets for banners, flags, etc.

Figure 5–68

Task 1 - Create Shared parameters.

1. Open the project /Structural/**Events-Plaza-S.rvt** found in your class files folder.

2. In the *Manage* tab>Project Settings panel, click (Project Parameters).

3. In the Project Parameters dialog box, click Add.

4. In the Parameter Properties dialog box, select the **Shared parameter** option and click Select....

5. If there is no existing shared parameter file, an alert box displays prompting you to select a shared parameter file. Click [Yes]. If the Shared Parameters dialog box opens, click [Edit...].

6. In the Edit Shared Parameters dialog box, click [Create...].

7. Save the new file as **Plaza-Parameters.txt** in the class files folder.

8. Create a new parameter group. In the *Groups* area, click [New]. Set the name as **Columns** and click [OK]. This becomes the current group, as shown in Figure 5–69.

Figure 5–69

9. In the *Parameters* area, click [New] and create three new shared parameters using the following information:

Name	Discipline	Type of Parameter
Bracket Type	Common	Text
Bracket Offset from Base	Common	Length
Bracket Finish	Common	Material

10. Click OK .

11. In the Shared Parameters dialog box, select **Bracket Type** as shown in Figure 5–70, and click OK .

Figure 5–70

12. In the Parameter Properties dialog box, in the *Parameter Data* area, group the parameter under **Other** and make it an **Instance** parameter. In the *Categories* area, filter the list based on **Structure** and select **Structural Columns,** as shown in Figure 5–71.

Figure 5–71

13. Click OK . **Bracket Type** is added to the shared parameters in the project.

14. Repeat the process to add **Bracket Offset from Base** and **Bracket Finish** to the Project Parameters list.

15. Click [OK] to finish creating the project parameters.

16. Save the project.

Task 2 - Create a Tag with Shared parameters.

---

1. Start a new family based on the **Generic Tag.rft** template found in the default library's *Annotations* folder.

2. Zoom in, read the information in red, and delete the note.

3. In the Properties panel, click ▦ (Family Category and Parameters).

4. In the Family Category and Parameters dialog box, set the *Family Category* to **Structural Column Tags**, as shown in Figure 5–72. Click [OK].

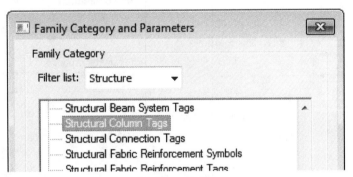

Figure 5–72

5. In the *Create* tab>Detail panel, click ╱ (Line). Draw a box, starting at the crossing of the two reference lines, as shown in Figure 5–73. Do not add the dimensions. They are for reference only.

Figure 5–73

---

6. In the *Create* tab>Text panel, click 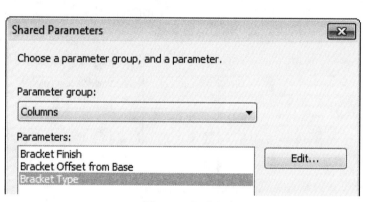 (Label).

7. Use the default type, **Label: 3/32"**.

8. In the *Modify | Place Label* tab>Format panel, set *Justification* to ≣ (Align Center) and ≡ (Align Top).

9. Click inside the box you just created.

10. In the Edit Label dialog box, which includes a list of the multi-category parameters supplied with the Autodesk Revit software, click (Add Parameter).

In this dialog box, you can only create shared parameters.

11. In the Parameter Properties dialog box, click Select... .

12. In the Shared Parameters dialog box, the shared parameters you created earlier should be available by default. Select **Bracket Type**, as shown in Figure 5–74, and click OK .

Shared Parameters

Choose a parameter group, and a parameter.

Parameter group:

Columns

Parameters:

Bracket Finish
Bracket Offset from Base
Bracket Type

Edit...

Figure 5–74

13. Click OK until you reach the Edit Label dialog box.

14. Select **Bracket Type** and click (Add parameter(s) to label). Click OK to insert the label into the family.

15. Click (Modify) and select the new label. Resize the outline of the text box so that it fits inside the box, and move the label so that it is top-centered in the box, as shown in Figure 5–75. Leave room for two more labels.

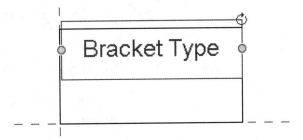

Figure 5–75

16. Repeat the steps for inserting a label, adding first **Bracket Offset from Base** and then **Bracket Finish**. The final tag should look similar to Figure 5–76.

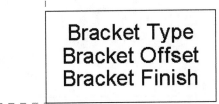

Figure 5–76

17. Save the new family with the name **Column-Bracket-Tag.rfa**.

18. Load the family into the project **Events-Plaza-S.rvt**.

19. The **Tag** command is automatically started. Tag one of the columns.

20. The tag is empty as shown in Figure 5–77, because no values have been added to the parameters.

Figure 5–77

21. Save the project.

Task 3 - Add Tags and modify information.

1. In the *Annotate* tab>Tag panel, click (Tag All).

2. In the Tag All Not Tagged dialog box, select the *Category* **Structural Column Tags** with the *Loaded Tags* set to **Column-Bracket-Tag.** Select **Leader**, click [OK], and click [OK]. All of the columns are tagged. The tags are blank but display question marks when selected, as shown in Figure 5–78. This is because the corresponding information has not been entered into the properties.

Figure 5–78

3. Select a column.

4. In Properties, scroll down to the *Other* area. The **Bracket Finish**, **Bracket Type**, and **Bracket Offset from base** parameters are available but have no information stored in them yet, as shown in Figure 5–79.

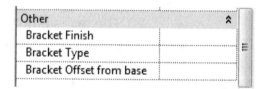

Figure 5–79

In this case, you will set the default values for all columns once.
Individual columns can be changed later.

5. Right-click on the column and select **Select All Instances> Visible in View**.

6. In Properties, set the *Bracket Offset from Base* to **12'-0"**, set the *Bracket Type* to **Banner**, and set the *Bracket Finish* to **Metal**.

7. Select two or three individual columns, and in Properties change the *Bracket Type* to **Sculptural** and the *Bracket Offset from Base* to **15'-0"**. The tags update only for those columns, as shown in Figure 5–80.

Figure 5–80

8. Save the project.

Task 4 - Create a Structural Column schedule.

1. Create a new building component schedule for structural columns.

2. In the Schedule Properties dialog box, in the *Fields* tab, add the **Column Location Mark** parameter and then add **Mark**, **Bracket Type**, **Bracket Offset from Base**, and **Bracket Finish**, as shown in Figure 5–81.

Figure 5–81

3. Sort by the Column Location Mark and modify the other schedule properties as required. Click [OK] when finished. The schedule should display the information you entered in the column's properties, as shown in Figure 5–82.

<Structural Column Schedule>				
A	**B**	**C**	**D**	**E**
Column Location M	Mark	Bracket Type	Bracket Offset fro	Bracket Finish
A-1	1	Banner	12' - 0"	Metal
A-2	2	Sculptural	15' - 0"	Metal
A-3	3	Banner	12' - 0"	Metal
A-4	4	Sculptural	15' - 0"	Metal
A-5	5	Banner	12' - 0"	Metal
A-6	6	Sculptural	15' - 0"	Metal
A-7	7	Banner	12' - 0"	Metal

Figure 5–82

4. Save the project.

Chapter Review Questions

1. An in-place family is created whenever you need a custom family that is:

   a. Not available in your library.

   b. Built using profiles.

   c. Directly connected to elements within the project.

   d. Requires shared parameters.

2. Which of the following are examples of elements for which you can create profiles? (Select all that apply.)

   a. Wall reveals.

   b. The top rail of railings.

   c. In-place Sweeps.

   d. Curtain Wall mullions.

3. At what size should you create the tag family elements, as shown in Figure 5–83?

Figure 5–83

   a. Full scale to match the size of the tagged element in the project.

   b. Full scale to match the size of the annotation on the sheet.

   c. One size for each scale.

   d. It varies according to the type of annotation.

4. Where are shared parameters, as shown in Figure 5–84, stored?

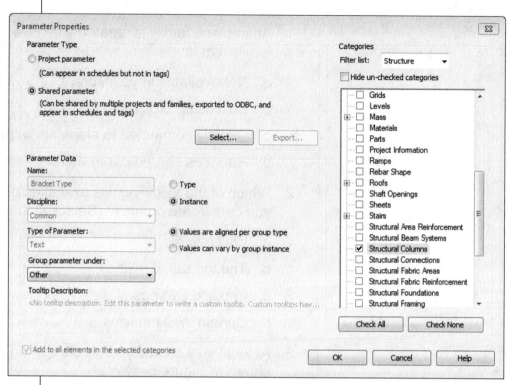

Figure 5–84

a. In a text file.

b. In the current project.

c. In a shared project.

d. In the family file.

Command Summary

Button	Command	Location
	Annotation Symbol	• **Application Menu:** expand New
	Model In-Place	• **Ribbon:** *Architecture* tab>Build panel> expand Component • **Ribbon:** *Structure* tab>Model panel> expand Component • **Ribbon:** *Systems* tab>Model panel> expand Component
	Project Parameters	• **Ribbon:** *Manage* tab>Project Settings panel
	Shared Parameters	• **Ribbon:** *Manage* tab>Project Settings panel

Chapter 6

Creating Architectural Specific Families

In this chapter you learn to create custom doors and windows. Using profiles and in-place families, you learn to create angled cornices and copings. You also learn how to create baluster and baluster panel families, and apply them to a railing type.

This chapter contains the following topics:

- **Creating Custom Doors and Windows**
- **Creating Angled Cornices and Copings**
- **Creating Custom Railings**
- **Families for Railings, Balusters, and Panels**

6.1 Creating Custom Doors and Windows

Autodesk Certification Topics & Objectives

Pro.   User

Modeling

• Edit a model element's material   ✓

 Learning Objective

> • Create custom doors and windows by starting from an existing
>   family or a template.

You can create families, including custom door and window families, by basing them on existing families or by using a template designed for the family type that comes with the Autodesk® Revit® software.

Starting from an Existing Family

If you start from an existing family, you can modify its various elements to create a new design. As with existing families, the custom family can then be used in projects. You can also add reference planes, as shown in Figure 6–1, parameters, and formulas to control the custom families.

New Ref Planes

EQ EQ

Figure 6–1

Starting From a New Template

If you start a family based on a template, you need to add the components for the family. Some components are included in the templates, such as the window with trim templates shown in Figure 6–2. However, you need to add most of the elements, including glass for the windows.

Figure 6–2

Practice 6a

Create Custom Doors

Learning Objectives

- Create a custom door type based on an existing door.
- Add reference planes and dimensions.
- Set formulas for the window size within the door.

Estimated time for completion: 20 minutes

In this practice you will work through the steps for creating a new door family based on an existing door family, and then use it in a project, as shown in Figure 6–3.

Figure 6–3

Task 1 - Modify a copy of an existing family.

1. In the default Autodesk Revit Library/Doors folder, open the family file **Single-Glass 2.rfa**.

2. In the Application Menu, expand ![Save As icon] (Save As) and click ![Family icon] (Family). Save the file in your class files folder with the name **Single-Glass-Square.rfa**.

3. Select the **Panel : Extrusion**, as shown in Figure 6–4.

Figure 6–4

4. In the *Modify | Panel* tab>Mode panel, click (Edit Extrusion).

5. Delete the four openings at the bottom of the door, as shown in Figure 6–5. Click (Finish Edit Mode) and click in empty space to finish the command.

Delete these
openings

Figure 6–5

6. Hover your cursor over one of the lines left over from the previous step and press <Tab> until **Glass : Extrusion** is displayed. Edit it as you did the **Panel : Extrusion**.

7. Click (Finish Edit Mode)

8. Open the Elevations (Elevation 1)>**Back** view. It displays the reference planes and dimensions used to constrain the door.

9. Delete the dimensions shown in Figure 6–6.

Delete these dimensions

Figure 6–6

Task 2 - Add reference planes and dimensions.

---

1. Delete the horizontal reference planes connected to the removed openings.

2. Add a reference plane midway between the existing muntin lines. Dimension and lock them as equal, as shown in Figure 6–7.

Zoom in close so you can lock both dimensions.

New ref plane

Figure 6–7

3. Create and lock the **7"** dimension at the top of the window, as shown in Figure 6–8.

Figure 6–8

4. Create a dimension string connecting the top, middle, and bottom reference planes of the window. Set the dimensions to be equal (**EQ**), as shown in Figure 6–9.

5. Create a dimension from the bottom to the top reference planes of the window.

6. Click ⬚ (Modify) to finish the command.

7. Select the new dimension. Create a label named **Window Height**, set it as a **Type parameter**, and assign it to this dimension, as shown in Figure 6–9.

Figure 6–9

Task 3 - Set formulas for the window size.

1. In the *Create* or *Modify* tab>Properties panel, click ⬚ (Family Types).

2. In the Family Types dialog box, set the value of the new *Window Height* label to **2'-2"**.

3. Click [OK].

4. Dimension the window (not the reference planes). Create a label named **Window Width** in the *Dimensions* group, as shown in Figure 6–10.

Figure 6–10

5. Erase the **Window Width** dimension.

6. Click [] (Family Types).

7. Add the formulas shown in Figure 6–11. The *Window Width* formula is **Width - (2 * Stile Width)**. The *Window Height* formula is **Window Width**. (Remember that formulas are case-sensitive.)

Dimensions		
Window Width	2' 2"	= Width - (2 * Stile Width)
Window Height	2' 2"	= Window Width

Figure 6–11

8. In the Family Types dialog box, select one of the sizes from the Name drop-down list, as shown in Figure 6–12. Click [Apply] to change the sizes and make sure the window moves within the door as expected. When you are finished flexing the dimensions, click [OK].

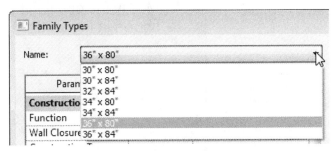

Figure 6–12

9. Open the 3D Views>**View 1** view.

10. Save the family and load it into a project (the exact one does not matter) to verify that it works correctly.

Practice 6b

Create Custom Windows

Learning Objectives

- Create a custom window family based on a template.
- Add trim and glass to the window.

Estimated time for completion: 20 minutes

In this practice you will work through the steps for creating a new window family based on a family template. You will modify the existing opening, trim it, and add materials and glass to the window, as shown in Figure 6–13.

Figure 6–13

Task 1 - Create a Custom Window family.

1. Create a new family based on the **Window with Trim.rft** template found in the Autodesk Revit Library.

2. Save the family to your class folder as **Arched Window with Trim.rfa**.

3. Open the Elevations>**Exterior** view. Select the Opening Cut (press <Tab> to toggle through the various elements) and click ✎ (Edit Sketch).

4. Modify the opening to add an arc and remove the top line, as shown in Figure 6–14.

Figure 6–14

5. Click ✓ (Finish Edit Mode).

6. Add a dimension to the arc and label it **Radius**.

7. Select the Trim: Extrusion element and click ⬜ (Edit Extrusion).

8. Modify the sketch so it matches the new arc opening. Remove the top of the trim and the associated dimension.

   Use ⇥ (Trim) to clean up the connections, as shown in Figure 6–15.

Figure 6–15

9. Click ✓ (Finish Edit Mode).

10. In the *Create* or *Modify* tab>Properties panel, click ⬛ (Family Types) and modify the **Radius** parameter to use the formula **Width/2**. Flex the model by trying different widths.

11. Set the final *Width* to **3'-0"** and click ⬛ OK to close the Family Types dialog box.

12. Save the family.

13. Click ⬛ (Load into Project) and test it in the same project as the door you just created.

Task 2 - Add a material to the window trim.

1. View the project with the door(s) and window(s) in a 3D view.

2. Set the *Visual Style* to (Shaded). The door has glass in the windows and materials applied to it, but the window does not have glass or materials, as shown in Figure 6–16.

Figure 6–16

3. Select one of the windows. In the *Modify | Windows* tab> Mode panel, click (Edit Family).

4. In the Family Editor, open the Elevations>**Exterior** view.

5. Set the *Visual Style* to (Shaded).

6. Select the **Trim Projection : Extrusion**.

7. In Properties, next to the **Materials** parameter, select **<By Category>**. Click (Browse) at the end of the row.

8. In the Materials Browser, under *Autodesk Materials*, select **Wood** and click (Add material to document), as shown in Figure 6–17.

Click here if the Autodesk Materials library pane does not display

Figure 6–17

9. Select the new material. In the *Graphics* tab, in the *Shading* area, select **Use Render Appearance**, as shown in Figure 6–18.

By default this material only displays when the Visual Style is set to Realistic. By using the Render Appearance, the color displays when the Visual Style is set to Shaded or Consistent Colors.

Figure 6–18

10. Close the Material Browser.

11. Save the window family file.

Task 3 - Add glass to the window.

1. Open the Floor Plans>**Ref. Level** view.

2. Draw a reference plane **1"** from the exterior face of the window and lock it in place, as shown in Figure 6–19.

Figure 6–19

3. Select the new reference plane. In Properties, set the *Name* to **Glass** and click [Apply].

4. Open the Elevations>**Exterior** view.

5. In the *Create* tab>Work Plane panel, click ⊞ (Set).

6. In the Work Plane dialog box, select the new reference plane **Glass** and click [OK].

7. In the *Create* tab>Form panel, click ⬚ (Extrusion).

8. Sketch the outline of the glass inside the window.

9. In Properties, set the *Extrusion End* to **1/2"**.

10. Set *Material* to **Glass, Clear Glazing** found in the Material Browser under the *AEC Materials>Glass*. Select **Use Render Appearance** so that it displays when the Visual Style is set as **Shaded**.

11. Close the Material Browser.

12. In Properties, click [Apply].

13. Click ✓ (Finish Edit Mode). The glass material displays.

14. Save the family file.

15. Click ⬆ (Load into Project) and select **Overwrite the existing version and its parameter values**. The new glass and trim material display in the project.

6.2 Creating Angled Cornices and Copings

Learning Objective

- Use in-place families to create angled cornices, fascias, and copings.

You might have tried to add a wall sweep to a wall at an angle, and found that it does not work. The **Wall Sweep** command only works horizontally or vertically. For example, to add a cornice to the top of a wall following the angled profile, as shown in Figure 6–20, you need to use a workaround, such as an in-place family using a solid sweep. A solid sweep can also be used to create a coping on the top of a short wall running beside steps.

Attempting to place a wall sweep   *In-place solid sweep family*

Figure 6–20

Creating Fascias

Another way to create profiles along an angle is to use a workaround to create a roof fascia on a model line, as shown in Figure 6–21. Typically, a fascia is applied to a roof edge but it can also be applied to a model line placed anywhere in a project.

Figure 6–21

- In the default architectural template at least one Fascia type is included.

How To: Create a Fascia Type

1. Load the profile for the fascia. (In the *Insert* tab>Import panel, click (Load Family). In the Load Family dialog box, navigate to the appropriate folder in which your profile is stored. For example, in the Autodesk Revit library, in the *Profiles>Roofs* folder, select **Fascia Built-up.rfa** and click Open .)

2. In the *Architecture* tab>Build panel, expand (Roof) and click (Fascia).

3. In Properties, click (Edit Type).

4. In the Type Properties dialog box, click Duplicate... .

5. In the Name dialog box, type a name and click OK .

6. In the Type Properties dialog box, select the appropriate profile, as shown in Figure 6–22.

Figure 6–22

7. Click OK and the new fascia type is ready to be used.

- The process is similar for creating new Gutter types.

How To: Add a Fascia using Model Lines

1. In the *Architecture* tab>Work Plane panel, click ▦ (Set) and select the appropriate work plane.

2. In the *Architecture* tab>Model panel, click ⌇ (Model Line).
3. Draw the model lines on the face of the wall where you want to add a fascia.

4. In the *Architecture* tab>Build panel, expand ◳ (Roof) and click ▽ (Fascia).
5. Select the model lines.

Hint: Object Style Subcategories

When creating an in-place family, you might want the family member to be modified in Visibility/Graphic Overrides separately from the main component. For example, if you are creating a cornice or coping for a wall and want to be able to turn it off separately from the wall, you can create an Object Style subcategory.

1. In the *Manage* tab>Settings panel, click ⊞ (Object Styles).
2. Click [New] in the *Modify Subcategories* area.
3. In the New Subcategory dialog box, type a *Name* and select the category it is going to be a *Subcategory of*, as shown in Figure 6–23.

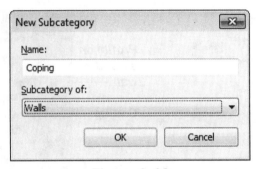

Figure 6–23

4. Click [OK] twice to finish the command.
5. Select the object you want to change and edit the Type Properties. Select a *Subcategory* under *Identity Data*, as shown in Figure 6–24, and click [OK].

Figure 6–24

The object style is now available in Visibility/Graphic Overrides, as shown in Figure 6–25.

Figure 6–25

Practice 6c

Create Angled Cornices and Copings

 Learning Objectives

- Create a coping using an in-place family.
- Use Model Lines and Roof Fascia to add a Profile to a Sloped Wall.

Estimated time for completion: 15 minutes

In this practice you will create a coping using an in-place family with a solid sweep. You will then add a profile to a sloped wall using the **Roof: Fascia** command and a model line, as shown in Figure 6–26.

Profile on sloped wall —

Coping —

Figure 6–26

Task 1 - Create a coping using an in-place family.

1. Open the project /Architectural/**Plaza-A.rvt** found in your class files folder. This is the beginning of a site design consisting of two slabs with retaining walls connected by a stair.

2. Open the Floor Plans>**Site** view. This project has three sections to help you draw additional elements.

3. Open the Sections>**East-West Site Section** view and zoom in on the lower wall, where you are going to add a stone coping to the top of the wall.

You are placed in the Family Editor with the corresponding Ribbon tabs.

4. In the *Architecture* tab>Build panel, expand ⬜ (Component) and click ⬜ (Model In-Place).

5. In the Family Category and Parameters dialog box, select **Walls** and click [OK].

6. Name the family **Coping**.

7. In the *Create* tab>Forms panel, click 🔄 (Sweep).

8. In the *Modify | Sweep* tab>Sweep panel, click ✏️ (Sketch Path).

9. In the Work Plane dialog box, select **Pick a plane** and click [OK]. Select the face of the concrete retaining wall.

10. Draw the path, as shown in Figure 6–27.

Figure 6–27

11. Click ✓ (Finish Edit Mode).

12. In the Sweep panel, click ✏️ (Edit Profile).

13. In the Go To View dialog box, select **Section: Wall Section** and click [Open View].

14. Zoom in and draw the profile, as shown in Figure 6–28.

Figure 6–28

15. Finish the profile, sweep, and model.

16. Switch to a 3D view to see the coping in place.

Task 2 - Use Model Lines and Roof Fascia to add a profile to a Sloped Wall.

1. Open the Sections>**East-West Site Section** view and zoom in on the upper plaza.

2. In the *Insert* tab>Load from Library panel, click   (Load Family and load the profile /Architectural/**Wall-Profile-A.rfa** found in your class files folder.

3. In the *Architecture* tab>Model panel, click   (Model Line).

4. In the Work Plane dialog box, select **Pick a Plane** and click OK and select the face of the concrete retaining wall.

5. Draw a model line **7"** down from the top of the retaining wall.

6. In the *Architecture* tab>Model panel, expand   (Roof) and click   (Roof: Fascia).

7. In Properties, click   Edit Type .

8. In the Type Properties dialog box, create a new fascia type named **Wall Sweep** using the profile you loaded earlier, and set the *Material* to **Masonry-Stone**, as shown in Figure 6–29.

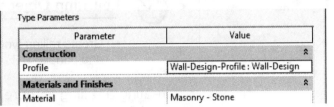

Figure 6–29

9. Once you have finished creating the **Roof Fascia** type, select the model line to place it in the project, as shown in Figure 6–30.

Figure 6–30

10. Save the project.

6.3 Creating Custom Railings

 Learning Objective

- Create railing types by specifying the rails, balusters, posts, and panels.

Creating a railing is more complex than creating a family; it consists of several preset families for the rails, balusters, posts, and panels, as shown in Figure 6–31. Once you have these ready, you can create a Railing type and set up the Rail Structure, Baluster Placement, Top Rail, Handrails, and other parameters.

Figure 6–31

- Additional elements include supports and terminations and are added to the Top Rail and Handrail types.

How To: Create a Railing Type

1. Create all of the components of a Railing type (such as rails, handrails, top rails, posts, balusters, and panels) before starting to create the type.
2. Select an existing railing.
3. In Properties, click ⊞ (Edit Type).
4. In the Type Properties dialog box, create a duplicate type.
5. Set up the Type Parameters as needed, as shown in Figure 6–32.

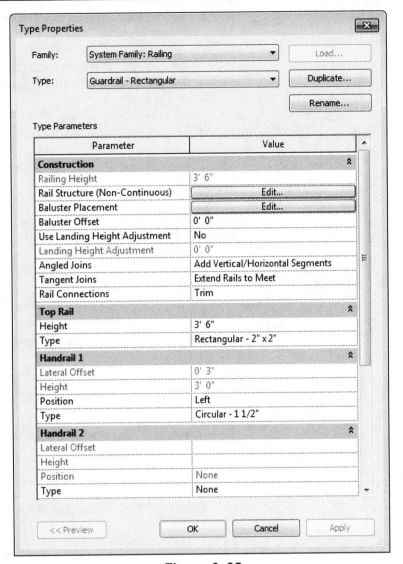

Figure 6–32

6. Click [OK] to close the dialog box.

How To: Set the Rail Structure (Non-Continuous)

1. Create a new Railing type or modify an existing one.
2. In the Type Properties dialog box, next to the **Rail Structure (Non-Continuous)** parameter, click [Edit...].

3. In the Edit Rails (Non-Continuous) dialog box, click

Insert to add a new rail to the list. You can have a single rail or multiple rails in a Railing type, as shown in Figure 6–33 with the **Handrail-Pipe** type.

Figure 6–33

4. Fill out the information about the rails as needed:

Name	The name of the individual railing component. Select the name to modify it.
Height	The height for each rail from the base height.
Offset	The distance from the rail sketch line.
Profile	Select a profile in the drop-down list. You need to have the profile loaded before you can use it. (This is just a profile family, not a rail type as is needed when you specify the top rails and handrails.)
Material	Specify a material for the rail. This does not display as a parameter in either the instance or type.

5. Click Up and Down to move the rail to the correct location in the group.

6. Click OK to finish the command.

- If there are no horizontal members other than the Top Rail and Handrail, this dialog box remains empty.

- If you want the non-continuous horizontal elements to have a material, you need to specify it here.

How To: Set up the Baluster Placement

When you have established the horizontal members of a railing, you can add the vertical members (i.e., balusters).

1. Create a new Railing type or modify an existing one.
2. In the Type Properties dialog box, next to the **Baluster Placement** parameter, click [Edit...]. The Edit Baluster Placement dialog box has two main areas: *Main pattern* and *Posts*, as shown in Figure 6–34.

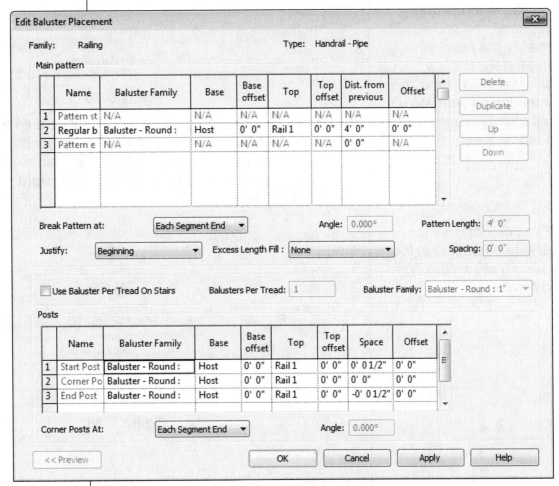

Figure 6–34

3. In the *Main pattern* area, add the baluster family and its sizes, such as the distance from the previous baluster. You can also add panels in this area.
4. If you are using a baluster on stairs and want a specific number per tread, select the **Use Baluster Per Tread On Stairs** option and specify the number per tread.
5. In the *Posts* area, specify the profiles for the *Start*, *Corner*, and *End* posts, and then specify their dimensions and locations.

How To: Set the Top Rail and/or Handrail

1. Create a new Railing type or modify an existing one.
2. Open the Type Properties dialog box.
3. In the Top Rail area, specify the *Height* and *Type* as shown in Figure 6–35. The *Type* is a separate Top Rail type that needs to be set up before you get to this point in the Railing type creation.

If you are creating a guardrail railing type, this is the top of the guardrail and you would specify the handrail separately. If it is a handrail railing type, this is the top rail and you do not specify a separate handrail type.

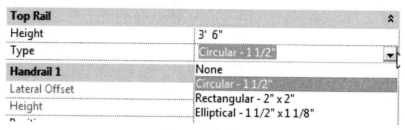

Figure 6–35

4. If you are creating a guardrail, you also need to specify the *Type* and *Position* of the handrail. The handrail can be set to **Left**, **Right**, or **Left and Right** of the main railing as shown in Figure 6–36. The **Lateral Offset** and **Height** are read-only parameters.

*If you do not want to include a handrail in the railing type, set the Type to **None**.*

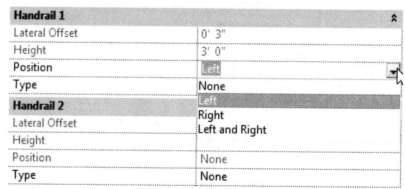

Figure 6–36

6.4 Families for Railings, Balusters, and Panels

 Learning Objectives

- Create rail profile families.
- Create families for balusters, posts, and panels.

To make a completely custom Railing type, you first need to create individual families for the rails, top rails, hand rails, posts, balusters, and panels, as shown in Figure 6–37.

Rail Profile   *Post*   *Baluster*   *Panel*

Figure 6–37

- All types of rails use profiles. Profiles for these elements must be loaded into the project before you create the new railing, Top Rail or handrail type.

- Several rail and baluster profiles are found in the *Revit Library Profiles* folder. Create custom profiles for railings using the **Profile-Rail.rft** template. There are three baluster templates: for standard balusters, for posts, and for panels.

Creating Rail Profile Families

A rail profile only consists of 2D elements, not solid elements. The program uses the profile as the base of a sweep following the railing lines.

Only a few rail styles are supplied with the Autodesk Revit software. Therefore, when you are doing custom work, you need to create custom rail profiles. The template **Profile-Rail.rft** is specifically created for railings. The template indicates where to start drawing the outline, as shown in Figure 6–38.

Figure 6–38

Top Rail and Handrail types need to be created before you add them to the overall Railing type. For example, you often need to have the handrail extend from the stair as shown in Figure 6–39. This is done in the Handrail type, rather than in the Railing type.

Figure 6–39

How To: Create a Top Rail or Handrail Type

1. In the Project Browser, expand Families>Railings>Handrail Type or Top Rail Type, as shown in Figure 6–40, and select one of the existing types.

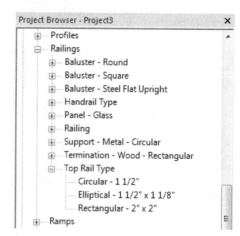

Figure 6–40

2. Right-click and select **Type Properties** or double-click on the name.
3. Duplicate and name a new type.
4. In the Type Properties dialog box, select a profile and set up the other **Construction** and **Material** parameters as shown in Figure 6–41.

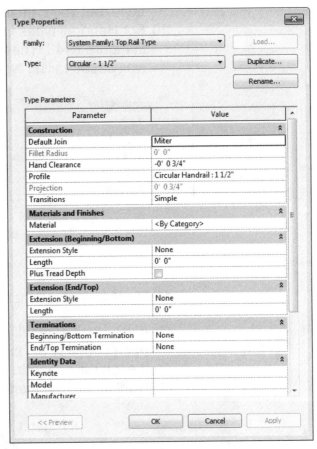

Figure 6–41

5. In the *Extension (Beginning/Bottom)* area, set the *Extension Style*. The options are **None**, **Wall**, **Floor**, and **Post** as shown in Figure 6–42.

Wall

Floor

Post

Figure 6–42

6. Set the *Length* and select **Plus Tread Depth** if required by the local codes.

7. Click [Apply] to check the addition.

8. Repeat the process for *Extension (End/Top)*.

9. A Termination can be added if needed. The default rectangular termination works best with the Floor Extension Style, but you can also create custom ones.

10. For Handrail types you can also specify *Supports*, as shown in Figure 6–43. These are typically used if you are creating a wall based railing type.

Supports		⤢
Family	Support - Metal - Circular	
Layout	Align With Posts	▾
Spacing	None	
Justification	Fixed Distance	
Number	Align With Posts	
	Fixed Number	
Identity Data	Maximum Spacing	
Keynote	Minimum Spacing	

Figure 6–43

11. Make any other changes and click [OK] to finish.

• If you want to modify a continuous railing type after it has been added to the project, in a 3D view, hover the cursor over the top rail or handrail. Press <Tab> until top rail or handrail is highlighted and then select it as shown in Figure 6–44

Top Rails : Top Rail Type : Rectangular - 2" x 2"

Figure 6–44

Creating Baluster, Post, and Panel Families

Balusters and posts are created from solid elements made with extrusions and/or revolves. Having the correct reference planes is important for flexibility. Standard balusters also require void elements to cut the angle on stair railings. There are three baluster templates: **Baluster.rft** (for standard balusters), **Baluster-Post.rft**, and **Baluster-Panel.rft**.

When you are creating a family, verify that you can modify an existing one to suit your needs. This is much faster than creating one from scratch and helps you learn how to construct the specific family.

- The example in Figure 6–45 shows a custom baluster modified from an existing baluster family supplied with the Autodesk Revit software.

Baluster-Custom1.rfa   **Modified Baluster**

Figure 6–45

The templates for these families include reference planes for the slope angles, as shown for a baluster panel in Figure 6–46. Lock the solid elements to these angles for stair railings so that they respond to the slope of the stair.

Figure 6–46

Adding Custom Posts

Posts are the point at which railings come together. In many cases, this is the area in which railings need to change pitch and extend into adjacent railings, creating an integral, non-interrupted system. Designing a post the first time is not easy. It is critical to have a good grasp of creating custom families and to want to experiment. An example is shown in Figure 6–47.

Figure 6–47

Post Categories vs. Generic Models

If you create a post as an actual post family, you cannot insert it as an independent component in the model. However, if you create a post as a generic model, you cannot use it in the Baluster dialog box and add it to a rail system. You should create the post family as an actual post and then save a copy as a generic model (recommended). This gives you the option of using the post in any situation.

Hint: Additional Cleanup Options

When railings are not cleaning up as expected, verify that the Stair Properties are correct. For example, the *Rail Connections* can be set to **Trim**, as shown in Figure 6–48, or **Weld**. The **Weld** option forces a miter joint rather than a butt joint.

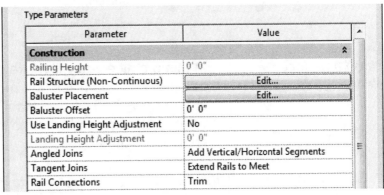

Figure 6–48

When a straight rail joins an arc rail, the Autodesk Revit software tends to distort the geometry. Select the segment of a rail in the railing's Sketch mode and modify the *Height Correction* in the Options Bar, as shown in Figure 6–49.

Figure 6–49

Practice 6d

Create Custom Railings

Learning Objectives

- Duplicate and modify existing baluster and baluster panel families.
- Create a custom railing type using the baluster and baluster panel families.

Estimated time for completion: 25 minutes

In this practice you will make copies of existing baluster and baluster panel families and modify them slightly. You will also create new Top Rail and Handrail types. You will then use the various families and types to create a new Railing type, as shown in Figure 6–50.

Figure 6–50

Task 1 - Set the material of a baluster family.

1. Open the project **/Architectural/ Modern-Hotel-Railings-A.rvt** from your class files folder.

2. Open the 3D Views>**Hall Balcony** view. This is the railing style you are going to use to create a new railing style.

3. Switch to the Floor Plans>**Floor 2** view. Families cannot be opened when you are in a 3D camera view.

4. In the Application Menu, expand 🗁 (Open) and click 🗐 (Family).

5. In the Library, expand the *Railings>Balusters* folder and open **Baluster-Round.rfa**.

6. Save the file as **Baluster-Round-Wood.rfa** in your class files folder.

7. In the Baluster family file, in the *Manage* tab>Settings panel, click ⬡ (Materials). A short list of materials is available in the family and no wood materials are available.

8. In the Material Browser, expand Autodesk Materials and select **Wood** as shown in Figure 6–51.

Figure 6–51

9. In the selection set next to **Birch**, select **Adds material to document** as shown in Figure 6–52.

Figure 6–52

In the *Project Materials* area, select the **Birch** material and in the *Graphics* tab, select **Use Render Appearance**, as shown in Figure 6–53.

Figure 6–53

10. Click [OK].

11. In the *Create* tab>Properties panel, click 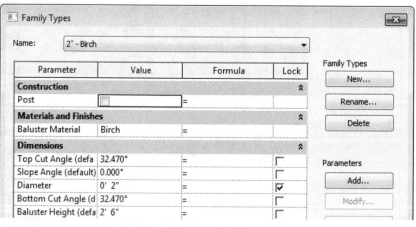 (Family Types).

12. In the Family Types dialog box, change the current type to **2"**.

13. In the *Family Types* area, click [New...] and name the new type **2" - Birch** and click [OK].

14. Set the *Baluster Material* to **Birch**, as shown in Figure 6–54.

The material for balusters cannot be set in the railing style, only in the family.

Figure 6–54

15. Click [OK].

16. In the View Control Bar, set the *Visual Style* to ⬛ (Consistent Colors) and then to ⬛ (Realistic) to display the new wood shade.

17. Save the baluster file.

18. In the *Create* tab>Family Editor panel, click 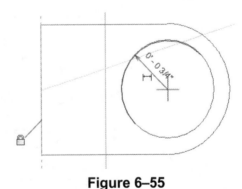 (Load into Project).

19. If the Modern Hotel project is the only one you have open, the family automatically loads and switches to the project file. If you have others open, select the Modern Hotel project from the list and click OK .

20. Switch back to the Baluster file and close it.

Task 2 - Modify a baluster panel family.

1. Open the family file **Baluster Panel - Glass w Brackets.rfa** and save it as **Baluster Panel - Glass with Open Brackets.rfa** in your class files folder.

2. Open the Elevations>**Left** view.

3. Zoom in on one of the brackets and select it.

4. In the *Modify | Extrusion* tab>Mode panel, click (Edit Extrusion).

5. Sketch a **3/4"** radius circle inside the bracket, as shown in Figure 6–55. This creates a hole in the extrusion.

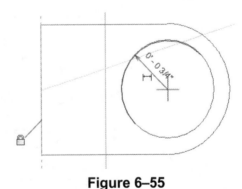

Figure 6–55

6. Click (Finish Edit Mode).

7. Repeat the process with the other three brackets.

8. Open the 3D Views>**View 1** view and set the *Visual Style* to (Consistent Colors). The panel displays with the opening in the brackets, as shown in Figure 6–56.

Figure 6–56

9. In the *Modify* tab>Properties panel, click ⊞ (Family Types).

10. In the Family Types dialog box, in the *Family Types* area, click New... .

11. Name the new type **36" w 1" Gap**.

12. In the Family Types dialog box, change the *Width* to **3'-0"**.

13. Click Apply . The panel updates, as shown in Figure 6–57. Click OK .

Figure 6–57

14. Save the baluster panel and load it into the Modern Hotel project.

Task 3 - Create Top Rail and Handrail types.

1. In the Modern Hotel project, in the Project Browser, expand Families>Railings>Top Rail Type and select **Circular - 1 1/2"**.

2. In the Type Properties dialog box, duplicate the type, and name it **Circular - 1 1/2" - Birch**.

3. Change the *Material* to **Birch**, and click OK.

4. In the Project Browser, expand the Handrail Type and click on **Circular - 1 1/2"**.

5. In the Type Properties dialog box, duplicate the type and name it **Circular - 1 1/2" - Birch**.

6. Change the *Material* to **Birch**.

7. Set the *Extension (Beginning/Bottom)* and *Extension (End/Top)* to **Wall**.

8. Click OK.

9. Save the project.

Task 4 - Create custom Railing types.

1. In the Modern Hotel project, open the 3D Views>**Hall Balcony** view.

2. Select the railing.

3. In Properties, click (Edit Type).

4. In the Type properties dialog box, click Duplicate and name the new railing type **Hotel Balcony Guardrail - Glass Panel**.

5. Next to the **Rail Structure (Non-Continuous)** parameter, click Edit...

6. In the Edit Rails dialog box, delete all of the Rails and click
OK .

7. Click OK twice. The new railing displays with wooden guardrail and handrail and existing posts, as shown in Figure 6–58.

Figure 6–58

8. Select the railing and edit the Railing type again.

9. Next to the **Baluster Placement** parameter, click
Edit... .

10. In the *Main pattern* area, next to *Regular Baluster* (in the *Baluster Family* column), change the type to **Baluster-Round-Wood: 2"-Birch**, as shown in Figure 6–59.

Figure 6–59

11. Click Duplicate... .

12. In row 2, change the *Name* to **Panel** and the *Baluster Family* to **Baluster Panel-Glass w Open Brackets: 36" w 1" Gap**.

13. Click [OK] twice and view the railings. The panel displays, but it is not in the correct location in relation to the posts, as shown in Figure 6–60.

Figure 6–60

Distances between balusters is measured from center to center.

14. Edit the type again and open the Edit Baluster Placement dialog box. In the *Dist. from Previous* column, you can see that the settings are now **4'-0"** for both the baluster and the panel. Therefore, the baluster and panel placement is spread out.

It took time to figure out exactly what would work best for this situation.

15. Set the *Dist. from Previous* to **1'-7 1/8"** for both the baluster and panel.

16. Set *Justify* to **Beginning** and *Excess Length Fill* to **None**, as shown in Figure 6–61.

Main pattern

	Name	Baluster Family	Base	Base offset	Top	Top offset	Dist. from previous	Offset
1	Pattern sta	N/A	N/A	N/A	N/A	N/A	N/A	N/A
2	Panel	Baluster Panel - Gla	Host	0' 0"	Top Rai	0' 0"	1' 7 1/8"	0' 0"
3	Regular ba	Baluster - Round -	Host	0' 0"	Top Rai	0' 0"	1' 7 1/8"	0' 0"
4	Pattern en	N/A	N/A	N/A	N/A	N/A	0' 0"	N/A

Delete
Duplicate
Up
Down

Break Pattern at: Each Segment End ▼   Angle: 0.000°   Pattern Length: 3' 2 1/4"

Justify: Beginning ▼   Excess Length Fill : None ▼   Spacing: 0' 0"

Figure 6–61

17. While still in the Edit Baluster Placement dialog box, in the *Posts* area, change the *Baluster Family* for all of the posts to **Baluster - Round - Wood: 2" - Birch** and click .

18. In the Type Properties dialog box, change the *Top Rail Type* to **Circular - 1 1/2" - Birch** and *Handrail 1* to the same.

19. Close the dialog boxes and view the new Railing type. This time, the baluster to panel fit is better, as shown in Figure 6–62.

Figure 6–62

20. Save the project.

Chapter Review Questions

1. The door family shown in Figure 6–63 does not exist in the default library. Which one of the following methods should you use to create the door family?

Figure 6–63

a. Start a new door family based on the default door template and build it from there.

b. Copy the existing **Single-Flush.rfa** family as the base and draw the panel outlines using detail lines.

c. Copy an existing panel-style family and modify the panel extrusions.

d. Start a new door family based on the **Single-Panel.rfa** template and modify the panel extrusions.

2. Based on the information in the Family Types dialog box (shown in Figure 6–64), if you changed the Trim Projection Ext value, would the Trim Projection Int also update?

Figure 6–64

a. Yes

b. No

3. Which of the following must be in place before you can add a fascia to an angled wall? (Select all that apply.)

a. A profile.

b. A fascia type.

c. A wall sweep.

d. A model line.

4. Which of the following parts of a railing type (shown in Figure 6–65) is created by a profile?

Figure 6–65

a. Rail

b. Post

c. Baluster

d. Baluster panel

5. What is the main difference between a Baluster family and a Post Family?

a. A Baluster is created using a profile and a Post is created using solid forms.

b. A Baluster has top and bottom angles programmed into the family, while a Post does not have any angles.

c. Balusters can be placed on stair treads, but posts can only be placed on landings.

d. Balusters are typically placed 4" apart, and Posts are placed 3'-0" apart.

Chapter 7

Creating MEP Specific Families

In this chapter, by working through practices, you learn how to upgrade an architectural plumbing fixture to use connectors, create a custom light fixture, and create a data device with annotation options. For an advanced challenge you can also create a pipe fitting flange. Select the practices that you find most helpful to your work.

Practice 7a

Upgrade an Architectural Plumbing Fixture to MEP

 Learning Objective

- Upgrade an existing architectural toilet fixture with pipe sizes and connectors for use in a MEP project.

Estimated time for completion: 15 minutes

In this practice you will upgrade an existing Autodesk® Revit® Architectural toilet fixture to be used in the Autodesk® Revit® MEP software. You will create parameters for pipe sizes. You will also add connectors for cold water and Sanitary systems, as shown in Figure 7–1.

Connector Element : Connector 1 : Domestic Cold Water

Connector Element : Connector 2 : Sanitary

Figure 7–1

Task 1 - Create parameters for pipe sizes.

1. Open the file /MEP/**Toilet-Commercial-Wall-3D.rfa** found in your class files folder.

2. In the Family Types dialog box, create the following **Family Type** parameters grouped under **Dimensions**:

Name	Discipline	Type of Parameter
Sanitary Radius	Piping	Pipe Size
Cold Water Radius	Piping	Pipe Size

The related diameter parameters need to be Shared because they are often used in plumbing fixture schedules.

3. Set *Sanitary Radius* to **2"** and *Cold Water Radius* to **1/2"**. **Lock** the parameters.

4. In the Family Types dialog box, in the *Parameters* area, click Add... .

5. In the Parameter Properties dialog box, in the *Parameter Type* area, select **Shared parameter** and click Select... .

6. In the Shared Parameters dialog box, click Create... .

7. In the Create Shared Parameter File dialog box, navigate to the *MEP* folder in your class files folder (it should already be there because you started the family in this folder). Create a new file named **MEP** and click Save .

8. In the Shared Parameters dialog box, in the *Groups* area, click New... . (You must create at least one group before you can create a shared parameter.)

9. In the New Parameter Group dialog box, name it **Piping** and click OK .

10. In the *Parameters* area, click New... .

11. In the Parameter Properties dialog box, set the following information as shown in Figure 7–2.

Name	Discipline	Type of Parameter
Sanitary Diameter	Piping	Pipe Size

Figure 7–2

12. Click .

13. Create another parameter using the following information:

Name	Discipline	Type of Parameter
Cold Water Diameter	Piping	Pipe Size

14. Click [OK] in each of the dialog boxes until you return to the Family Types dialog box.

15. Create formulas for *Sanitary Diameter* and *Cold Water Diameter* based on the corresponding radius parameters, as shown in Figure 7–3.

Dimensions			
Sanitary Radius	2"	=	☑
Sanitary Diameter	4"	= Sanitary Radius * 2	☑
Cold Water Radius	1/2"	=	☑
Cold Water Diameter	1"	= Cold Water Radius * 2	☑
Mounting Height	1' 3"	=	☑

Figure 7–3

• Hint: Parameters can be organized using [Move Up] and [Move Down]. You can also change the sorting order by clicking [Ascending] or [Descending].

16. Click [OK] .

Task 2 - Add connectors.

1. Rotate the view so that the back of the toilet is displayed. (If the wall displays, hide it temporarily or set the *Visual Style* to **Wireframe** while you are adding connectors.)

2. In the *Create* tab>Connectors panel, click (Pipe Connector).

3. In the Options Bar, select **Domestic Cold Water**.

4. Hover over the face of the pipe opening, as shown in Figure 7–4 and click to place the connector.

Figure 7–4

5. Click ⌨ (Modify) and select the Connector.

6. In Properties, set the following values for parameters:

    *   **Flow Configuration:** Fixture Units
    *   **Fixture Units:** 2.5
    *   **Flow Direction:** In
    *   **Allow Slope Adjustments:** clear

7. Scroll down to the *Dimensions* area, and next to *Diameter*, click ⬚ (Associate Parameter).

8. In the Associate Family Parameter dialog box, select **Cold Water Diameter**, as shown in Figure 7–5, and click .

Figure 7–5

9. The connector resizes to fit the correct pipe size.

10. Add a Pipe Connector for a Sanitary system to the back of the fixture.

11. Select the connector and set the following properties.

- **System Classification:** Sanitary
- **Flow Configuration:** Fixture Units
- **Fixture Units:** 4
- **Flow Direction:** Out
- **Allow Slope Adjustments:** select
- **Diameter:** Associate with **Sanitary Diameter** parameter

12. Add any other parameters or values required to make this a more useful MEP fixture.

13. Save the family.

14. Test the fixture in a project.

Practice 7b | Create a Custom Lighting Fixture Family

 Learning Objectives

- Modify the light source.
- Add elements for pendant and glass shade.
- Apply a power connector.
- (Optional) Create family types with different materials for the pendant and glass shade.

Estimated time for completion: 20 minutes

In this practice you will create a new lighting fixture family, modify the light source, create geometry for a pendant and glass shade, and apply a connector, as shown in Figure 7–6. If you have time you can load materials and create family types using different materials.

Figure 7–6

Task 1 - Setup a new light fixture family.

1. Create a new family based on the **Lighting Fixture ceiling based.rft** template found in the Autodesk Revit Library.

2. Save the family to your class folder as **Pendant Light.rfa**.

3. Open the Elevations>**Front** view. It includes reference planes for the Ceiling and Light Source, a ceiling element, and the Ref. Level as shown in Figure 7–7.

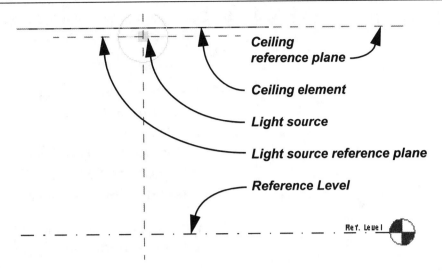

*Ceiling
reference plane*

Ceiling element

Light source

Light source reference plane

Reference Level

Ref. Level

Figure 7–7

4. Select the light source. In the *Modify | Light Source* tab> Lighting panel, click ⛺ (Light Source Definition).

5. In the Light Source Definition dialog box, change the Light distribution to ◮ (Photometric Web), as shown in Figure 7–8 and click [OK].

Figure 7–8

6. Open the Family Types dialog box and set the following values for the parameters:

- **Lamp:** CF42TRT
- **Apparent Load:** 44.21 VA
- **Tilt Angle:** 90

- **Photometric Web File (click):** spot_ideal.ies
- **Light Loss Factor:** 0.85
- **Initial Intensity:** Luminous Flux, 3200

7. In the Family Types dialog box, add two Type parameters for **Pendant Material** and **Glass Material.**

8. Save the family.

Task 2 - Create the fixture geometry.

1. Zoom in on the area near the light source.

The light source is temporarily hidden in these graphics.

2. Add reference planes as needed to help you create two revolves for a pendant and glass shade, similar to that shown in Figure 7–9.

Sketch for Pendant   *Sketch for Glass*

6"

4"

7 1/2"

Figure 7–9

3. Select the pendant revolve. In Properties, in the *Materials and Finishes* area, for **Materials** parameter, click ▯ (Associate Family Parameter).

4. In the Associate Family Parameter dialog box, select **Pendant Material** and click OK .

5. Repeat this with the glass shade revolve.

6. Save the project.

Task 3 - Add a connector.

1. Open a 3D view and set the *Visual Style* to **Wireframe**.

2. In the *Create* tab>Connectors panel, click ⚡ (Electrical Connector).

3. In the Options Bar, select **Power - Balanced**.

4. Attach the connector to the face of the pendant at the point where the pendant touches the ceiling, as shown in Figure 7–10.

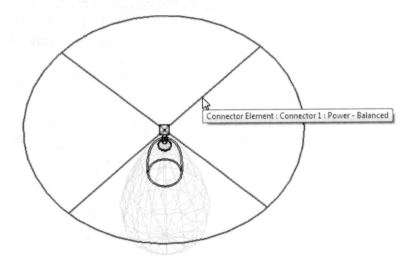

Figure 7–10

5. Click ⌖ (Modify) and select the connector.

6. In Properties specify the values for the following parameters:

   - **Power Factor:** 0.95
   - **System Type:** Power - Balanced (verify)
   - **Apparent Load:** Associate with the Apparent Load parameter
   - **Voltage:** 277
   - **Load Classification:** Lighting

7. Save the family.

Task 4 - (Optional) Add materials and create Family types.

1. In the *Manage* tab>Settings Panel, click ⬡ (Materials). Note that in the Materials Browser there are not many materials to select from. Close the dialog box.

2. Open the family /MEP/**Light-Fixture-Sample- Materials.rfa** found in your class files folder. (This is a finished version of the light fixture with several materials added.)

3. Switch back to your new light fixture family.

4. In the *Manage* tab>Settings panel, click ⬓ (Transfer Project Standards).

5. In the Select Items to Copy dialog box, verify that *Copy from* is set to **Light-Fixture-Sample-Materials.rfa** and clear everything but **Materials**, as shown in Figure 7–11.

Figure 7–11

6. Click [OK]. The materials are copied into the current family.

7. In the Family Types dialog box, assign materials to the **Glass Material** and **Pendant Material** parameters.

8. If you have time, create several Family Types that use different colors of glass and different pendant materials.

9. Save the family.

Practice 7c

Create an Data Device with Annotation Parameters

Learning Objective

- Create a data device with both solid elements and annotation elements.

Estimated time for completion: 20 minutes

In this practice you will create a data device using reference planes, extrusions, and connectors. You will then add an annotation symbol to the family with its related parameters, as shown in Figure 7–12. You will also test the family in a project.

Figure 7–12

Task 1 - Setup Reference planes.

1. Create a new family based on the **Data Device Hosted.rft** template found in the Autodesk Revit Library.

2. Save the family to your class folder as **Data Receptacle Type C.rfa**.

3. In the Floor Plans>**Ref. Level** view, set the *View Scale* to **3"=1'-0"**.

4. Zoom in closer to the intersection of the reference planes.

5. Create and dimension the reference planes, as shown in Figure 7–13. You do not need to label these dimensions as all of the data receptacles are the same size.

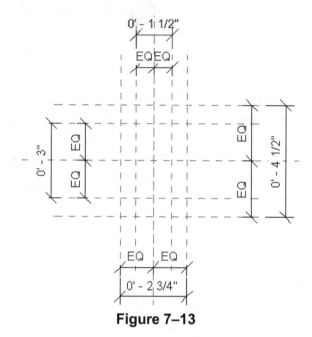

Figure 7–13

6. Save the family.

Task 2 - Create the model extrusions.

1. Using the intersections of the reference planes, create a **1 1/2" x 3"** extrusion and set *Extrusion End* to (negative) **-2 1/8"**.

2. Create another extrusion on the top of the first extrusion for the face plate **4 1/2" x 2 3/4" x 3/16"**.

3. Open a 3D view and set the *Visual Style* to **Wireframe**. The finished view displays as shown in Figure 7–14.

Figure 7–14

4. In the *Create* tab>Connectors panel, click ✣ (Electrical Connector).

5. In the Options Bar, select **Data**.

6. Select the face of the top extrusion.

7. Click ⬚ (Modify) and select both extrusions.

8. In the *Modify | Extrusion* tab>Mode panel, click ⬚ (Visibility Settings).

9. In the Family Element Visibility Settings dialog box, clear **Front/Back**, **Coarse**, and **Medium**. Click [OK] .

    *   This causes the 3D elements to display only at the Fine detail level where it is often used to coordinate the placement of items by their real dimensions. At the Coarse and Medium detail levels the tag is more useful.

10. Return to the **Ref. Level** view.

11. Save the family.

Task 3 - Create an Annotation symbol.

---

1. Create a new family based on the **Generic Annotation.rft** template found in the Autodesk Revit Library.

2. Save the family to your class folder as **Data Device Annotation.rfa.**

3. Read and delete the red note. You will not modify the Family Category in this case because you need it to remain a generic annotation.

Do not add the dimensions, they are for information only.

4. Draw the sketch as shown in Figure 7–15.

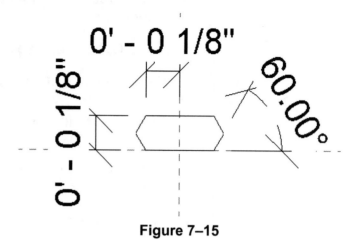

Figure 7–15

5. In the *Create* tab>Text panel, click (Label).

6. Click inside the new symbol sketch.

7. In the Edit Label dialog box there are no parameters listed. Click (Add Parameter).

8. Create an Instance parameter named **Label**, set *Type of Parameter* as **Text**, and set *Group parameter under* as **Identity Data**.

9. Back in the Edit Label dialog box, add the parameter to the label and set the *Sample Value* to **A1**, as shown in Figure 7–16 and click ___OK___ .

Figure 7–16

10. Select the new label and, in Properties, click (Edit Type). In the Type Properties dialog box, set the *Background* to **Transparent** and click ___OK___ .

11. Relocate the label to fit inside the symbol sketch.

12. With nothing selected, in Properties, select **Rotate with component** and **Keep text readable.**

13. Save the annotation family and load it into the data receptacle family.

Task 4 - Add the Label Family to the Data Receptacle.

---

1. In the data receptacle family, place a copy of the Label family at the center of the elements, as shown in Figure 7–17.

Generic Annotations : Label : Label

Figure 7–17

2. In the Family Types dialog box, create an Instance parameter named **Label**. Set *Type of Parameter* as **Text** and *Group parameter under* as **Identity Data**.

3. Set the *Value* to **C7**, as shown in Figure 7–18.

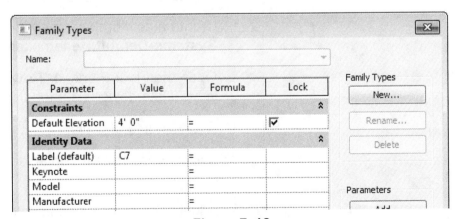

Figure 7–18

4. Close the dialog box. The **Label** parameter in the data receptacle family is not linked to the one in the Label family.

5. Select the instance of the Label family.

6. In Properties, use Associate Family Parameter to link the **Label** parameter to the one in the data receptacle family.

7. When you finish, the label displays as C7, as shown in Figure 7–19.

Figure 7–19

8. If you have time you can create Family Types for C1, C2, C3, C4, C5, C6, and C7. Change the value of the **Label** parameter for each of these as required.

9. Save the family.

Task 5 - Test the family.

---

1. Create a new project using the **Electrical-Default.rte** or **Systems-Default.rte** template.

2. Open the Floor Plans>**1- Power** view and close the **1-Mech** view. (Data devices do not display in Mechanical views.)

3. Add a couple of walls.

4. Switch to the data receptacle family and load it into the project.

5. Add it several times using different types if you have created them.

6. Save the project and the family and close the files.

Practice 7d

Create a Pipe Fitting Flange (Advanced)

7–19

Learning Objectives

- Create reference planes, dimensions, and labels to set up parameters including formulas.
- Draw single-line representations for Coarse and Medium detail levels.
- Extrude solids and voids of the flange for the Fine detail level.
- Create and apply Family Types.

Estimated time for completion: 90-120 minutes

In this practice you will create a family file based on a template and create reference planes, dimension them, label the dimensions, and use a formula in parameters. You will then create the flange components: a single-line representation for Coarse and Medium Detail Levels, extruded solids and voids for Fine Detail Level, as shown in Figure 7–20. You will then create and apply Family Types.

Figure 7–20

Task 1 - Open a Family template.

1. Create a new family based on the **Plumbing Fixture.rft** template found in the Autodesk Revit Library.

2. Save the family to your class folder as **Pipe Fitting Flange.rfa.**

3. In the *Create* tab>Properties panel, click 🔲 (Family Category and Parameters).

4. In the Family Category and parameters dialog box, set the *Filter list* to **Piping** and in the *Family Category* area, select **Pipe Fittings**.

5. In the *Family Parameters* area, set the following options:

   - Clear the **Work Plane-Based** option.
   - Select **Always Vertical**.
   - For the *Part Type*, select **Transition**.
   - Clear the **Shared** option.

6. Click [OK].

7. Type **UN** to open the Project Units dialog box.

8. Set the *Discipline* to **Piping** and change the *Pipe Size* format *Rounding* to the nearest **1/16"**.

9. Click [OK].

10. Save the family.

Task 2 - Create parameters.

1. In the *Create* tab>Properties panel, click 🔲 (Family Types).

2. In the *Parameters* area, click [Add].

3. In the Parameter Properties dialog box, in the *Parameter Type* area, select **Family Parameter** (if it is not already selected) and specify the following:

   - **Name:** NomRad
   - **Discipline:** Piping
   - **Type of Parameter:** Pipe Size
   - **Group Parameter Under:** Dimensions
   - Select the **Type** option.

4. Click [OK].

5. Repeat the steps, creating parameters named **NomDia**, **FlgRad**, **FlgDia**, **PipeOD**, **PipeOR**, **RFD**, **RFR**, **RFT**, **FT**, **LTH**, **HT**, and **HubRad**. Define the parameters as follows:

   - **Parameter Type:** Family Parameter
   - **Discipline:** Piping
   - **Type:** Pipe Size
   - **Group Parameter Under:** Dimensions
   - Select the **Instance** option.

6. In the Family Types dialog box, specify the following values:

   - **RFT:** 1/16"
   - **NomRad:** 2"
   - **FlgDia:** 9"
   - **PipeOD:** 4 1/2"
   - **FT:** 3/4"
   - **RFD:** 7"
   - **LTH:** 5"

7. In the Family Types dialog box, enter the following formulas for the parameters:

   - **NomDia:** NomRad * 2
   - **FlgRad:** FlgDia / 2
   - **PipeOR:** PipeOD / 2
   - **HubRad:** PipeOR * 1.5
   - **RFD:** FlgDia - 2"
   - **RFR:** RFD / 2
   - **HT:** LTH - (FT + RFT)

The final information displays as shown in Figure 7–21.

Parameter	Value	Formula	
Graphics			
Mechanical			
Dimensions			
RFT (default)	1/16"	=	
RFR (default)	3 1/2"	= RFD / 2	
RFD (default)	7"	= FlgDia - 0' 2"	
PipeOR (default)	2 1/4"	= PipeOD / 2	
PipeOD (default)	4 1/2"	=	
NomDia (default)	4"	= NomRad * 2	
NomRad	2"	=	
LTH (default)	5"	=	
HubRad (default)	3 3/8"	= PipeOR * 1.5	
HT (default)	4 3/16"	= LTH - (FT + RFT)	
FlgRad (default)	4 1/2"	= FlgDia / 2	
FlgDia (default)	9"	=	
FT (default)	3/4"	=	
OffsetHeight (default)		=	
OffsetWidth (default)		=	

Family Types: New..., Rename..., Delete

Parameters: Add..., Modify..., Remove, Move Up, Move Down

Sorting Order: Ascending, Descending

Figure 7–21

8. Click OK.

9. Save the family.

Task 3 - Create Plan View Reference Planes.

1. Continue working in the family file **150 WN Flange.rfa**.

2. Maximize the **Ref. Level** view.

3. Select the vertical reference plane. It is named **Center Left/Right**.

4. Press <Esc> to clear the plane.

5. In the *Create* tab>Datum panel, click (Reference Plane).

6. In the *Modify | Place Reference Plane* tab>Draw panel, click (Pick Lines).

7. In the Options Bar, set *Offset* as **2"**.

8. Hover over the vertical reference plane so that the dashed line is displayed on the left side. Click to create a new reference plane.

9. Repeat on the right of the same reference plane and again to the right of the new plane to create a total of 4 reference planes, as shown in Figure 7–22.

Figure 7–22

10. Click ↳ (Modify) or press <Esc> to end the command.

11. Select the extreme left vertical plane.

12. In Properties, set the *Name* to **Weld** and set *Is Reference* to **Not a Reference**.

13. Repeat the steps for the two remaining planes, setting *Name* to **Flange Thickness** (third from left) and **Gasket** (far right), as shown in Figure 7–23.

Figure 7–23

14. Click ✐ (Aligned) dimension.

15. Select the Gasket vertical reference plane and then select the Flange Thickness reference plane to its immediate left.

16. Move the cursor up and click to place the dimension above the ends of the reference planes.

17. Click ⌖ (Modify) to end the command.

18. Select the dimension. In the Options Bar, select the arrow in the Label box and select **RFT** as shown in Figure 7–24. The two planes move so that they are **1/16"** apart.

Figure 7–24

19. Repeat the steps to place a dimension between the Center (Left/Right) and Flange Thickness planes.

20. Select the dimension. In the Options Bar, select the arrow in the Label box and select **FT**.

21. Repeat the steps to place a dimension between the Weld (far left) and Gasket (far right) planes.

22. Select the dimension. In the Options Bar, select the arrow in the Label box and select **LTH**. The final result should be displayed as shown in Figure 7–25.

Figure 7–25

23. Save the family.

Task 4 - Create model lines.

---

1. Continue working in the family file **150 WN Flange.rfa**.

2. Type **VG**.

3. In the Visibility Graphics dialog box, in the *Model* tab, click
   Object Styles... .

4. In the Object Styles dialog box, click Select All and change
   the *Projection Line Weight* to **5** for all objects, as shown in
   Figure 7–26.

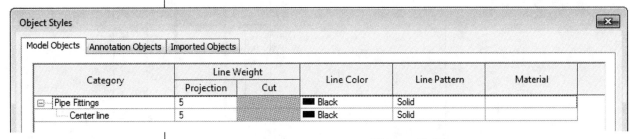

Figure 7–26

5. Click OK twice to close the dialog boxes.

6. In the *Create* tab>Model panel, click ⌐ (Model Line).

7. In the *Place Model Lines* tab>Draw panel, click ✎ (Line).

8. In the Options Bar, clear **Chain**.

9. Draw a vertical line (no particular length) on the far left reference plane. Start the line below the horizontal reference and end above it. Draw another vertical line on the far right reference plane.

   • It is critical that the lines are directly on the reference planes. When drawing the lines, either use object snap overrides or drag the lines slightly off to the side of the planes, and use the **Align** tool to place them.

10. Draw a horizontal line from the intersection of the horizontal plane and far left plane to the intersection of the horizontal and far right plane.

11. Add dimensions as shown in Figure 7–27.

   • To dimension from end to end of a line, hover over the end of a line and press <Tab> until you see a small circle then click to select the end.
   • The overall length of the line does not matter in this step.
   • Change the view scale as needed to display the dimensions.

Figure 7–27

12. Select the overall dimension on the far left.

13. In the Options Bar, in the Label drop-down list, select **PipeOD**.

14. Select the overall dimension on the far right.

15. In the Options Bar, in the Label drop-down list, select **FlgDia**. The result displays as shown in Figure 7–28.

Figure 7–28

16. Clear the dimension and select only the three lines.

17. In the *Modify | Lines* tab>Visibility panel, click (Visibility Settings).

18. In the Family Element Visibility Settings dialog box, in the *Detail Levels* area, clear the **Fine** option. Leave all of the others selected, as shown in Figure 7–29. This enables the selected elements to be visible only at the Coarse and Medium detail levels.

Figure 7–29

19. Click ⬚ OK ⬚.

20. Test the *Detail Levels* ending on **Medium**.

21. Save the family.

Task 5 - Create the Raised Face and Flange extrusions.

1. In the Project Browser, open the Elevations>**Left** view.

2. Select the model lines and temporarily hide the elements.

3. In the *Create* tab>Forms panel, click (Extrusion).

4. In the *Modify | Create Extrusion* tab>Work Plane panel, click (Set).

5. In the Work Plane dialog box, in the Name drop-down list, select **Reference Plane: Flange Thickness**, as shown in Figure 7–30 and click [OK]

Figure 7–30

6. In the *Modify | Create Extrusion* tab>Draw panel, click (Circle).

7. In the Options Bar, select **Radius** and type **3 1/2"**.

8. Select the intersection of the horizontal and vertical reference planes. Use the **SI** (intersection object snap override if required).

9. Click (Modify).

10. Select the circle and click the icon to make the temporary dimension permanent.

11. Click (Modify).

12. Select the dimension line. In the Options Bar, in the Label drop-down list, select **RFR**.

13. Click (Modify) to release all selections.

14. In Properties, in the *Extrusion End* row, click the button as shown in Figure 7–31.

Figure 7–31

15. In the Associate Family Parameter dialog box, select **RFT** as shown in Figure 7–32 and click [OK].

Figure 7–32

16. In the *Modify | Create Extrusion*>Mode panel, click

    ✓ (Finish Edit Mode) and click in the view to release the selection.

17. Click ⬜ (Extrusion) again.

18. Set the Work Plane to **Reference Plane: Center (Left/Right)** and click [OK].

19. Draw a circle at the same intersection using a radius of **4 1/2"**.

20. Make the temporary dimension permanent and label it as **FlgRad**.

21. In the *Extrusion End* row, click the button. In the Associate Family Parameter dialog box, select **FT** and click [OK].

22. Click ✓ (Finish Edit Mode) and click in the view to release the selection.

23. Save the family.

Task 6 - Create the Pipe Connection Blend.

1. In the *Create* tab>Forms panel, click ⬛ (Blend).

2. In the *Modify | Create Blend Base Boundary* tab>Work Plane panel, click 🔲 (Set).

3. In the Work Plane dialog box, select **Reference Plane: Weld** and click [OK].

4. In the Draw panel, click ⊘ (Circle).

5. In the Options Bar, select **Radius** and type **2 1/4"**. Place the center at the intersection of the horizontal and vertical reference planes.

6. Make the temporary dimension permanent and label it **PipeOR**.

7. In the *Modify | Create Blend Base Boundary* tab>Mode panel, click (Edit Top).

8. Draw another circle at the intersection of the reference planes with a radius of **3 3/8"**.

9. Make the temporary dimension permanent and label it **HubRad**.

10. In Properties, for *Second End*, associate the parameter with **HT**.

11. Click ✓ (Finish Edit Mode).

12. Open the 3D Views>**View 1** view.

13. Change the Scale to **3"=1'-0"** so you can see the elements rather than the dimension, as shown in Figure 7–33.

Figure 7–33

14. Select the three model lines and temporarily hide them. You can also do this with the dimensions if required.

15. Save the family.

Task 7 - Create the Pipe Bore.

---

1. Open the Elevations>**Left** view.

2. In the *Create* tab>Forms panel, expand ⬜ (Void Forms) and click ⬜ (Void Extrusion).

3. Set the Work Plane to **Reference Plane: Weld** and click OK .

4. Draw a circle with the *Radius* of **2"** at the intersection of the reference planes.

5. Make the temporary dimension permanent and Label it **NomRad**.

6. In Properties, for *Extrusion End,* associate it with **LTH** parameter.

7. Click (Finish Edit mode).

8. Open the 3D Views>**View 1** view and shade the view. You can see the hole created by the void form, as shown in Figure 7–34.

Figure 7–34

You can only select one extrusion or void form at a time when changing the Visibility Settings.

9. Select one of the extrusion or void forms and click (Visibility Settings).

10. In the Family Element Visibility Settings dialog box, clear the **Coarse** and **Medium** options and verify that the **Fine** option is selected. This enables the selected elements to be visible only at the Fine detail level.

11. Click OK .

12. You might need to switch to the 3D view to select the pipe bore (void form).

13. Repeat the steps for the remaining extrusion or void forms.

14. Save the family.

Task 8 - Add connectors.

1. Continue working in the **View 1** view.

2. In the *Create* tab>Connectors panel, click 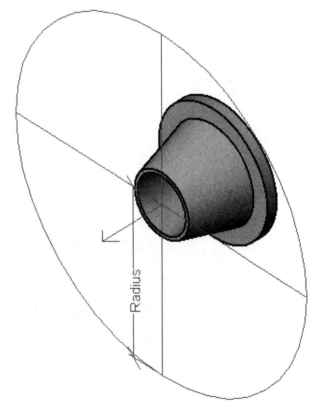 (Pipe Connector).

3. In the *Modify | Place Pipe Connector* tab>Placement panel, verify that (Face) is selected.

4. In the Options Bar, in the System type drop-down list, select **Hydronic Supply**.

5. Press <Tab> as required to highlight the small face of the blend and click to add the connector.

6. The arrow of the connector should be pointing outward from the flange object, as shown in Figure 7–35. If the arrow is pointing inward, click the **Flip** control.

Figure 7–35

- The connector arrow does not indicate flow direction. Instead, it points in the direction from which the pipe is going to connect into it.

7. Spin the view so that the raised face is visible and apply another connector to that face as shown in Figure 7–36.

Figure 7–36

8. Click ⌖ (Modify).

9. Select the first connector. In the *Modify | Connector Element* tab>Connector Links panel, click 🔗 (Link Connectors).

10. Click the second connector to link it to the first.

11. Click ⌖ (Modify).

12. Select both connectors.

13. In Properties, for *Radius,* associate it with the **NomRad** parameter and click ⸤ OK ⸥.

14. The connectors are resized as shown in Figure 7–37.

Figure 7–37

15. Save the family.

Task 9 - Create family types.

1. Continue working in the family file **150 WN Flange.rfa**.

2. In the Properties panel, click ⊞ (Family Types).

3. In the Family Types dialog box, in the *Family Types* area, click ⎡ New ⎤.

4. In the Name dialog box, type **4"** and click ⎡ OK ⎤.

5. Click ⎡ New ⎤ again. In the Name dialog box, type **6"**.

6. In the *Dimensions* area, change the parameter values according to the following:

   - **PipeOD:** 6 5/8"
   - **NomRad:** 3"
   - **LTH:** 3 1/2"
   - **FlgDia:** 11"
   - **FT:** 15/16"

7. Drag and move the Family Types dialog box so that the flange is visible.

8. Click [Apply]. The flange changes size according to the new parameter values, as shown in Figure 7–38.

Figure 7–38

9. In the Name drop-down list, select **4"**.

10. Click [Apply] again. The flange returns to its original size.

11. Click [OK] to close the dialog box.

12. Save the family.

Task 10 - Test the flange in a project.

1. Start a new project and switch back to the family.

2. In the Family Editor panel, click (Load into Project).

  • If you have one project open, the new family loads directly into it. If you have more than one project open, select the right one(s) in the dialog box.

3. You are returned to the project.

4. In the Project Browser, expand the *Families* area and the *Pipe Fittings* area. The **150 WN Flange** family is listed. Expand the **150 WN Flange** family, as shown in Figure 7–39.

Figure 7–39

5. Drag an instance of each type into the drawing area of the project.

6. Zoom in to display the plan view of the flanges at a Coarse Detail level, as shown on the left in Figure 7–40.

7. Change the *Detail Level* to **Fine** and the flanges display in detail at full size, as shown on the right in Figure 7–40.

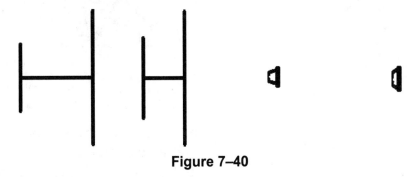

Figure 7–40

8. Open a 3D view.

9. Zoom in on the flanges and turn on ![icon] (Thin Lines) as required.

10. Change Detail Level to **Fine** and type **SD** to shade the view.

11. Spin the view to examine the flanges from all sides.

12. Save the project file.

13. Close the project and family files. Save any changes you want to keep.

Chapter Review Questions

1. The architect has requested that you use a vanity design that is not setup to work with MEP systems, such as the one shown in Figure 7–41. What do you need to do to upgrade it?

Figure 7–41

a. Add pipes to the family where you want the project pipes to tie in.

b. Add connectors to the family where you want the project pipes to tie in.

c. Create a separate MEP specific vanity and use **Copy/Monitor** to add it to the project.

d. Import an existing sink designed to work with MEP systems into the family.

2. Which of the following Light Source Definition distribution options enables you to specify an IES file?

a. (Spherical)

b. (Hemispherical)

c. (Spot)

d. (Photometric Web)

3. If you want to include an annotation element, such as a label that references a parameter in a family, you can only do so by creating a separate annotation tag.

a. True

b. False

4. How do you have a family display different elements when you change the *Detail Level* from *Coarse* to **Fine**?

a. In the project file, select the family and in Properties change the detail level.

b. In the family file, select the elements and modify the Visibility Settings.

c. In the family file, in the View Properties, set the detail level.

d. In the project file, set the Visibility Settings for the view.

5. In the Family Types dialog box shown in Figure 7–42, if the *Pump Length* changed to **2'-0"**, what would the value of *Radius 2* be?

Figure 7–42

a. 5'-0"

b. 4'-0"

c. 4'-11"

d. 5'-1"

Chapter 8

Creating Structural Specific Families

In this chapter you learn to create structural specific families by working through a series of practices including a parametric gusset plate, an in-place stiffener plate, an in-place slab depression, a built-up column, a tapered concreted column, a truss family, a pre-cast hollow core slab and a tapered moment frame. Select the ones that are most helpful in your work.

Practice 8a

Parametric Gusset Plate

Learning Objectives

- Create reference planes, dimensions, and parameters.
- Create solid geometry for the plates.
- Modify Visibility Settings and create Family Types.

Estimated time for completion: 30 minutes

In this exercise you will create a family file based on a template and create reference planes. You will then create gussets as a mass, create material parameters, and apply Family Types. Finally, you will turn off the visibility of the gusset plate from the coarse detail to all views, as shown in Figure 8–1.

Figure 8–1

Task 1 - Start a New Family using a template and add reference planes.

1. Create a new family based on the **Structural Stiffener.rft**. template found in the Autodesk Revit Library.

2. Save the family to your class folder as **Parametric Gusset Plate.rfa.**

3. Open the Elevations (Elevation 1)>**Left** view.

The exact location is not required yet. Make sure that the diagonal reference plane being added crosses the intersection of the two default (existing) reference planes.

4. Create three new reference planes, as shown in Figure 8–2.

Figure 8–2

5. Add another reference plane **8"** from the 45 degree reference plane and add dimensions between each reference plane, as shown in Figure 8–3. Set the *vertical* and *horizontal* dimensions to **8"** each. Then offset the diagonal reference plane **8"** down and add a dimension starting from the original reference plane.

Figure 8–3

6. Select one of the dimensions to create new family type labels. Select the dimension. In the Options Bar, in the Label drop-down list, select <**Add parameter...**>.

7. In the Parameter Properties dialog box, add a new type parameter named **Width**, as shown in Figure 8–4.

Figure 8–4

8. Click [OK].

9. Select the other dimensions. In the Options Bar, add the **Width** labels, as shown in Figure 8–5.

Width = 0' - 8"

Figure 8–5

10. In the *Create* tab>Properties panel, click (Family Types). Test the dimensions by changing the distance of the *Width* in the Family Types dialog box. Do the other reference planes remain in place?

Task 2 - Create Front View Reference Planes.

1. Switch to the Elevations>**Front** view and create two reference planes, **1/4"** on either side of the existing vertical plane and add dimensions, as shown in Figure 8–6.

Figure 8–6

2. Label the overall dimension as **Thickness**.

3. In the *Create* tab>Properties panel, click ⊞ (Family Types). Test the dimensions by changing the distance of *Thickness* in the Family Types dialog box. Verify that all of the reference planes are moving together. Click ⟨ OK ⟩.

4. Save the family.

Task 3 - Creating Family Geometry.

1. Switch to Elevations>**Left** view.

2. In the *Create* tab>Forms panel, click ⬕ (Extrusion). In the Options Bar, set the *Depth* to **1/2"**.

3. Draw individual lines across the outside intersections of the reference planes, and lock all five lines to the reference planes, as shown in Figure 8–7.

*Use the **Align** command to help lock the lines to the reference plane.*

Figure 8–7

4. Click ✔ (Finish Edit Mode).

5. Switch to the Elevations>**Front** view. Align the left and right sides of the extrusion with the reference planes you created earlier and lock them.

6. Switch to a 3D view.

7. In the *Create* tab>Properties panel, click (Family Types) to flex the model to verify that everything is working together. The model displays as shown in Figure 8–8.

Figure 8–8

8. Save the family.

Task 4 - Add Material Parameters.

1. Open the Family Types dialog box.

2. In the *Parameters* area, click [Add].

3. Create an Instance parameter named **Material** and set the *Type of Parameter* to **Material**. The Group automatically updates to Materials and Finishes, as shown in Figure 8–9. Click [OK].

*Setting the parameter as an **Instance** makes it easier to modify it in the project file.*

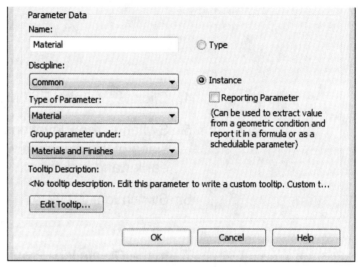

Figure 8–9

4. In the 3D view, select the plate.

5. In Properties, in the *Materials and Finishes* area, in *Material* row, click ⬚ (Associate Family Parameter).

6. In the Associate Family Parameter dialog box, select **Material** as shown in Figure 8–10 and click [OK].

Figure 8–10

7. In Properties, the **Material** parameter is now marked with the **=** sign, as shown in Figure 8–11. Therefore, when the family is loaded into a project, you can control its material using Properties.

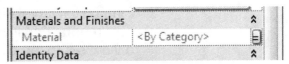

Figure 8–11

Task 5 - Change the Visibility Settings in a Family.

1. Select the extrusion.

2. In the *Modify | Extrusion* tab>Mode panel, click (Visibility Settings).

3. In the Family Element Visibility Settings dialog box, clear the **Coarse** option as shown in Figure 8–12, so that the gusset plate does not display at a Coarse detail level.

Figure 8–12

4. Click [OK].

5. Press <Esc> to clear the selection.

6. Change the *Detail Level* to **Coarse**, **Medium**, and **Fine**. The outline of the Gusset Plate remains dark in the Medium and Fine Detail Levels but turns gray in the **Coarse** Detail Level. This means that it will not display in a project when inserted in a view set to the Coarse Detail Level.

7. Save the family.

Task 6 - Create Family Types.

1. Open the Family Types dialog box.

2. In the *Family Types* area, click [New]. Type **10"** for the name and click [OK].

3. Set the *Width* to **10"** and the *Thickness* to **1/2"**. Click [Apply].

4. Repeat Steps 2 and 3. Set the name of the new family as **12"** and set the *Width* to **12"**. Leave the *Thickness* as **1/2"**.

5. Click [OK].

6. Save the family.

7. In the Family Editor panel, click ⬆ (Load into Project).

   - If you have only one project open, the family will load into it directly.
   - If you have more than one project open, using the menu, select which one(s) to load the family into.
   - If no projects are open, an alert box opens. Open a new project and try the process again.

8. The family file **Parametric Gusset Plate.rfa** loads into the project.

9. The **Component** command is automatically started. Insert one of each Plate type into the project.

10. Switch to a 3D view to see the differences.

11. Shade the view (shortcut: **SD**).

12. Select one of the Plates and in Properties, apply a material to it. Repeat with the others using different materials.

13. Save the family and project.

Practice 8b

Estimated time for completion: 15 minutes

Column Stiffeners (In-Place Family)

 Learning Objective

- Create an in-place family in a detail view

In this practice you will create a stiffener plate to strengthen a column's flange, as shown in Figure 8–13.

Figure 8–13

Task 1 - Create an in-place family in a detail view.

1. Open the file /Structural/**Column-Stiffeners-S.rvt** found in your class files folder. The file opens in the Structural Plans> **Level 2** view.

2. In the Project Browser, open **Detail Views: Detail 0**. It displays a column supporting a beam and concrete on metal deck slab, as shown in Figure 8–14.

Figure 8–14

3. The column requires stiffeners to strengthen its flanges. In the *Structure* tab>Model panel, expand 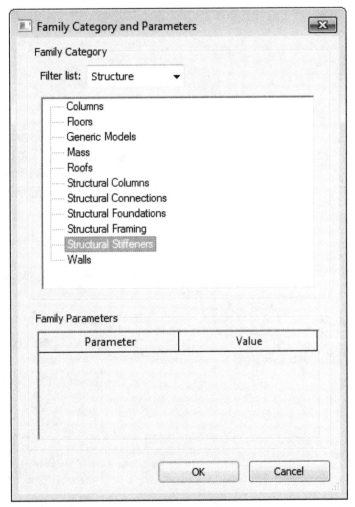 (Component) and click (Model In-Place).

4. In the Family Category and Parameters dialog box, set the *Filter list* to **Structure** and select **Structural Stiffeners**, as shown in Figure 8–15. Click ⌐OK⌐.

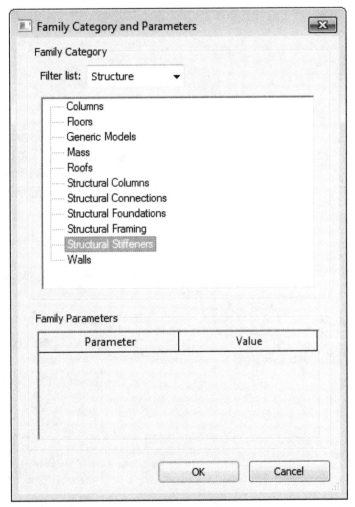

Figure 8–15

5. Enter a name for the stiffener plate, as shown in Figure 8–16.

Figure 8–16

6. You are now in the In-Place Editor. In the **Detail 0** view, draw two horizontal reference planes, as shown in Figure 8–17. These reference planes assist in locating the stiffener plates. One reference plane indicates the **Top of Beam** and the second indicates the **Bottom of Beam**.

Figure 8–17

7. Select the Top of Beam reference plane. In Properties, in the *Identity Data* area, for the *Name* value, type **Top of Beam** as shown in Figure 8–18. Repeat the procedure to name the second reference plane, **Bottom of Beam**.

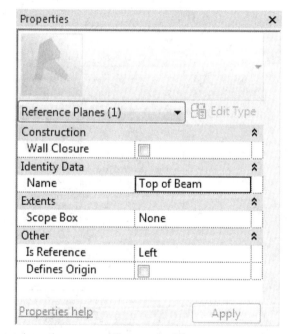

Figure 8–18

8. In the *Create* tab>Forms panel, click ⬚ (Extrusion).

9. The Work Plane dialog box opens enabling you to select a new Work Plane for the location of the stiffener plate. In the drop-down list, select **Reference Plane: Top of Beam**.

10. Click [OK].

11. In the Go To View dialog box, select **Structural Plan: Level 2**. This view is used to draw the stiffener plate.

12. Click [Open View].

13. In the Structural Plans>**Level 2** view, zoom into the grid intersection **1/A**.

14. In the *Modify | Create Extrusion* tab>Draw panel, click

    ✏️ (Pick Lines). In the Options Bar, select **Lock**. This ensures that the stiffener edges adjust to any changes to the column size.

15. Select and trim the perimeter of the inside face of the column, as shown in Figure 8–19.

Figure 8–19

16. In Properties, set the *Extrusion End* value to (negative) **-1"**, as shown in Figure 8–20.

Figure 8–20

17. Click ✔️ (Finish Edit Mode).

18. Switch to the **Detail 0** view. Note that the stiffener plate is located under the **Top of Beam** reference planes.

19. Select the stiffener plate and click (Copy). In the Options Bar, clear the **Constrain** option. Select the starting point as the bottom of the stiffener plate and copy it halfway down between the two reference planes.

20. Select the copied stiffener plate.

21. In the *Modify | Extrusion* tab>Work Plane panel, click **Edit Work Plane**.

22. In the Work Plane dialog box, select **Reference Plane: Bottom of Beam** and click ⬚ OK ⬚. The plate moves into a new position.

23. The stiffener plate thickness must be adjusted upward. Select the new stiffener plate and change the *Extrusion End* to **1"**.

24. The new plate now moves with the **Bottom of Beam** reference plane, as shown in Figure 8–21.

Figure 8–21

25. In the In-Place Editor panel, click ✓ (Finish Model).

26. In the project file, navigate through the different views to see the stiffener plates.

27. Save the project.

Practice 8c

In-Place Slab Depression

Learning Objectives

- Create a floor-based family by setting up the parametric framework.
- Create a void form for a depression in the floor.
- Apply the family in a project.

Estimated time for completion: 15 minutes.

Slab depression family is an important host-based family that you need to modify for your projects. In this practice, you will create a slab depression using a template file and apply it in a project, as shown in Figure 8–22.

Figure 8–22

Task 1 - Create a family and add reference planes, insertion points, and dimensions.

1. Create a new family based on the **Generic Model floor based.rft** template found in the Autodesk Revit Library.

2. Save the family to your class folder as **Slab Depression Component.rfa**.

3. In the *Create* tab>Datum panel, click ✎ (Reference Plane).

4. Add the horizontal and vertical reference planes and dimensions, as shown in Figure 8–23.

Figure 8–23

5. Label the horizontal dimension as **Slab Depression Length** and the Vertical dimension as **Slab Depression Width**. In both cases set the parameter to **Instance**. The parameters display as shown in Figure 8–24.

Figure 8–24

6. Open the Elevations>**Front** view where you create the depth of the depressed slab.

7. Add another reference plane **3"** down from the reference level. Add a dimension between the reference level and the new reference plane. Label the dimension as **Slab Depression Depth**, as shown in Figure 8–25.

Figure 8–25

8. Save the family.

Task 2 - Create the depressed area for the slab.

---

1. Now you will create the depressed area for the slab by creating a void form and locking it to the reference planes. Switch to the Floor Plans>**Ref. Level** view.

2. In the *Create* tab>Forms panel, expand ⬚ (Void Forms) and

   click ⬚ (Void Extrusion).

3. In the Draw panel, click ⬚ (Rectangle).

4. Add the rectangle by clicking at the top left corner of the intersecting reference planes and then the bottom right corner. Click the lock controls to constrain the void form to the reference planes, as shown in Figure 8–26.

Figure 8–26

5. Click ✓ (Finish Edit Mode).

6. Press <Esc> to clear the extrusion selection.

7. Open the Elevations>**Front** view.

8. In the *Modify* tab>Modify panel, click ⬚ (Align).

9. Select the lower reference plane first and then pick the bottom of the void form, as shown in Figure 8–27. Select the lock control to constrain the bottom of the void form to the reference plane.

Figure 8–27

10. Still in the **Align** command, select the reference level and pick the top of the void form. Select the lock control to constrain the top of the void form to the reference level.

11. In the *Modify* tab>Geometry panel, click $\overset{\text{⟋}}{}$ (Cut Geometry) and pick the void form and the slab object. (The order of the selection does not matter.)

12. Open a 3D view to see the depression within the slab object. Type **SD** to shade the view, as shown in Figure 8–28.

Figure 8–28

13. Use the Family Types dialog box to flex the depression.

14. Close the dialog box.

15. Save the Depressed Slab component family file. Do not close the family file.

Task 3 - Test the component family file.

---

1. Create a new project and save the file as **Depressed Slab Example.rvt**.

2. In the *Structure* tab>Foundation panel, click ⬭ (Foundation Slab). Create an **8" Concrete Slab** in the new project.

3. When the slab has been created in the project file, return to the **Slab Depression Component.rfa** family file.

4. In the Family Editor panel, click 🔲 (Load into Project).

5. The Autodesk Revit software automatically switches to the **Depressed Slab Example.rvt** file as long as there are no other files open and the appropriate command is started.

6. Pick a location for the slab depression. The insertion is based on the origin within the family file. In the family file you based the insertion point at the center of the recessed slab.

7. Select different views to display the depression. Cut some sections through it.

8. To change the size of slab depression, return to the Floor Plans>**Level 2** view, and select the component.

9. In Properties, change the values to any required size, as shown in Figure 8–29. Click [OK].

Figure 8–29

10. Return to the 3D view and Section view to see the new shape of the depressed slab.

11. Save and close the project and family files.

Practice 8d

Built-Up Column

Estimated time for completion: 15 minutes.

The analytical line is already incorporated into the family in the structural system family template. Therefore, it is not required to be created in the new family.

Learning Objectives

- Set up the parametric framework for a column
- Use extrusions to create the sides of the column.

The Autodesk® Revit® Structure software has an extensive structural columns library to meet many standard types and sizes in the industry. However, there is still a need for built-up (custom) made columns. In this practice you will create a built-up column from steel plates, as shown in Figure 8–30.

Figure 8–30

Task 4 - Set up reference planes and dimensions.

1. Create a new family based on the **Structural Column.rft** template found in the Autodesk Revit Library.

2. Save the family to your class folder as **Built-Up Column.rfa**.

3. In the Structural Plans>**Lower Ref. Level** view, add reference planes to the inside of the four exterior reference planes using ⚲ (Pick Lines) with an *Offset* of **2"**, as shown in Figure 8–31.

Figure 8–31

4. Delete the vertical **EQ** dimensions to prevent over-constraining and re-insert new vertical EQ dimensions at the inner reference planes, as shown in Figure 8–32.

Figure 8–32

5. Place single dimensions horizontally and vertically above the EQ dimensions, as shown in Figure 8–33.

Figure 8–33

*The **Instance** option permits the value to be modified per element.*

6. Select the horizontal dimension and label it. Set the *Name* to **Primary Plate Length** and select **Instance**, as shown in Figure 8–34.

Figure 8–34

7. Follow the same procedures for the vertical dimension, naming it **Secondary Plate Length**.

8. Add four more dimensions, as shown in Figure 8–35. Set the parameters for these new dimensions to determine the thickness of the primary and secondary plates.

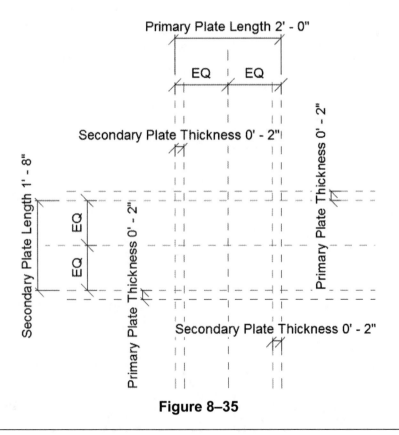

Figure 8–35

Task 5 - Create the plates.

1. In the *Create* tab>Forms panel, click ⬜ (Extrusion) to create the plates. Only one plate can be created at a time because each extrusion must be a closed loop.

2. Sketch the rectangle, based on the start and end points shown in Figure 8–36. Also lock the lines to the reference planes. Leave the **Extrusion Start** and **Extrusion End** parameters as default. The column height is adjusted later by aligning with other reference planes.

Figure 8–36

3. Click ✓ (Finish Edit Mode).

4. Select the primary plate created and mirror it using the center line as the axis of reflection.

5. Repeat the steps to create the secondary plate shown in Figure 8–37.

Figure 8–37

6. Open the Elevations>**Front** view. You will establish the height of the column.

7. Use (Align) to align the four plates to the Upper Ref. Level. Select the **Upper Ref. Level** and then the top of a plate and lock it in place. Repeat this procedure until all four plates are locked to the **Upper Ref. Level** and **Lower Ref. Leve**l, as shown in Figure 8–38.

Figure 8–38

8. Set the *Visual Style* of the view to **Hidden Line**. Note that the secondary plates behind the primary plates disappear.

9. Use Symbolic Lines to display the secondary plates with hidden lines. In the *Annotate* tab>Detail panel, click (Symbolic Line).

10. In the *Modify | Place Symbolic Lines* tab>Subcategory panel Type Selector, select **Hidden Lines (Projection)**.

11. In the Options Bar, verify that the **Chain** option is cleared. Draw a line from the intersection of the Upper Ref. Level and the inside reference planes on both sides of the column, as shown in Figure 8–39. Lock these lines to both the Upper and Lower Ref. Levels.

Figure 8–39

12. To test the Built-Up Column, open a new project and load the **Built-Up Column** family into the new project. Insert a column (as shown in Figure 8–40), and navigate from one view to another to see the new column.

Figure 8–40

13. Save the family.

Practice 8e

Tapered Concrete Column

Learning Objectives

- Create Reference Planes and Parameters as the framework of the column family.
- Create geometry using a solid blend.

Estimated time for completion: 15 minutes

In this practice you will create a tapered concrete column using a column family template. You will create its geometry using a solid blend and add a taper parameter that can be modified as shown in Figure 8–41.

Figure 8–41

Task 1 - Create Reference Planes and Parameters,

1. Create a new family based on the **Structural Column.rft** template found in the Autodesk Revit Library.

2. Save the family to your class folder as **Tapered-Concrete-Column.rfa**

3. In the *Create* tab>Datum panel, click (Reference Plane) and add one horizontal reference plane offset **2'-0"** from the lower existing horizontal plane. Add a **2'-0"** dimension as shown in Figure 8–42.

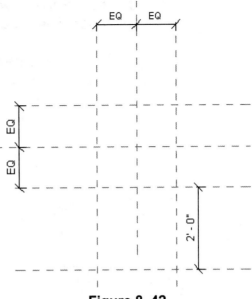

Figure 8–42

4. Select the new reference plane. In Properties, name the reference plane **Taper** as shown in Figure 8–43.

Figure 8–43

5. Select the **2'-0"** dimension. In the Options Bar, in the Label drop-down list, select **<Add parameter...>**.

6. In the Parameter Properties dialog box, set the *Name* to **Taper**, select the **Dimensions** group and **Type** parameter, as shown in Figure 8–44, and click ☐ OK ☐.

Figure 8–44

7. Add dimensions to the outer horizontal and vertical reference planes representing the base of the column. Label the horizontal and vertical dimensions as **Base Width** and **Base Length**, respectively, as shown in Figure 8–45. Add the parameters to the **Dimensions** group and set them as **Type** parameters.

Figure 8–45

8. Save the family.

Task 2 - Create geometry.

1. In the *Create* tab>Forms panel, click (Blend).

   (Blend icon shown inline with the step text.)

2. The Base profile needs to be established first. In the *Modify | Create Blend Base Boundary* tab>Draw panel, click
   (Rectangle). Draw a square along the Base reference planes. Lock the lines to the reference planes, as shown in Figure 8–46.

Figure 8–46

3. After completing the outline of the base of the column, the Top of the profile needs to be established. In the *Modify | Create Blend Base Boundary* tab>Mode panel, click
   (Edit Top).

4. In the Draw panel, click (Rectangle). Draw a **2'x 4'** rectangle along the full extents of the reference planes as shown in Figure 8–47, and lock them.

Figure 8–47

5. In the Blend panel, click ✓ (Finish Edit Mode).

6. Open the **Front** elevation view.

7. In the *Modify* tab>Edit panel, click ⊡ (Align). Select the **Upper Ref. Level**, pick the top of the column, and lock it into place with the reference level, as shown in Figure 8–48. This is to ensure that the top of the column is always constrained to the Upper Ref. Level.

Figure 8–48

8. Open the **View 1** 3D view and rotate it to display the constructed version of the tapered concrete column. You can also shade it as shown in Figure 8–49.

Figure 8–49

9. In the Properties panel, click (Family Types) and test the parameters by changing the values as shown in Figure 8–50.

Figure 8–50

10. Reset the default values and close the Family Types dialog box.

11. Save the family.

12. If you have time you can create Family Types using various dimensions and test them in a project.

Practice 8f

Truss Family

 Learning Objectives

- Start a truss family and add reference planes and labels.
- Add Top Chord, Bottom Chord, and Web layout lines.

Estimated time for completion: 40 minutes

In this practice you will create a truss using a truss family template, add reference planes, create parameters, and add chords and webs to form the structure of the trusses as shown in Figure 8–51.

Figure 8–51

Task 1 - Add Reference Planes and Labels.

1. Create a new family based on the **Structural Trusses.rft** template found in the Autodesk Revit Library.

1. Save the family to your class folder as **Custom Truss.rfa**

2. In the *Create* tab>Datum panel, click (Reference Plane).

3. In the Draw panel, click (Pick Lines).

4. In the Options Bar, set the *Offset* to **10'-0"**.

5. Add a vertical reference plane to each side of the center vertical reference plane as shown in Figure 8–52.

Figure 8–52

6. Dimension as shown in Figure 8–52. Label the overall dimension as **Top Chord Length**. When you create the parameter, create it as an **Instance** parameter as shown in Figure 8–53.

Figure 8–53

7. Open the Family Types dialog box and scroll down to the *Dimensions* area. Add the formula *Top Chord Length* = **Truss Length / 3**, as shown in Figure 8–54.

Dimensions			
Top Chord Length (default)	20' 0"	=	Truss Length /3
Truss Length (default)	80' 0"	=	
Truss Height (default)	10' 0"	=	

Figure 8–54

8. Click OK.

Task 2 - Add the Top Chord, Bottom Chord, and Web layout lines.

1. In the *Create* tab>Detail panel, click ⋈ (Top Chord).

2. In the Options Bar, verify that the **Chain** option is cleared so that you can lock each line as it is created.

3. Starting from the left vertical reference plane, draw the top chord from **4'-0"** above the bottom reference plane to the intersection of the next vertical and top horizontal reference planes. Click the two 🔒 to lock the sketch to the reference planes as shown in Figure 8–55.

Use temporary dimensions to locate the start point or draw an additional reference plane 4'-0" above the bottom reference plane.

Figure 8–55

4. Continue drawing the chord across the top of the truss and then down to the right vertical reference plane, locking as you go, shown in Figure 8–56. The exact angle for the last web will be fixed later.

Figure 8–56

5. While you are still in the contextual tab in the Draw panel, click (Bottom Chord). (Alternatively, in the *Create* tab> Detail panel, click (Bottom Chord).)

6. Draw the bottom chord, beginning from the far left reference plane along the bottom reference plane to the far right reference plane. Remember to lock the bottom chord sketch line in place, as shown in Figure 8–57.

Figure 8–57

7. Add dimensions from the bottom reference plane to the intersection of the far left reference plane and the starting point of the top chord line and repeat on the right. Then create new labels for *End Height (Left)* and *End Height (Right)*, as shown Figure 8–58. When you create the parameter, set it as an **Instance** parameter. Adjust the *End Height (Right)* to **4'-0"** in the Family Types dialog box.

Figure 8–58

8. In the *Create* tab>Detail panel, click (Web). In the Options Bar, verify that the **Chain** option is not selected.

9. Draw vertical web lines along each vertical reference plane, as shown in Figure 8–59. Start at the far left reference plane and work over to the right. The webs at the two far ends of the truss should go from the bottom reference plane to the intersection of the top chord line. The three web lines along the middle three vertical reference planes should go from the top reference plane to the bottom reference plane. Lock all of the web lines to their respective reference planes as shown in Figure 8–59.

Figure 8–59

10. Draw two new vertical web lines and dimension them so that they are equal, as shown in Figure 8–60.

Figure 8–60

• Ensure that you dimension to the vertical reference planes where available or the truss will not flex correctly.

11. Draw one vertical web from the top to the bottom reference planes between the left **Truss Chord Length** reference plane and the center reference plane and dimension it to be equal as shown in Figure 8–61.

Figure 8–61

12. Repeat the steps to create vertical webs for the right side of the truss. (DO NOT mirror the Web lines as this might cause undesirable results or errors in the truss family.) The final outcome should be as shown in Figure 8–62.

Figure 8–62

13. Add diagonal web members to the left of the truss, from the top chord to the bottom chord. Start from the far left side working toward the center of the truss. Repeat the process from the other direction. The final outcome is shown in Figure 8–63. DO NOT mirror the web lines, as this might cause errors when the truss is loaded into a project.

Figure 8–63

14. Using the Family Types dialog box, flex the geometry using the parameters found in the *Dimensions* area.

15. Reset the values to the original dimensions.

16. Save the family.

Practice 8g

Precast Hollow Core Slab

 Learning Objectives

- Create a family using the Structural Framing - Beams and Braces template.
- Use a CAD file to modify the sketch of an extrusion.
- Assign a material to the extrusion.
- Set visibility settings for Medium and Fine detail levels along with simple geometry for the Coarse detail level.

Estimated time for completion: 20 minutes

In this practice you will use the **Structural Framing - Beams and Braces.rft** file as the base of the hollow core slab. You will modify an existing extrusion and import a CAD drawing to assist in setting up the new profile. You will assign a material to the extrusion and establish the visibility settings for Medium and Fine Detail Levels. You will then draw a second extrusion with a simple rectangular profile, assign the material and set the visibility settings so that it only displays at a Coarse Detail Level as shown in Figure 8–64.

Detail Level: Coarse

Detail Level: Medium and Fine

Figure 8–64

Task 1 - Import a CAD file into a family template to create the hollow core geometry.

---

1. Create a new family based on the **Structural Framing - Beams and Braces.rft** template found in the Autodesk Revit Library.

2. Save the family to your class folder as **Precast-Hollow-Core-Slab.rfa**

3. Close any other projects or family files that you might have open.

4. Open the Floor Plan>**Ref Level**, Elevation>**Front**, Elevation> **Left**, and 3D View>**View 1** views.

5. Type **WT** (Window Tile) and then **ZA** (Zoom All to Fit). The layout should be similar to that shown in Figure 8–65. This helps you to develop the precast hollow core slab.

Figure 8–65

6. In the Elevation>**Left** view, zoom in on the geometry.

7. Select the extrusion. In the *Modify | Extrusion* tab>Mode panel, click ![edit icon] (Edit Extrusion).

8. Select the outline geometry (as shown in Figure 8–66) and the reference planes that are part of the extrusion and delete them from the view.

Figure 8–66

In this example, a CAD drawing is used to create the geometry of the hollow core slab.

9. In the *Insert* tab>Import panel, click 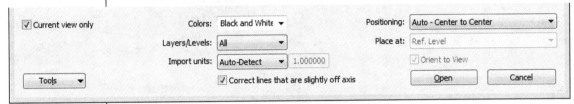 (Import CAD).

10. In the Import CAD Formats dialog box, navigate to your class files folder, select **Precast-Hollow-Core-Slab.dwg**, and set the following options as shown in Figure 8–67:

   - **Select** Current View Only
   - **Colors:** Black and White
   - **Layers:** All
   - **Import units:** Auto-Detect
   - **Positioning:** Auto - Center to Center

Figure 8–67

11. Click .

12. A message box opens prompting you about exploding import instances. Click [Yes] to continue. The family now includes the sketch lines from the AutoCAD drawing as shown in Figure 8–68.

Figure 8–68

13. To select the material for the hollow core slab, in Properties, in the *Materials and Finishes* area, select **<By Category>**, and then click (Browse), as shown Figure 8–69.

Figure 8–69

14. In the Material Browser, select **Concrete-Precast Concrete** as shown in Figure 8–70.

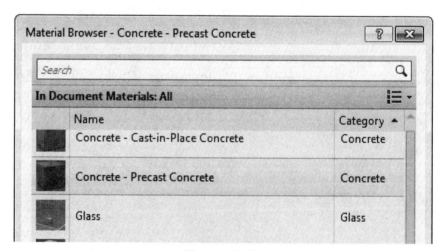

Figure 8–70

15. Click [OK] to close the dialog boxes. The Material is assigned.

16. In the *Modify | Edit Extrusion* tab>Mode panel, click (Finish Edit Mode).

17. Click in empty space to release the selection.

18. In the 3D view, zoom out as needed to display the slab. Set the *Visual Style* to (Shaded) to display the new slab with the concrete material applied, as shown in Figure 8–71.

Figure 8–71

19. Save the file.

Task 2 - Establish visibility settings.

1. Select the new extrusion.

2. In the *Modify | Extrusion* tab>Mode panel, click (Visibility Settings).

3. In the Family Element Visibility Settings dialog box, in the *Detail Levels* area, verify that **Coarse** is cleared as shown in Figure 8–72.

Figure 8–72

4. Click OK .

5. Clear the extrusion and test the Detail Levels. In the Coarse detail level, the extrusion should display in gray. This is only true in the family file. When inserted into a project this extrusion will not display at a Coarse detail level.

6. Activate the Elevation>**Left** view.

7. In the *Create* tab>Forms panel, click ⬛ (Extrusion).

   - If a Work Plane dialog box opens, verify that **Pick a plane** is selected, and click [OK]. Click the face of the existing extrusion to select it as the work plane.

8. In the *Modify | Create Extrusion* tab>Draw panel, click ⬜ (Rectangle) and draw a rectangle around the perimeter of the hollow core slab starting at the lower left corner. (When you are near the upper right corner, press <Tab> once to force the 4'-0" temporary dimension.) Lock all of the lines in place with the padlock icons. (There might only be three, as shown in Figure 8–73.)

Figure 8–73

9. In Properties, set the *Extrusion End* to (negative) **-8'-0"** and the *Material* to **Concrete - Precast Concrete**.

10. Click ✓ (Finish Edit Mode).

11. Activate the Floor Plan>**Ref. Level** view.

12. Use the **Align** command to align the new extrusion to the **Member Left** reference plane as shown in Figure 8–74.

Figure 8–74

13. Repeat and align the other end to the **Member Right** reference plane.

14. Select the new rectangular extrusion.

15. In the *Modify | Extrusion* tab>Mode panel, click ▢ (Visibility Settings).

16. In the Family Element Visibility Settings dialog box, in the *Detail Levels* area, clear **Medium** and **Fine** as shown in Figure 8–75.

Figure 8–75

17. Click ▢ OK ▢ .

18. Release the selection and try the different Detail Levels.

Task 3 - Add hidden lines.

---

1. Activate the Floor Plans>**Ref. Level** view.

2. In the View Control Bar, set the *Visual Style* to ▱ (Hidden Line).

This line graphically represents the beam on coarse detail plan views. Because you are creating a slab system rather than a beam, the model line is not required.

3. Select the heavy model line in the middle of the slab as shown in Figure 8–76 and delete it.

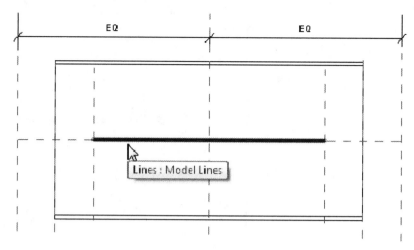

Figure 8–76

4. In the View Control Bar, set the *Visual Style* to (Wireframe).

5. In the *Annotate* tab>Detail panel, click (Symbolic Lines).

6. In the *Modify | Place Symbolic Lines* tab>Subcategory panel, set the *Subcategory* to **Hidden Lines [projection]**.

7. In the *Modify | Place Symbolic Lines* tab>Draw panel, click (Line). In the Options Bar, clear the **Chain** option.

8. Draw hidden lines horizontally along the edges as shown in Figure 8–77. You cannot see them as you draw because they are in the same location as the elements displayed through the wireframe view.

Figure 8–77

9. In the View Control Bar, set the *Visual Style* to (Hidden Line). The hidden lines should be displayed.

10. Click ⟋ (Modify).

11. Select the 12 hidden lines that you just created.

12. In the *Modify | Lines* tab>Visibilitypanel, click ⬚ (Visibility Settings).

13. Set the visibility of only the lines to the **Medium** and **Fine** *Detail Levels*.

14. Save the family in your class files folder.

15. Load the family into a project.

16. Using ⬗ (Beam) draw a beam using the new **Precast-Hollow-Core-Slab** family.

17. Test the visibility settings in the plan and elevation views.

18. Close but do not save the project.

19. Save and close the family.

Practice 8h

Tapered Moment Frame

 Learning Objectives

- Setup reference planes and parameters as the framework of the family.
- Create geometry for the columns and beams of the family.

Estimated time for completion: 40 minutes

In this practice you will use the family template file **Structural Column.rft** as the basis of the Tapered Moment Frame. You will create reference planes and parameters and then create the geometry for the columns and tapered beam using both solid sweeps and extrusions, as shown in Figure 8–78.

Figure 8–78

Task 1 - Set up the reference planes and parameters.

1. Create a new family based on the **Structural Column.rft** template found in the Autodesk Revit Library.

2. Save the family to your class folder as **Tapered-Moment-Frame.rfa**

3. Draw dimensions and add labels for **Length** and **Column Width** to the existing reference planes as shown in Figure 8–79. Create them as **Type** parameters.

Figure 8–79

4. Open the Family Types dialog box

5. In the Family Types dialog box, change the values of *Length* to **26'-0"** and *Column Width* to **1'-0"** as shown in Figure 8–80, and click [OK].

Figure 8–80

6. Zoom out and extend the horizontal reference planes beyond the new vertical reference planes as shown in Figure 8–81. To extend the **Front/Back** reference plane you need to unpin it. When finished, select it again and click on the **Pin** icon to pin it back in place so that it will not move when you add dimensions and labels.

Figure 8–81

7. Add two new horizontal reference planes with associated dimensions and labels to represent the **Beam Width** as shown in Figure 8–82. Create this as a **Type** parameter.

Figure 8–82

8. Open the Elevations>**Front** view.

9. Change the *elevation* of the Upper Ref. Level to **13'-0"**.

10. Extend the reference planes and levels so that they all overlap as shown in Figure 8–83.

Figure 8–83

11. On the left side of the view add two short vertical reference planes, dimensions, and labels, as shown in Figure 8–84. These are for the **Column Top** (2'-0") and **Column Base** (1'-0"). Create these as **Type** parameters.

Figure 8–84

12. Select the two new reference planes along with their labeled dimensions and mirror them across to the other side. The following reference planes should be established, as shown in Figure 8–85.

Figure 8–85

13. Add a reference plane **10'-0"** above the Lower Ref. Level for the knee height of the tapered moment frame. Dimension the new reference plane from the Lower Ref. Level and create a parameter named **Knee Height** as shown in Figure 8–86. Create this as a **Type** parameter.

Figure 8–86

Levels are datum elements and you cannot attach (lock) to a level.

14. Place another horizontal reference plane on top of the Upper Ref. Level and lock it into the level. This will be used to dimension the beam angle reference plane created in the following steps.

15. Add a reference plane at a **5** degree angle. Dimension it using the **Angular Dimension** command (ensure that you select the horizontal reference plane and not the Level) and create a label named **Beam Angle** as shown in Figure 8–87. This reference plane determines the slope of the top of the moment frame. Create them as **Type** parameters.

The beam angle should always be larger than 0 degrees.

Figure 8–87

This reference plane determines the maximum height of the tapered beam's bottom plate at the center of the moment frame.

16. Mirror the new angular reference plane along the center vertical reference plane. Dimension it and apply the Label.

17. Add one final reference plane **12'-0"** above the Lower Ref. Level. Dimension and label it **Beam Middle Height**. The reference planes and dimensions in the Front Elevation view should be similar to those shown in Figure 8–88. Create this as a **Type** parameter.

Figure 8–88

18. Save the family file.

Task 2 - Create the geometry for the Tapered Column.

---

1. In the *Create* tab>Forms panel, click (Sweep).

2. In the *Create* tab>Work Plane panel, click (Set).

3. In the Work Plane dialog box, select **Reference Plane: Center (Front/Back)** as shown in Figure 8–89.

Figure 8–89

4. In the *Modify | Sweep* tab>Sweep panel, click 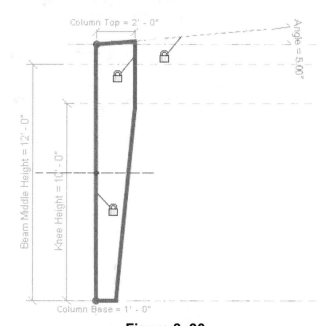 (Sketch Path).

5. In the Draw panel, ✏ (Line) is selected by default. In the Options Bar, verify that the **Chain** option is selected.

6. Sketch the path for the column of the moment frame. Align the two vertical and one angular sketch lines to their parallel reference planes and lock them in place, as shown in Figure 8–90.

Draw the left vertical sketch first. The profile is drawn in this plane.

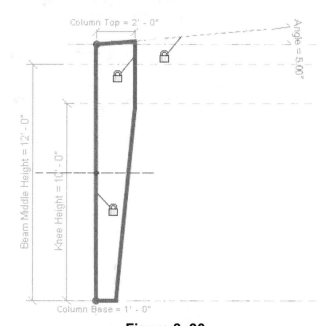

Figure 8–90

7. In the Mode panel, click ✔ (Finish Edit Mode).

8. In the *Modify | Sweep* tab>Sweep panel, click 🖉 (Edit Profile).

9. When the Go To View dialog box opens, select **Floor Plan: Lower Ref. Level**. Click [Open View] .

10. Expand the Reference lines to the ends if you have not already done so.

11. Zoom in on the Profile target and draw a rectangle **3/4" x 1'-0"**. Lock it to the reference planes as shown in Figure 8–91.

Figure 8–91

12. Click ✔ (Finish Edit Mode) twice to finish the Profile and the Sweep.

13. Open the 3D Views>**View 1** view. Rotate and shade it to display the column up to this point as shown in Figure 8–92.

Figure 8–92

14. Return to the Elevations>**Front** view.

15. Click 🗍 (Extrusion) and set the *Work Plane* to **Reference Plane: Center (Front/Back)**.

16. In the *Modify | Create Extrusion* tab>Draw panel, click ⚲ (Pick Lines). In the Options Bar, select the **Lock** option.

17. Zoom into the sweep that was created earlier and select all of the interior lines, as shown in Figure 8–93.

*The lines are automatically locked to the selected lines because you selected the **Lock** option.*

Figure 8–93

18. In Properties, set the values of the *Extrusion End* to **3/8"** and *Extrusion Start* to (negative) **-3/8"**, as shown in Figure 8–94.

Figure 8–94

19. Click ✓ (Finish Edit Mode)

20. Display the column profile in a shaded 3D View and return to the Elevations>**Front** view.

21. Mirror the new tapered column (both extrusion and sweep) along the center vertical reference plane, as shown in Figure 8–95.

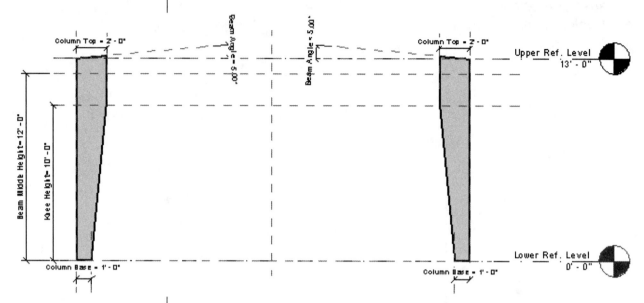

Figure 8–95

22. Save the family file.

Task 3 - Create the geometry for the Tapered Beam.

1. Start the **Sweep** command and draw a path for the beam's top flange of the moment frame as shown in Figure 8–96. Align and lock the lines to the reference planes.

Verify that you are aligning to the reference planes and not other elements. Press <Tab> to cycle through the options. The name of the selected element is displayed in the Status Bar.

Figure 8–96

2. Click (Finish Edit Mode).

3. In the *Modify | Sweep* tab>Sweep panel, click (Edit Profile).

4. In the Go To View dialog box, select **Elevation: Left** and click Open View .

5. Zoom in on the sweep target and draw a rectangle **3/4"x 8"** from the upper left corner of the reference plane. Lock the top, left, and right profile lines to their parallel reference planes, as shown in Figure 8–97.

Figure 8–97

6. Click ✓ (Finish Edit Mode) twice to finish the Profile and the Sweep.

7. Display the top plate of the beam profile in a 3D View, as shown in Figure 8–98.

Figure 8–98

8. Return to the Elevations>**Front** view and create another sweep for the beam's bottom flange using the sketch for the path shown in Figure 8–99 and the sketch for the profile shown in Figure 8–100.

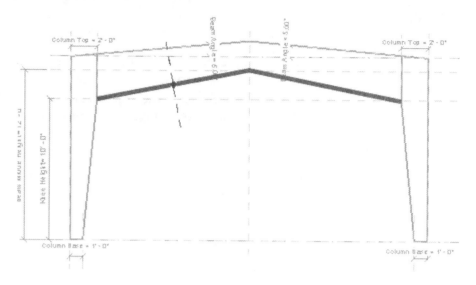

Figure 8–99

The profile location is based on the path target.

Figure 8–100

9. The final 3D view should display as shown in Figure 8–101.

Figure 8–101

10. Return to the Elevations>**Front** view and add an extrusion using the interior of the previously created sweeps as shown in Figure 8–102. Set the *Extrusion End* to **3/8"** and *Extrusion Start* to (negative) **-3/8"**.

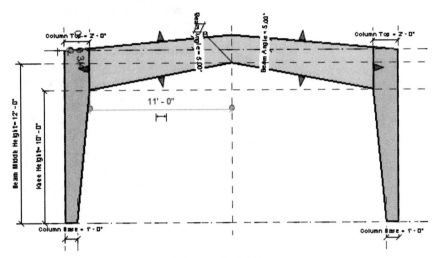

Figure 8–102

11. Open the 3D view and move it to one side. Open the Family Types dialog box and flex the geometry of the **Tapered Moment Frame** parameters as shown in Figure 8–103.

Figure 8–103

12. Save the family file.

Chapter Review Questions

1. How do you change a standard dimension to a parameter-based dimension, as shown in Figure 8–104?

Figure 8–104

  a. In the Type Selector, select a parameter-based type.

  b. In Properties, change the *Value*.

  c. In the Options Bar, expand the Label options and select **<Add parameter...>**.

  d. In the Family Types dialog box, in the *Parameters* area click Add .

2. Why would you create an in-place family rather than a component family?

  a. An in-place family can be used several times in the current project only.

  b. An in-place family is used once in the current project for a specific location and size.

  c. A component family cannot be modified to fit the specific location.

  d. A component family cannot be joined to other elements in the project.

3. Which of the following Generic Model family templates would you use to create a slab depression?

   a. **Generic Model wall based.rft**

   b. **Generic Model face based.rft**

   c. **Generic Model line based.rft**

   d. **Generic Model floor based.rft**

4. In a truss family, is the highlighted element shown in Figure 8–105 a Chord or a Web?

Figure 8–105

   a. Chord

   b. Web

5. When assigning material to a solid form you can select the **Associate Family Parameter** option. The option to select the material is greyed out as shown in Figure 8–106. Where do you assign the material?

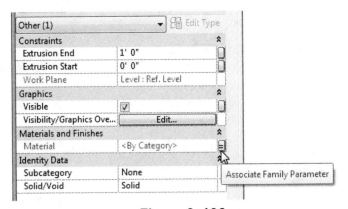

Figure 8–106

   a. In the Family Types dialog box, select the associated parameter and select the material.

   b. In the *Manage* tab>Settings panel, click (Materials) and select the material.

   c. In the *Modify* tab>Geometry panel, click (Paint).

   d. In the Family Category and Parameters dialog box, specify the material in the *Family Parameters* area.

Appendix A

Additional Management Tools

In this chapter you learn how to create object styles, including line weight, line color, line pattern, and line style as well as how to create fill patterns and materials. You also learn how to do basic user interface customization by modifying keyboard shortcuts, double-click functions, and the Project Browser organization.

This chapter contains the following topics:

- **Creating Object Styles**
- **Creating Fill Patterns**
- **Creating Materials**
- **Basic User Interface Customization**

A.1 Creating Object Styles

Learning Objective

- Create object styles for components, including line weight, color, pattern, and material.

Every element in the Autodesk® Revit® software contains object styles that control how its components display in various views. For example, the *Doors* element includes the *Elevation Swing*, *Frame/Mullion*, *Glass*, *Hidden Lines*, *Opening*, *Panel*, and *Plan Swing* as components, as shown in Figure A–1. The *Elevation Swing* is set to a light line weight, displayed in black with a dashed line pattern. It does not have any material attached to it, but the *Glass* component does.

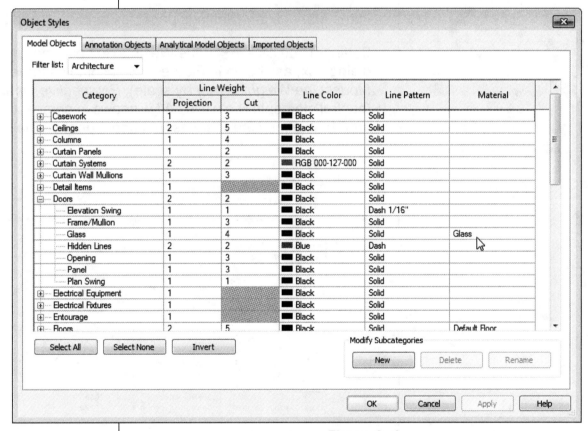

Figure A–1

- In the *Manage* tab>Settings panel, click (Object Styles) to open the Object Styles dialog box.

- To modify an object style, select the element to change and then select an option in the appropriate column in the drop-down list or dialog box.

Line Weights

Line weights for model elements can be set for a **Projection** (in elevations) or **Cut** (in section and plan). For example, a wall displays a heavy line weight while the door and window cuts are lighter, as shown in Figure A–2.

Figure A–2

- Annotation elements are only set for projection.

Hint: Setting Line Weights

In the *Manage* tab>Settings panel, expand 🔧 (Additional Settings) and click ☰ (Line Weights) to open the Line Weights dialog box, as shown in Figure A–3. It contains three tabs: *Model Line Weights* (vary by scale), *Perspective Line Weights* (control elements like walls and windows in perspective views), and *Annotation Line Weights* (not dependent on the scale).

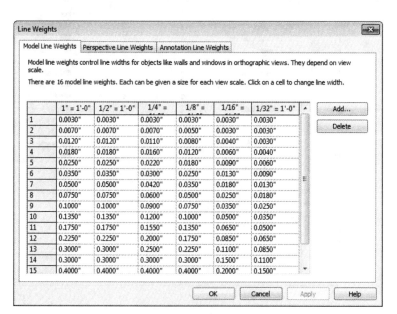

Figure A–3

You can customize the line weights in each tab and add scales as needed for the model line weights.

Line Color

When you select the **Line Color** option in Object Styles or elsewhere, the Color dialog box opens, as shown in Figure A–4.

Figure A–4

You can select from thousands of colors, including options from the Pantone color system, as shown in Figure A–5. Typically, most elements in the Autodesk Revit software are black for printing purposes. When you shade and render, the elements take on the color of the assigned material. Therefore, these dialog boxes are opened when you create materials.

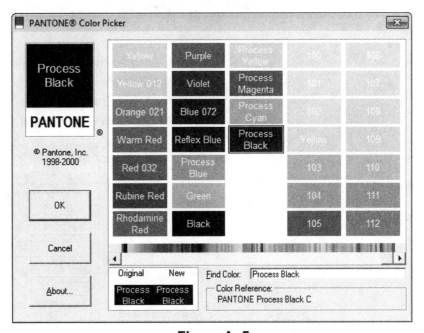

Figure A–5

Line Patterns

Line Patterns can be specified for various components in the Object Styles dialog box. In the example shown in Figure A–6, the line pattern **Dash** is used for the elevation door swing and the line pattern **Dash dot** is used for the callout bubble.

Figure A–6

How To: Create Line Patterns

A wide variety of patterns are supplied with the Autodesk Revit software and you can create your own with a series of dashes, spaces, and dots.

1. In the *Manage* tab>Settings panel, expand (Additional Settings) and click (Line Patterns) to open the Line Patterns dialog box.

2. In the Line Patterns dialog box, click New .

3. In the Name dialog box, type a name for the pattern and click OK .

4. In the Line Pattern Properties dialog box, add a list of dashes, spaces, and/or dots and specify their values, as shown in Figure A–7. *Space* is always the option after a dash or dot. You do not have to enter a value for dots.

Figure A–7

Line Styles

Line styles are a specific type of object style used with the sketching tools. They are not part of the Object Styles dialog box, but are created in a similar way.

In the *Manage* tab>Settings panel, expand 🔧 (Additional Settings) and click ▦ (Line Styles). In the Line Styles dialog box (shown in Figure A–8), specify the *Line Weight*, *Line Color*, and *Line Pattern* for each line style.

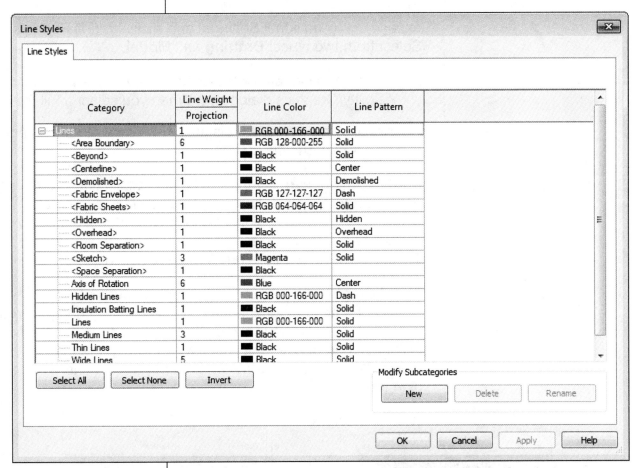

Figure A–8

A.2 Creating Fill Patterns

 Learning Objective

- Create patterns used in the **Filled Region** command and for cut and surface patterns in materials.

Fill patterns are used by the various **Filled Region** commands and material specifications. In the *Manage* tab>Settings panel, expand 🔧 (Additional Settings) and click ▨ (Fill Patterns). Select from two types: **Drafting** and **Model**.

- Fill Patterns can also be created while you are working in the Visibility/Graphics dialog box. When you select a Fill Pattern override, the dialog box displays ⌊...⌋ (Browse), which opens the Fill Patterns dialog box.

Drafting patterns are symbolic. The view scale controls the size of the pattern. Basic patterns include hatching and cross-hatching, as well as designs that display material (such as aluminum or concrete), as shown on the left in Figure A–9. These are used in details and in plan or section cuts.

Model patterns are full scale to the actual elements they represent. They do not change if the view scale changes. You can select brick, various sizes of tile, lines that are a specific distance apart, roof shakes, etc., as shown on the right in Figure A–9. These patterns are primarily used in elevation and plan views.

Drafting Fill

Model Fill

Figure A–9

How To: Create a New Simple Fill Pattern

1. In the *Manage* tab>Settings panel, expand (Additional Settings) and click (Fill Patterns).
2. In the New Pattern dialog box, select the type of pattern you want to create: **Drafting** or **Model**.
3. Click New .
4. In the New Pattern dialog box, specify the required **Orientation in Host Layers** option and select the *Simple* pattern style, as shown in Figure A–10.

Figure A–10

5. Type a name for the new pattern.
6. Type values for the *Line angle* and *Line spacing*, and select the **Parallel lines** or **Crosshatch** option.
7. Click OK to finish. The pattern can now be used to create a filled region type or used in a material.

• Filled regions can have either **Opaque** or **Transparent** backgrounds. This is set up in the Type Properties of the filled region.

How To: Create a New Custom Fill Pattern

1. In the *Manage* tab>Settings panel, expand ✏ (Additional Settings) and click ▨ (Fill Patterns).
2. In the Fill Patterns dialog box, select the type of pattern you want to create: **Drafting** or **Model**.
3. Click ⌊ New ⌋.
4. In the New Pattern dialog box, select the **Custom** option, as shown in Figure A–11.

Figure A–11

5. Click ⌊ Import... ⌋ and select a PAT file. This file can be created specifically for the Autodesk Revit software or it can be based on an AutoCAD® PAT file.
6. Once the file is imported, a list of available patterns is displayed. Select the pattern. The name is automatically assigned. You can change the name after it has been selected.
7. Set the *Import Scale* as needed.
8. Click ⌊ OK ⌋ to finish.

Importing Patterns from AutoCAD

Pattern files (PAT) can be imported from the AutoCAD® software, such as the Escher pattern shown in Figure A–12.

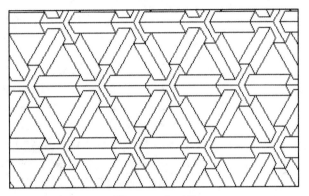

Figure A–12

One change must be made in the pattern file for it to be usable in the Autodesk Revit software. Open the PAT file and add the following line after the title of a custom hatch, as shown in Figure A–13.

```
*AR-HBONE, Standard brick herringbone pattern @ 45 degrees
;%TYPE=MODEL
45,        0,0,         4,4,                    12,-4
135,       2.828427125,2.828427125,   4,-4,     12,-4
```

Figure A–13

- A line with a semicolon in front it is ignored by the AutoCAD software, while the type is specified for the Autodesk Revit software.

- Any pattern in the **Acad.pat** file can be automatically brought in as a drafting pattern. However, you must add the string above to specify model patterns.

A.3 Creating Materials

Learning Objective

- Create materials and material libraries that can be used in multiple projects.

When you shade or render Autodesk Revit models, their appearance depends on the materials that have been associated with the elements, as shown in a shaded view in Figure A–14. Materials also include information that can be used in material takeoff schedules and in energy and structural analysis. You can use materials supplied with the Autodesk Revit software or create custom materials.

Figure A–14

- Materials can be assigned in several ways: using (Paint) on faces, setting it in the layers of system families (such as walls and floors), and in object styles. You also assign materials when you create other component families, such as doors and furniture.

- Materials consist of 2D graphic settings for shading, surface, and cut patterns and the 3D rendering appearance, as well as physical and thermal properties. You can also include identity data, such as manufacturer, model, and keynotes.

Material Libraries

Materials are stored in libraries, which can be shared between Autodesk Revit projects and the AutoCAD, Autodesk® Inventor®, Showcase and Autodesk® 3ds Max® software. Before creating custom materials it is recommended that you create a custom library. Materials can be copied between the current project and the library.

*   You can also use Transfer Project Standards to bring in all the materials from another project into the current project.

How To: Create a Material Library

1. In the *Manage* tab>Settings panel, click ⬡ (Materials).

2. At the bottom of the Material Browser, expand ▣ (Creates, opens and edits user-defined libraries) and select **Create New Library** as shown in Figure A–15.

Figure A–15

3. In the Select File dialog box, navigate to the appropriate folder, type a *File name* and save the library. The Material Library displays in the Library list without any materials displayed.

4. Create new materials as needed in the current project. Then drag and drop both new and existing materials from the project materials into the new library as shown in Figure A–16.

Libraries that come with the Autodesk Revit software are locked. You can copy materials from them but cannot add or change materials in them.

Figure A–16

How To: Create a Material

1. In the *Manage* tab>Settings panel, click ⬡ (Materials).

2. In the Material Editor, expand ⊕ (Creates or duplicates a material), and select either **Create New Material** or **Duplicate Material** as shown in Figure A–17. If you are duplicating a material, select an existing material similar to what you want to use first.

*You can also right-click on an existing material in the Material Browser and select **Duplicate**.*

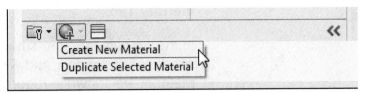

Figure A–17

3. A new material is added to the current project. Modify the name of the material or right-click on the Material name in the Material Browser and select **Rename**. Duplicated materials include all of the properties of the existing material as shown for a new Aluminum material in Figure A–18.

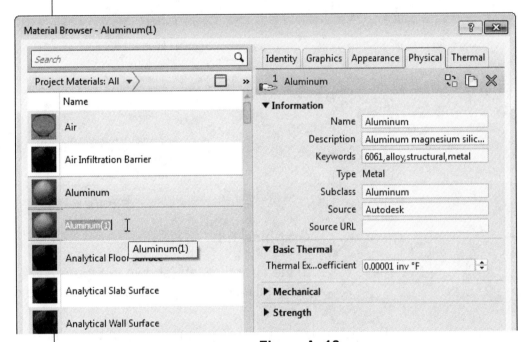

Figure A–18

4. In the *Identity* tab, set up information, such as the related keynote, model, manufacturer, and other schedule-related items.

5. In the *Graphics* tab, set up the *Shading*, *Surface Pattern*, and *Cut Pattern* as required.

6. In the *Appearance* tab, set up the rendering design, including the properties of the elements to be rendered.

7. In the *Physical* tab, specify the physical properties of the material including, **Basic Thermal**, **Mechanical**, and **Strength** properties, if applicable.

8. In the *Thermal* tab, specify the advanced thermal physical properties of the material.

9. Click Apply and add additional materials as required.

10. Click OK when you are finished.

Appearance, Physical, and Thermal parameters can be stored in Assets. Instead of making changes directly in these tabs, investigate the existing assets to determine whether you can swap one asset for another.

Identity Tab

In the *Identity* tab, you set up the *Descriptive Information*, *Product Information*, and *Revit Annotation Information* for the material, as shown in Figure A–19. This information can be used in material takeoff schedules.

Figure A–19

Graphics Tab

In the *Graphics* tab (shown in Figure A–20), you set how a material displays in shaded or hidden line mode.

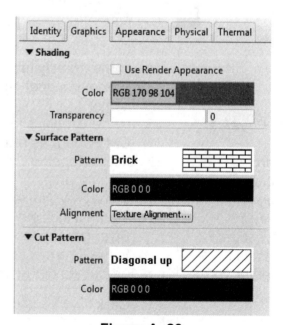

Figure A–20

- The *Shading* area controls how the material displays when an element is shaded. If you want the shaded view to resemble the rendered view, select the **Use Render Appearance** option. The color and other options are modified to match the Render Appearance selection. Alternatively, you can set up a color and transparency ratio. Only use this if the render appearance would be too dark or otherwise not suit the use.

- The *Surface Pattern* and *Cut Pattern* areas enable you to select a fill pattern and color to display on a surface or in a section cut. Surface patterns stay true to size. Cut patterns are drafting patterns, which change size according to the view scale.

Appearance Tab

In the *Appearance* tab, you can set different aspects of a rendered material, including **Information**, the type of material (in this example Masonry is selected as shown in Figure A–21) and other parameters depending on the type of material you are working with.

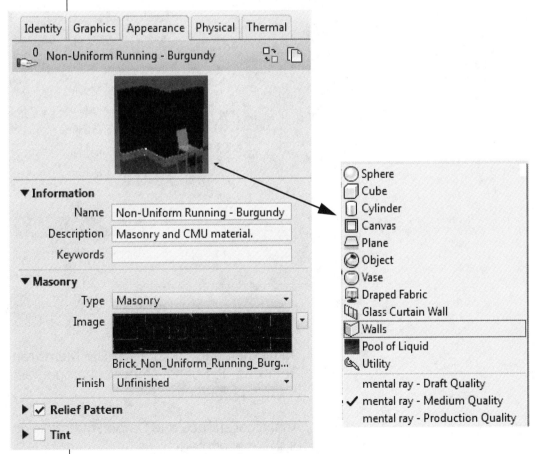

Figure A–21

- You can select how to display the preview of the material by expanding the list next to the graphic as shown in Figure A–21.

Physical Tab

In the *Physical* tab, you can specify information about the physical properties of the material. The options vary by material type, as shown in Figure A–22,

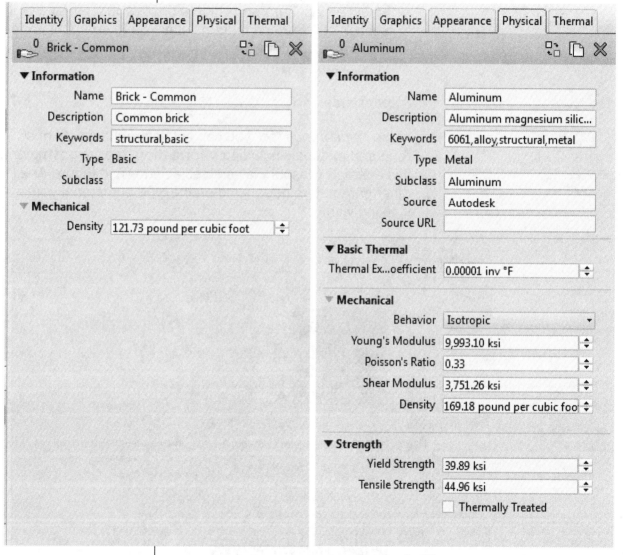

Figure A–22

- Some materials, such as **EPDM Membrane** or **Vapor Retarder**, do not have physical properties, but do have thermal properties.

- Analytical surface and Default materials do not have physical or thermal properties.

Working with Assets

Physical Assets contain preset parameters for materials. These assets are available in the *Appearance*, *Physical* and *Thermal* tabs. Autodesk provides an extensive library of assets that are divided by material type as shown in Figure A–23. You can modify and add assets to materials depending on the variables needed in the project.

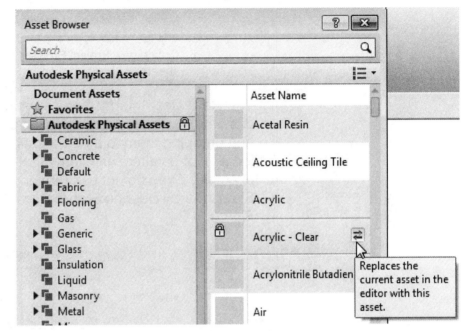

Figure A–23

How To: Replace an Asset for a Material

1. In the Material Browser, select the material that you want to modify.
2. In the *Appearance*, *Physical*, or *Thermal* tab, click

   (Replaces this asset).
3. In the Asset Browser, hover over the required asset and click

   (Replaces the current asset in the editor with this asset) as shown in Figure A–23,
4. Close the Asset Browser.

• The assets are filtered by type. Therefore, you need to modify the Appearance asset by clicking through the *Appearance* tab, etc.

• You can create new assets by duplicating an existing one and then modifying the parameters.

A.4 Basic User Interface Customization

Learning Objectives

- Modify the keyboard shortcuts and double-click function for the mouse.
- Create new Project Browser organization layouts for views and sheets.

The Revit User Interface has a variety of features that can be customized. From moving Ribbon panels around by dragging and dropping them to a new location, to the activation and location of palettes, and items that display on the status bar. For example, if you do not use Design Options you can clean up the Status Bar by clearing **Status Bar - Design Options** as shown in Figure A–24.

Figure A–24

You can also customize other parts of the Autodesk Revit software, including customizing keyboard shortcuts, specifying how the double-click functions work and setting up the Project Browser organization.

Customizing Shortcuts

A helpful customization is to set up the keyboard shortcuts for frequently used commands. These are not saved by project, but on each computer. To display the shortcuts that are already available, hover the cursor over a tool, such as **Wall**, to display the tool tip that displays the associated shortcut, as shown in Figure A–25.

When you type keyboard shortcuts, you do not need to press <Enter> or the <Spacebar>.

Figure A–25

How To: Customize the Keyboard Shortcuts

1. In the *View* tab>Windows panel, expand (User Interface), and click (Keyboard Shortcuts) or, in the Application Menu, click Options . In the Options dialog box, in the *User Interface* pane, in the *Configure* area, next to *Keyboard shortcuts:* click Customize... .

2. In the Keyboard Shortcuts dialog box, use the **Search** or **Filter** options to narrow the search, as shown in Figure A–26.

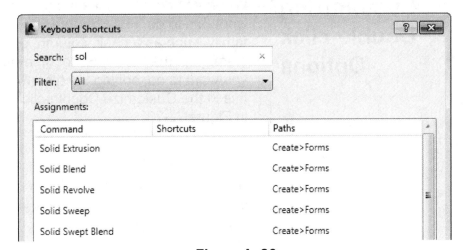

Figure A–26

3. Select the command that you want to add or modify.

4. In the Press new keys edit box, type the shortcut that you want to use (as shown in Figure A–27), and click .

If a shortcut has already been assigned, you can still use it. Press the <Spacebar> to cycle through the options.

Figure A–27

5. Click OK when you have finished.

- To remove shortcuts, select the shortcut, and click ⬛ Remove.

- You can import or export the shortcut file to be used in other stations of the Autodesk® Revit® software than the one on which they were created. When you export to XML, all of the commands are exported. You can then add the required shortcuts to the XML file and import them into your program.

Customizing Double-click Options

When you double-click on elements, you can specify what you want this to do. For example, by default, double-clicking on a family, such as a chair, column, or plumbing fixture, opens the element in the Family Editor. In most cases that is not something you want to do, editing the type would be better. You can change this in the Customize Double-click Settings dialog box as shown in Figure A–28.

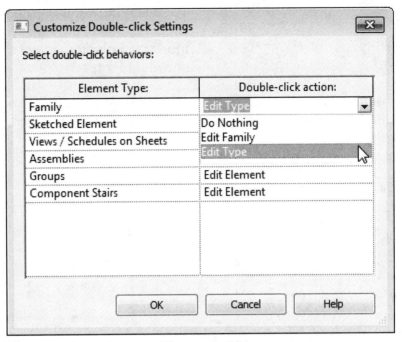

Figure A–28

How To: Customize Double-Click Options

1. In the Application Menu, click Options .
2. In the Options dialog box, in the *User Interface* pane, in the *Configure* area, next to *Double-click Options:* click

    .

3. Select the method that you want to use for each of the element types.

Customizing the Browser Organization

The Project Browser is the heart of the Autodesk Revit software. It is where you access all of the different views, sheets, family types, etc. When working with complex projects, it can help to organize the views and sheets so that it is most useful to the methods used in your firm. It is easy to switch between different organizations and you can create custom ones to suit your work.

- To switch between existing organization types, in the Project Browser, select the **View** node at the top of the palette, and in the Type Selector, select the type that you want to use as shown in Figure A–29.

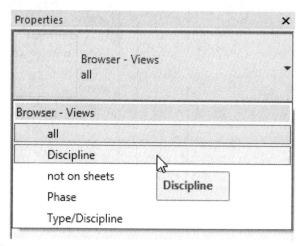

Figure A–29

- You can also switch sheet organizations by selecting the *Sheets* node and changing the type in the Type Selector.

How To: Customize the Browser Organization

1. In the *View* tab>Windows panel, expand (User Interface), and click (Browser Organization) or, in the Project Browser, right-click on the *Views* or *Sheets* node and select **Browser Organization**.

2. In the Browser Organization dialog box, select the *Views* or *Sheets* tab, and click 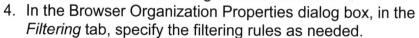.

3. Name the new browser organization and click [OK].

4. In the Browser Organization Properties dialog box, in the *Filtering* tab, specify the filtering rules as needed.

5. In the *Grouping and Sorting* tab, assign the various groups as needed. The example shown in Figure A–30 is by discipline, an organization that is used most often in the MEP templates.

Figure A–30

6. Click [OK] to finish the property changes.
7. In the Browser Organization dialog box, you can continue to create the new organization and then select the current organization. Click [Apply] between sets if you are creating multiple organizations. Click [OK] when you have finished.

- In the Options dialog box, in the *General* tab, in the *View Options* area, you can set the *Default view discipline* that is used when you create new views, such as sections, callouts, and elevations, as shown in Figure A–31.

Figure A–31

- When you duplicate a view, it automatically assumes the discipline and other view properties of the original view.

Command Summary

Button	Command	Location
	Browser Organization	• **Ribbon:** *View* tab>Windows panel> expand User Interface • **Application Menu:** Options>*User Interface* tab
	Fill Patterns	• **Ribbon:** *Manage* tab>Settings panel> expand Additional Settings
	Keyboard Shortcuts	• **Ribbon:** *View* tab>Windows panel> expand User Interface • **Application Menu:** Options>*User Interface* tab
	Line Patterns	• ***Ribbon:*** *Manage* tab>Settings panel> expand Additional Settings
	Line Styles	• **Ribbon:** *Manage* tab>Settings panel> expand Additional Settings
	Line Weights	• **Ribbon:** *Manage* tab>Settings panel> expand Additional Settings
	Materials	• **Ribbon:** *Manage* tab>Settings panel
	Object Styles	• **Ribbon:** *Manage* tab>Settings panel

Appendix B

Autodesk Revit 2015 Certification Exam Objectives

This appendix lists the Autodesk Revit 2015 Certification Exam Objectives for both the Professional and User exams.

This chapter contains the following topics:

- **Autodesk Certified Exam Objectives**

B.1 Autodesk Certified Exam Objectives

The following table will help you to locate the exam objectives within the chapters of the *Autodesk Revit 2015 Architecture Fundamentals* training guide to help you prepare for the Autodesk Revit 2015 Certified Professional (Pro.) and Autodesk Revit 2015 Certified User exams.

Pro.	User	Exam Objectives	Training Guide & Chapter
User Interface			
	✓	Change the view scale	• **Fundamentals:** Ch. 1
	✓	Identify file types	• **Fundamentals:** Ch. 1
	✓	Identify primary parts of the User Interface (UI)	• **Fundamentals:** Ch. 1
✓	✓	Use the Project Browser	• **Fundamentals:** Ch. 1
Collaboration			
✓		Copy and monitor elements in a linked file	• **Collaboration Tools:** Ch. 2
✓		Import DWG and image files	• **Fundamentals:** Ch. 3 • **Collaboration Tools:** Ch. 3
✓		Use worksharing	• **Collaboration Tools:** Ch. 4
Documentation			
	✓	Create a title sheet	• **Fundamentals:** Ch. 13
✓		Create and modify filled regions	• **Fundamentals:** Ch. 16
✓		Place detail components and repeating details	• **Fundamentals:** Ch. 16
✓		Set the colors used in a color scheme legend	• **Conceptual Design and Visualization:** Ch. 2
✓	✓	Tag elements (doors, windows, etc.) by category	• **Fundamentals:** Ch. 15
✓		Use dimension strings	• **Fundamentals:** Ch. 14
✓		Work with phases	• **Collaboration Tools:** Ch. 1

Pro.	User	Exam Objectives	Training Guide & Chapter
Elements			
✓		Change elements within a curtain wall	• **Fundamentals:** Ch. 6
✓		Create a new family type	• **Fundamentals:** Ch. 5 • **BIM Management:** Ch. 4
✓		Create a stacked wall	• **BIM Management:** Ch. 3
	✓	Create and modify walls	• **Fundamentals:** Ch. 4
✓		Create compound walls	• **BIM Management:** Ch. 3
✓		Differentiate system and component families	• **BIM Management:** Ch. 3 and 4
	✓	Edit doors	• **Fundamentals:** Ch. 5
	✓	Edit windows	• **Fundamentals:** Ch. 5
	✓	Trim objects	• **Fundamentals:** Ch. 2
✓		Work with family Parameters	• **BIM Management:** Ch. 4
Families			
✓		Assess review warnings in Revit	• **Fundamentals:** Ch. 12
✓		Use Family creation procedures	• **BIM Management:** Ch. 4
✓	✓	Work with families	• **Fundamentals:** Ch. 8
Modeling			
	✓	Add dimensions	• **Fundamentals:** Ch. 14
	✓	Add model text to a plan	• **Fundamentals:** Ch. 14
✓		Attach walls to a roof or ceiling	• **Fundamentals:** Ch. 11
✓		Change a generic floor/ceiling/roof to a specific type	• **Fundamentals:** Ch. 9, 10, and 11
✓		Create a building pad	• **Site and Structural Design:** Ch. 1
✓	✓	Create a stair with a landing	• **Fundamentals:** Ch. 12
✓		Create elements such as floors, ceilings, or roofs	• **Fundamentals:** Ch. 9, 10, and 11
✓		Define floors for a mass	• **Conceptual Design and Visualization:** Ch. 1
✓		Edit a model element's material	• **BIM Management:** Ch. 4 and 6

Pro.	User	Exam Objectives	Training Guide & Chapter
✓		Edit room-aware families	• **BIM Management:** Ch. 4
✓		Generate a toposurface	• **Site and Structural Design:** Ch. 1
✓	✓	Model railings	• **Fundamentals:** Ch. 12
	✓	Use grids	• **Fundamentals:** Ch. 3
Views			
✓		Control visibility	• **Fundamentals:** Ch. 7
✓		Create a duplicate view for a plan, section, elevation, drafting view, etc.	• **Fundamentals:** Ch. 7
	✓	Create a schedule and add schedule tags	• **Fundamentals:** App. B
✓		Create and manage legends	• **Fundamentals:** Ch. 14
	✓	Create section views	• **Fundamentals:** Ch. 7
✓		Define element properties in a schedule	• **Fundamentals:** Ch. 15
✓		Manage view position on sheets	• **Fundamentals:** Ch. 13
✓		Organize and sort items in a schedule	• **Fundamentals:** App. B • **BIM Management:** Ch. 2
✓	✓	Use levels	• **Fundamentals:** Ch. 3

Index